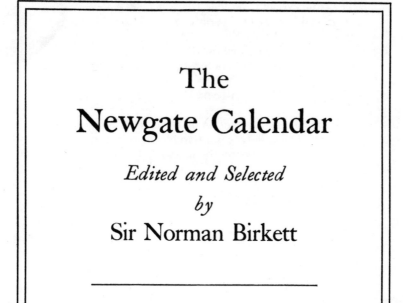

The
Newgate Calendar

Edited and Selected
by
Sir Norman Birkett

With Contemporary Engravings

Folio Press: J. M. Dent
London 1974

The extract from *The Diary of Dudley Ryder* is
reprinted here by kind permission of Messrs. Methuen.

Distributed for the Folio Press
202 Great Suffolk Street, London SE1 by
J. M. DENT & SONS LTD
Aldine House, Albemarle Street, London W1

Folio Society first edition of 1951, with letterpress
text and collotype illustrations, reprinted by
photolitho in 1974

ISBN 0 460 04155 X

PRINTED IN GREAT BRITAIN
by Redwood Burn Limited, Trowbridge & Esher
Set in Caslon Old Face type
Bound by J. M. Dent & Sons Ltd., Letchworth

List of Trials

3

Introduction

CRIMINAL trials have always exercised a great fascination over the minds of men. Wherein that fascination resides is not to be stated with any great certainty, though it is doubtless made up of many diverse elements. It was said of the late Lord Birkenhead's collection of *Famous Trials* that it displayed 'mankind under the microscope', and it may well be that that is the essence of the whole matter. It is not at all surprising therefore that a considerable literature exists upon the subject, for apart from the purely human interest of which I have spoken, the administration of the criminal law has always been recognised to be of supreme importance in the national life.

The period covered by the trials here recorded (1700–1780) has a very special importance. It was an age to which many people in our own day look back with longing as the age in which they would have liked to live, and it is sometimes spoken of as the 'gentle' eighteenth century. It was, of course, the age of Johnson and his circle, preserved for us in the pages of Boswell, of Gray and the famous *Elegy*, of Gibbon's *Decline and Fall*, of Sterne's *Tristram Shandy* and Henry Fielding's *Tom Jones*. But the temptation to compare past ages with our own, and to judge them by the standards of knowledge and experience we have so painfully acquired, is to be resisted. The purpose of this book is not in any sense critical or analytical. Its modest and, I think, useful purpose is to reproduce some of the criminal trials of the eighteenth century as recorded at the time, with the comments of the Editors, and thus to reveal a phase of life that is sometimes forgotten when the glories of that age are being considered. For let it be said at once that the trials here set out exhibit the criminal law in what we now regard as a barbaric and even savage state. The punishment of death was imposed almost as freely as a Magistrate now imposes a fine of forty shillings. In 1748, William York, a boy of ten, was sentenced to death, and the whole body of judges to whom the matter was referred said ' . . . the

5

sparing of this boy merely on account of his age will probably have a quite contrary tendency [to that of deterrence], and in justice to the public the law should take its course.' He was not executed in fact, the execution being postponed many times, but he was under sentence of death for nine years. Women were burnt alive in the most shocking circumstances; traitors suffered the terrible ordeal of being disembowelled; the bodies of those executed were hung about the countryside in chains; public executions at Newgate and Tyburn were carried out in the presence of great multitudes of people, when scenes of the most degrading and revolting character took place; and powerful voices still cried out for more severe and spectacular punishments. It is true that Blackstone in the famous *Commentaries on the Laws of England* (1765) stated that the burning of women and the disembowelling of traitors did not take place until the victims had been deprived of sensation by strangling. But this was barbarous enough in all conscience. It was this barbarity of the law with which the great reformers of the nineteenth century were chiefly concerned, and men like Eden and Romilly and Edmund Burke discussed the administration of the law with great insight and understanding, and particularly the place of punishment in the maintenance of public order and in the prevention and suppression of crime.

The publications of the eighteenth century make it plain that Retribution and Deterrence were the moving ideas of criminal legislation, and the volumes from which the present selection of trials has been taken were no exception. For nearly two hundred years books have been appearing from time to time with the title of *The Newgate Calendar*. That title has become part of our common speech, as when Dickens in *Our Mutual Friend* speaks of one 'committing all the crimes in the Newgate Calendar'. Calendar is a word in use to-day at every Assize or Quarter Sessions for the list of prisoners for trial, and Newgate is the name of the famous or infamous prison with a thousand years of history behind it, and about which a perfect library of books has been written. The present collection of trials is taken from a very remarkable book called *The Malefactor's Register or New Newgate and Tyburn Calendar*, published towards the close of the eighteenth century. The names of the authors are not stated : they preferred to call themselves The Editors. There can be no doubt that these volumes formed the basis of many editions of *The Newgate Calendar*. They contain a large number of cases, but no case concludes without a solemn and portentous homily, intended no doubt to justify the Frontispiece which is described as ' A Mother presenting *The Malefactor's Register* to her son and tenderly entreating him to regard the instructions therein recorded'. Those sons (if there were such) who received these volumes from a fond mother must have been heartily sick of them before they had finished reading them. The moralising is really too much. The volumes were dedicated to Sir John Fielding who died in 1780. He was the half-brother of the great Henry Fielding and was associated with him as a Magistrate. He was blind from birth and was said to have known three thousand thieves by their voices, though this sounds extremely unlikely. He was the author of many pamphlets dealing with his office and the prevention of crime. In the Dedication to him the Editors say of 'a plan [his] genius has suggested for the speedy detection of offenders' that 'if any single villain was properly apprised of the nature of this scheme, he would, from motives of fear only, be very cautious how he violated the laws of his country.' This is the authentic note of the eighteenth century. It is to put the offender in fear by the nature of the punishments devised. In our own day we have witnessed a great division of opinion on the question of abolishing Capital Punishment for the very few offences for which it is now imposed—Treason, Murder, Piracy with violence, and Setting Fire to Dockyards. But in the eighty years covered by these volumes, very many hundreds of offences were punishable by death, with no alternative punishment provided, many of them offences of the most trivial kind. Dr Radzinowicz in his *History of the Criminal Law* deals with the subject in the most detailed way, and the interested reader must be referred to that fascinating volume, for it is more interesting than any novel, and contains a wealth of information, drawn from every kind of source, showing the state of the criminal law then existing, and relating it to the social and political background of the times. This Introduction can only refer to one or two matters, and then only in the barest outline.

During the period with which we are concerned, the punishment of every felony was death. It will sound quite incredible to modern ears, but that was the state of the criminal law down to the year 1826. The distinction between felonies and misdemeanours was always rather artificial, but for all felonies there was only one sentence. Grand Larceny, for example, was to steal anything of the value of more than twelve pence, and that was a felony, and the penalty was death. Privately stealing in a shop to the value of five shillings also carried the death penalty. When in the nineteenth century Sir Samuel Romilly's Bill for abolishing the death penalty for this offence had passed the House of Commons, Lord Eldon, the Lord Chancellor of George the Third and George the Fourth, not only defended and indeed eulogised this state of the law, but induced the House of Lords to reject the Bill by a majority that included seven bishops.

There are one or two important and interesting matters to be remembered in considering the state of the criminal law in the eighteenth century. The first is that most extraordinary provision which went under the name of Benefit of Clergy. It sprang originally from the immunity of the cleric from the jurisdiction of the criminal courts, and goes back very many centuries. Clerics were supposed to be literate, and the only test of their literacy was whether they could read. To this day, after a man has been convicted of felony (but not misdemeanour) the Clerk of Assize still says to him—'Prisoner at the Bar, you have been convicted of felony. Have you anything to say why the sentence of the Court should not be passed upon you?' In cases of murder the words are added 'and why you should not die'. This is a direct survival of Benefit of Clergy, for it was at that point in the trial that it could be claimed. The test was the same for everybody. The convicted man was given a copy of the Scriptures and told to read the first verse of the fifty-first Psalm—'Have mercy upon me, O God, according to thy loving-kindness; according to the multitude of thy tender mercies, blot out my transgressions.' This verse was known for centuries as 'the necking verse' and it was always the verse selected for the test. There was a time when even the foulest murderer could go free if he could merely say these words, even though he had learnt them by heart, and, in truth, could not read at all. It is a wonderfully ironic thing to think of some savage murderer repeating these lovely words, without the slightest meaning for him, and in consequence going scot-free. Women, of course, could never be clerics, but a special Act of Parliament extended the privilege to them. In course of time, quite inevitably, the privilege was cut down. In the fifteenth century it was provided that when a man had succeeded in his claim to Benefit of Clergy he was to be branded on the thumb with M for murder and T for any other felony. Upon his next conviction, unless he was in fact a cleric, and in Holy Orders, he could not claim Benefit of Clergy. Some Clerks of Assize still say to the convicted prisoner 'Hold up your hand' before sentence is passed, and this is also a survival from the days when Benefit of Clergy was in force. In the sixteenth century, Benefit of Clergy was taken away from many offences such as Murder, Highway Robbery, Horse Stealing and similar felonies. But during the period covered by this book, a very large number of Statutes were passed creating felonies punishable by death without Benefit of Clergy, such as stealing in a dwelling house to the value of forty shillings, stealing in a shop to the value of five shillings, and picking pockets. Nevertheless it was the opinion of Mr Justice Stephen that even when all allowances had been made for the effect of Benefit of Clergy (which was not wholly abolished until 1827) the criminal law of the eighteenth century was not only of very great severity, but it was also utterly lacking in principle.

It must also be remembered that during the period of which we speak there was no proper police system in the country. There were constables and watchmen of course, but they were notoriously inefficient. It was not until 1753 that Henry Fielding took the first tentative step towards the establishment of a professional police force, and not until 1829 that Sir Robert Peel inaugurated the system which, with many amendments, is the system in force to-day. It is interesting to notice that much of the opposition to the establishment of a police force was the belief that it was destructive of the traditional liberties of Englishmen; and even to-day the powers of the police are severely limited because of the same feeling. The police are granted no more power than is necessary for the carrying out of their duties, and the Courts watch over the exercise of this power with the greatest vigilance. So recently as 1947, the House of Lords, the highest legal tribunal in the land, pronounced the act of a sergeant of police in Liverpool to be unlawful, when he had arrested a man, believing him to be a receiver of stolen goods, without informing the man of the reason for the arrest.

The prison system was equally defective. John Howard published his great work on *The State of Prisons* in 1777, and confirmed in the most striking way the views of earlier writers on the conditions existing in the gaols and the houses of correction. Those conditions were, to speak plainly, as bad as they could possibly be. Vice and corruption were everywhere to be found. The conditions at Newgate, for example, were utterly shocking, as a host of contemporary writers testify. Imprisonment, therefore, as an alternative to capital punishment, was not looked upon by the authorities with any favour, nor was transportation for a term of years, or even for life, regarded by many people as an effective punishment, though Henry Fielding strongly supported it. When the alternative punishments were in this unsatisfactory state, it is not surprising that the advocates of more and more capital punishment should find their advocacy rewarded in the manner I have described.

In these circumstances, when death was the commonest penalty, it is pitiful to recall the lot of prisoners charged with offences against the criminal law. They were almost defenceless unless the judges came to their aid. It was not until the year 1837 that a prisoner charged with felony was allowed to have counsel to examine and cross-examine the witnesses or to address the jury. His counsel could only speak on a point of law if the prisoner himself had raised it, and the Court agreed that it was a point of law. It was not until the year 1898 (incredible as it sounds) that a prisoner was allowed to go into the witness box and give evidence upon his own behalf. It was not until 1849 that the prisoner was allowed to have a copy of the depositions, that is, the evidence which had been taken down in writing in the Court where he had been committed for trial.

This rather dreadful state of affairs had some slight alleviations. There was, in the words of the late Lord Justice Mackinnon, 'a general conspiracy of benevolence on the part of judges, juries and counsel to mitigate the effects of the system by excessive technicalities of procedure.' For example, if a man's name was wrongly spelt in the Indictment, the Indictment was quashed, and he went out a free man, whatever the charge was against him. On charges of stealing to the value of forty shillings in a dwelling house or to the value of five shillings in a shop, juries entered into the general conspiracy with the approval of the judge, and found no difficulty in saying that the goods stolen were less than forty shillings, or five shillings, when it was quite obvious that the value was much in excess of those sums. All these things tended to bring the law into great disrepute and paved the way for the reforms of the next century. Those reforms have been extended in all subsequent years, and the recent Criminal Justice Act is the great contribution of the present generation to that wholesome and necessary work.

Perhaps I may conclude this Introduction with a little homily of my own, though not quite in the manner of the Editors of *The Malefactor's Register*. The cases in this book have been selected for their interest. Murder, Forgery, Perjury, Coining, Treason, Horse-Stealing, Bigamy, Larceny, Petit Treason, Piracy and offences against the Waltham Black Act—all make up a pretty gruesome Calendar. They exhibit human nature, as Burke once observed, in a variety of sombre circumstances. But they also show how closely allied are public opinion and the provisions of the criminal law. It is never true to say that the prevailing thought of the age is mirrored in the existing criminal law. Sometimes legislation lags behind public opinion, and sometimes it is a long way ahead of it. Problems of punishment, during the last two hundred years at least, have always been highly controversial. The major problems of criminal justice are, however, always the same in all ages, and they are two in number. What is the behaviour of the citizen which the community should make criminal, and what is to be done with the people who commit crimes ?

It is now generally recognised that crime cannot be prevented by punishment alone. It is either impossible or impracticable. The cases in this book show the lengths to which the dominating ideas of the eighteenth century were carried. Deterrence and Retribution were emphasised, though the idea of Reformation was not altogether absent. The concluding note by the Editors of *The Malefactor's Register*, which we reproduce, insists that the reformation of prisoners should be the great aim of the legislators, and to that end speaks of the existing state of the prisons and the reforms there urgently needed. The view most widely held to-day is that the criminal law should conform to what the public feels to be right and just. It should secure the law-abiding citizen from infractions of his liberties by wrong-doers. It should avoid all false sentiment in the punishments decreed, and particularly the view that extreme severity is all that is required. The criminal law of the eighteenth century was severe enough and yet it failed in its purpose. More and more will the idea of the reform of the offender, and most particularly the reform of the YOUNG offender, gather support, for it is now seen that although some offenders are beyond the reach of reform, nevertheless it is in reformation that the best hope lies of genuine and lasting advance in the campaign against crime.

Preface

IN an age abandoned to dissipation, and when the ties of religion and morality fail to have their accustomed influence on the mind, the publication of a New Work of this nature makes its appearance with peculiar propriety.

It has not been unusual, of late years, to complain of the sanguinary complection of our laws; and if there were any reason to expect that the practice of felony would be lessened by the institution of any laws less sanguinary than those now in force, it would be a good argument for the enacting of such laws.

Wise and virtuous legislators can wish nothing more ardently than the general welfare of the community; and those who have from time to time given birth to the laws of England, have indisputably done it with a view to this general welfare. But as the wisest productions of the human mind are liable to error, and as there is visibly an encreasing depravity in the manners of the age, it is no wonder that our laws are found, in some instances, inadequate to the purposes for which they were enacted: and, perhaps, if, in a few instances they were made more, and in others less severe than they are at present, the happiest consequences might result to the public.

It is with the utmost deference to the wisdom of their superiors, that the editors of this work offer the following hints for the improvement of the police of this country, and the security of the lives and properties of the subject: and,

1st. If his majesty would be graciously pleased to let the law operate in its *full force* against every convicted housebreaker, it would probably greatly lessen the number of those atrocious offenders; and consequently add to the repose of every family of property in the kingdom. What can be conceived more dreadful than a band of ruffians drawing the curtains of the bed at midnight, and presenting the drawn dagger, and the loaded pistol? The imagination will paint the terrors of such a situation, in a light more striking than language can display them.

13

2dly. If the same royal prerogative was exerted for the punishment of women convicts, it would indisputably produce very happy effects. It is to the low and abandoned women that hundreds of young fellows owe their destruction. They rob, they plunder, to support these wretches. Let it not seem cruel that we make one remark, of which we are convinced experience would justify the propriety. The execution of *ten* women would do more public service than that of an *hundred* men; for, exclusive of the force of example, it would perhaps tend to the preservation of more than an hundred.

3dly. Notorious defrauds, by gambling, or otherwise, should be rendered capital felonies by a statute; for, as the law now stands, after a temporary punishment, the common cheat is turned loose to make fresh depredations on the public.

4thly. Forgery, enormous as the crime is, in a commercial state, might perhaps be more effectually punished and prevented than at present, by dooming the convict to *labour for life* on board the ballast-lighters. Forgerers are seldom among the low and abandoned part of mankind. Forgery is very often the last dreadful refuge to which the distressed tradesman flies. These people then are sensible of shame, and perpetual infamy would be abundantly more terrible to such men than the mere dread of death.

5thly. Highwaymen, we conceive, might with propriety be punished by labouring on the high-way, chained by the legs, agreeable to a design we have given in a plate in this work. Many a young fellow is hardened enough to think of taking a purse on the highway, to supply his extravagancies, who would be terrified from the practice, if he knew he could not ride half a dozen miles out of London, without seeing a number of highwaymen working together, under the ignominious circumstances above-mentioned.

With regard to murderers, and persons convicted of unnatural crimes, we cannot think of altering the present mode of punishment. 'Him that sheddeth man's blood, by man shall his blood be shed:' as to the other wretches, it is only to be lamented that their deaths cannot be aggravated by every species of torment!

Having said thus much, we submit our labours to the candid revision of the public, nothing doubting that, on a careful perusal, they will be found to answer the purpose of guarding the minds of youth against the approaches of vice; and, in consequence, of advancing the happiness of the community. THE EDITORS

The Trials

THE
MALEFACTOR's REGISTER;
OR,
New NEWGATE and TYBURN CALENDAR.

CONTAINING THE

AUTHENTIC LIVES, TRIALS, ACCOUNTS OF EXECUTIONS, DYING SPEECHES, AND OTHER CURIOUS PARTICULARS,

Relating to ALL the moſt notorious

VIOLATERS OF THE LAWS OF THEIR COUNTRY;

WHO HAVE

Suffered DEATH, and other exemplary PUNISHMENTS, in *England*, *Scotland*, and *Ireland*, from the Commencement of the Year 1700, to the MIDSUMMER SESSIONS of next Year.

Together with

NUMEROUS TRIALS in EXTRAORDINARY CASES, where the Parties have been ACQUITTED.

This Work alſo comprehends all the moſt material Paſſages in the SESSIONS-PAPERS for *a long Series of Years*, and complete NARRATIVES of all the Capital TRIALS for

BIGAMY,	HIGH-TREASON,	RIOTS,
BURGLARY,	HORSE-STEALING,	STREET-ROBBERY,
FELONY,	MURDER,	UNNATURAL CRIMES,
FORGERY,	PETIT-TREASON,	And various other
FOOTPAD-ROBBERY,	PIRACY,	OFFENCES, and
HIGHWAY-ROBBERY,	RAPES,	MISDEMEANORS.

To which is added,

A *correct Liſt* of all the Capital *Convictions* at the *Old Bailey*, &c. &c. &c. ſince the Commencement of the *preſent Century*; which will be of the higheſt Uſe to refer to on many Occaſions.

The Whole tending, by a general *Diſplay* of the *Progreſs* and *Conſequence* of *Vice*, to impreſs on the Mind proper Ideas of the Happineſs reſulting from a Life of ſtrict *Honor* and *Integrity*: and to convince Individuals of the ſuperior Excellence of thoſe Laws framed for the Protection of our *Lives* and *Properties*.

Offered not only as an Object of *Curioſity* and *Entertainment*, but as a Work of *real* and *ſubſtantial Uſe*.

The Crimes *related* here *are* great *and* true,
The Subjects vary, *and the* Work *is* new:
By reading, learn *the Ways of Sin* to *ſhun*,
Be timely Taught, and you'll not be *undone*.

Dedicated to Sir JOHN FIELDING, Knight.

Embelliſhed with a moſt elegant and ſuperb Set of entire New Copper-Plates, finely engraved from original Deſigns, by SAMUEL WALE, Eſq. and others.

LONDON:
Printed, *by Authority*, only for ALEX. HOGG, at No. 16, Pater-noſter Row, and Sold by all Bookſellers in Town and Country.

FRONTISPIECE.

A Mother presenting The Malefactor's Register to her Son, and tenderly intreating him to regard the Instructions therein recorded.

Dodd delin   Goldar sculp.

The anxious Mother, with a Parents Care,
Presents our Labours to her future Heir;
"The Wise, the Brave, the Temperate, and the Just,
Who love their Neighbour, and in God who trust,
Safe through the Dang'rous paths of Life may steer,
Nor dread those Evils we exhibit Here".

Singular circumstances respecting the unhappy Case of Captain JOHN KIDD, with his Life, Piracies, Trial, and Execution.

THE case of captain Kidd, while in agitation, engaged the attention of the public in a very eminent degree, though the man himself was one of the most contemptible of the human race. The town of Greenock in Scotland gave birth to captain Kidd, who was bred to the sea, and having quitted his native country, he resided at New-York, where he became owner of a small vessel, with which he traded among the pirates, obtained a thorough knowledge of their haunts, and could give a better account of them than any other person whatever. He was neither remarkable for the excess of his courage, nor for his want of it. In a word, his ruling passion appeared to be avarice, and to this was owing his connection with the pirates.

When Kidd was in company with these abandoned people he used to converse and act as they did; yet at other times he would make singular professions of honesty, and intimate how easy a matter it would be to extirpate these people, and prevent their making future depredations.

His frequent remarks of this kind engaged the notice of several considerable planters, who forming a more favourable idea of him than his true character would warrant, procured him the patronage with which he was afterwards honoured. Before we enter into farther particulars respecting this man, it will be proper to say something of the situation of public affairs, previous to, and at the time he began to grow conspicuous.

Great complaints had been made, for years past, of the piracies committed in the West-Indies, which had been greatly encouraged by some of the inhabitants of North-America, on account of the advantage that could be made by the purchase of effects thus fraudulently obtained. This coming to the knowledge of king William the Third, he, in the year 1695, bestowed the government of New-England and New-York on the earl of Bellamont, an

Irish nobleman of distinguished character and abilities.

Soon after his Majesty had conferred this honour on lord Bellamont, his lordship began to consider of the most effectual method to redress the evils complained of, and he represented to colonel Levingston, a gentleman who had great property in New-York, that some proper steps should be taken to obviate the evils so long complained of. Just at this juncture captain Kidd was arrived from New-York, in a sloop of his own: him, therefore, the colonel mentioned to lord Bellamont, as a bold and daring man, who was very fit to be employed against the pirates, as he was perfectly well acquainted with the places they frequented.

This plan met with the fullest approbation of his lordship, who knowing how desirous the king was that this nest of pirates should be destroyed, mentioned the affair to his majesty, who greatly applauded the design, and recommended it to the notice of the board of admiralty. The commissioners likewise approved it; but such was then the hurry and confusion of public affairs, that, though the design was approved, no steps were taken towards carrying it into execution.

All that passed on this occasion being known to colonel Levingston, he made an application to lord Bellamont, and informed him that as the affair would not well admit of delay, it was worthy (though it had not met with public encouragement) of being undertaken by some private persons of rank and distinction, and carried into execution at their own expence.

His lordship approved of this project, but it was attended with considerable difficulty: at length, however, the lord chancellor Somers, the duke of Shrewsbury, the earl of Romney, the earl of Oxford, and some other persons, with colonel Levingston and captain Kidd, agreed to raise £6,000 for the expence of the voyage; and the colonel and captain were to have a fifth of the profits of the whole undertaking.

King William approved of this plan so highly, and thought it would produce such great advantages to his subjects, that he promised to contribute to its success; and therefore a reserve was agreed to be made of a tenth part of the effects seized from the pirates, for the use of his majesty: but after the contract was concluded, the king could not spare his share of the money, and therefore the whole was advanced by the persons above-mentioned.

Matters being thus far adjusted, a commission in the usual form was granted to captain Kidd, to take and seize pirates, and bring them to justice; but there was no special clause or proviso to restrain his conduct, or regulate the mode of his proceeding. Kidd was known to lord Bellamont, who once introduced him to the earl of Oxford, and another gentleman presented him to lord Romney. With regard to the other parties concerned, he was wholly unacquainted with them: and so ill was this affair conducted, that he had no private instructions how to act, but received his sailing orders from lord Bellamont, the purport of which were, that he should act agreeable to the letter of his commission.

A vessel was purchased and manned, and received the name of the Adventure Galley; and in this captain Kidd sailed for New-York, towards the close of the year 1695, and in his passage made prize of a French ship. From New-York he sailed to the Madeira Islands, thence to Bonavisto and St Jago, and from this last place to Madagascar. He now began to cruize at the entrance of the Red Sea, but not being successful in those latitudes, he sailed to Calicut, and there took a ship of one hundred and fifty tons burthen, which he carried to Madagascar, and there sold.

His prize being disposed of, he again put to sea, and at the expiration of five weeks took the Quedah merchant, a ship of above four hundred tons burthen, the master of which was an Englishman, named Wright, who had two Dutch mates on board, and a French gunner, but the crew, near ninety in number, consisted of Moors.

This ship he carried to St Mary's near Madagascar, where he burnt the Adventure Galley, belonging to his owners, and divided the lading of the Quedah merchant with his crew, taking forty shares to himself. They then went on board the last mentioned ship, and sailed for the

West-Indies. It is uncertain whether the inhabitants of the West-India islands knew that Kidd was a pirate; but he was refused refreshments at Anguilla and St. Thomas's, and therefore sailed to Mona, betwixt Porto Rico and Hispaniola, where, through the management of an Englishman named Bolton, he obtained a supply of provisions from Curassoa. He now bought a sloop of Bolton, in which he stowed great part of his ill-gotten effects, and left the Quedah merchant, with eighteen of his ship's company, in Bolton's care.

Kidd now sailed in the sloop, and touched at several places, where he disposed of a great part of his cargo, and then steered for Boston in New-England. In the interim Bolton sold the Quedah merchant to the Spaniards, and immediately sailed as a passenger in a ship for Boston, where he arrived a considerable time before Kidd, and gave information to lord Bellamont, then the resident governor, of what had happened.

On Kidd's arrival, therefore, he was seized by order of his lordship; when all he had to urge in his defence was, that he thought the Quedah merchant was a lawful prize, as she was manned with Moors; though there was no kind of proof that this vessel had committed any act of piracy.

Hereupon the earl of Bellamont immediately dispatched an account to England of the circumstances that had arisen, and requested that a ship might be sent for Kidd, who had committed several other notorious acts of piracy. On this the ship Rochester was sent to bring him to England; but this vessel, happening to be disabled, was obliged to return; a circumstance which greatly encreased a public clamour which had for some time subsisted respecting this business.

There is not the least doubt but that this clamour took its rise from party prejudice; yet it was carried to such a height, that the members of parliament for several places were instructed to move the house for an enquiry into the affair; and accordingly it was moved in the house of commons, that 'The letters patent, granted to the earl of Bellamont and others, respecting the goods taken from pirates, were dishonourable to the king, against the law of nations, contrary to the laws and statutes of this realm, an invasion of property, and destructive to commerce.' Though a negative was put on this motion, yet the enemies of lord Somers and the earl of Oxford continued to charge those noblemen with giving countenance to pirates; and it was even insinuated that the earl of Bellamont was not less culpable than his associates.

Accordingly another motion was made in the house of commons, to address his majesty, that 'Kidd might not be tried till the next sessions of parliament, and that the earl of Bellamont might be directed to send home all examinations and other papers relative to the affair.' This motion was carried, and the king complied with the request.

On Kidd's arrival in England he was sent for and examined at the bar of the house of commons, with a view to fix part of his guilt on the parties who had been concerned in sending him on the expedition: but nothing arose to criminate any of those distinguished persons. Kidd, who was in some degree intoxicated, made a very contemptible appearance at the bar of the house; on which a member, who had been one of the most earnest to have him examined, violently exclaimed, 'D——n this fellow, I thought he had been only a knave; but, unfortunately, he happens to be a fool likewise.'

At length Kidd was tried at the Old-Bailey, and was convicted on the clearest evidence: but neither at that time, nor afterwards, charged any of his employers with being privy to his infamous transactions.

Kidd was hanged at Execution-Dock on the 23rd day of May 1701; but a circumstance happened at his execution that will be worthy of recital. After he had been tied up to the gallows, the rope broke, and he fell to the ground; but being immediately tied up again, the ordinary, who had before exhorted him, desired to speak with him once more; and on this second application, entreated him to make the most careful use of the few farther moments thus providentially allotted him for the final preparation of his soul to meet its important change. These exhortations appeared to have the wished-for effect; and he was left, professing his charity to all the world, and his hopes of salvation through the merits of his redeemer.

Thus ended the life of captain Kidd, a man, who, if he had entertained a proper regard to the welfare of the public, or even to his own advantage, might have become an useful member of society, instead of a disgrace to it. The opportunities he had obtained of acquiring a compleat knowledge of the haunts of the pirates, rendered him one of the most proper men in the world to have extirpated this nest of villains; but his own avarice defeated the generous views of some of the greatest and most distinguished men of the age in which he lived. Hence we may learn the destructive nature of avarice, which generally counteracts all its own purposes. Captain Kidd might have acquired a fortune, and rendered a capital service to his country, in a point the most essential to its interests; but he appeared to be dead to all those generous sensations which do honour to humanity, and materially injured his country, while he was bringing final disgrace on himself.

The story of this wretched malefactor will effectually impress on the mind of the reader the truth of the old observation, that 'Honesty is the best policy.'

> Henceforth let honour's paths be trod,
>   Nor villains seek in vain
> To mock the sacred laws of God,
>   To give their neighbours pain.

Captain Kidd was in no sense a 'notable pirate', but his case has points of interest. The Lord Chancellor, Lord Somers, was the John Somers who was junior counsel in the great and famous case of the Seven Bishops. Macaulay's famous account of this trial will be well remembered. In the *History of England* he said: 'Somers had no advantages of birth or fortune; nor had he yet had any opportunity of distinguishing himself before the eyes of the public: but his genius, his industry, his great and various accomplishments were well known to a small circle of friends. . . . Somers rose last. He spoke little more than five minutes: but every word was full of weighty matter; and when he sat down his reputation as an orator and a constitutional lawyer was established.'

22

The usual place for the execution of pirates was Execution Dock at East Wapping. There was the usual public procession from New-gate to Wapping and the scaffold was erected at the very edge of the river. The hanging bodies of the dead pirates were left until they had been washed by several tides. This practice of exposing the bodies of criminals was widespread. Gibbets could be seen almost everywhere in London, for it was sometimes decreed that the criminal should be executed near the scene of his crime or at a cross-roads.

Singular Case of JOHN SMITH, called HALF-HANGED SMITH, who was convicted, but escaped Death in a most remarkable manner.

THIS malefactor was the son of a farmer at Malton about fifteen miles from the city of York, who bound him apprentice to a packer in London, with whom he served out his time, and afterwards worked as a journeyman. He then went to sea in a merchant-man, after which he entered on board a man of war, and was at the famous expedition against Vigo; but on the return from that expedition he was discharged.

He had not been long disengaged from the naval service when he enlisted as a soldier in the regiment of guards commanded by lord Cutts: but in this station he soon made bad connections, and engaged with some of his dissolute companions as a house-breaker.

On the 5th of December 1705, he was arraigned on four different indictments, on two of which he was convicted, and received sentence of death. While he lay under sentence he seemed very little affected with his situation, absolutely depending on a reprieve through the interest of his friends.

However, an order came for his execution on the 24th day of the same month, in consequence of which he was carried to Tyburn, where he performed his devotions, and was turned off in the usual manner; but when he had hung near fifteen minutes the people present cried out 'A reprieve!' Hereupon the malefactor was cut down, and being conveyed to a house in the neighbourhood, he soon recovered, in consequence of bleeding, and other proper applications.

When he perfectly recovered his senses he was asked what were his feelings at the time of execution; to which he repeatedly replied, in substance, as follows; that, 'when he was turned off, he, for some time, was sensible of very great pain, occasioned by the weight of his body, and felt his spirits in a strange commotion, violently pressing upwards: that having forced their way to his head, he, as it were, saw a great blaze or glaring light, which seemed to

24

go out at his eyes with a flash, and then he lost all sense of pain. That after he was cut down, and began to come to himself, the blood and spirits forcing themselves into their former channels, put him, by a sort of pricking or shooting, to such intolerable pain, that he could have wished those hanged who had cut him down.'

After this narrow escape from the grave, Smith pleaded to his pardon on the 20th of February: yet such was his propensity to evil deeds, that he returned to his former practices, and being again apprehended, was tried at the Old-Bailey for house-breaking; but some difficulties arising in the case, the jury brought in a special verdict, in consequence of which the affair was left to the opinion of the twelve judges, who determined in favour of the prisoner.

After this second extraordinary escape, he was a third time indicted; but the prosecutor happening to die before the day of trial, he once more obtained that liberty which his conduct shewed he had not deserved.

We have no account what became of this man after this third remarkable incident in his favour: but Christian charity inclines us to hope that he made a proper use of the singular dispensations of Providence evidenced in his own person.

History scarce affords a more extraordinary case than this of Smith: but let no one who reads this account of his triple escape from the gallows indulge a moment's inclination to the pursuit of illicit practices: since, in almost every instance but the present, the ways of vice assuredly lead to destruction; and we are not assured that they did not do so in his case; for the sequel of his life has not come to our knowledge.

This case is remembered solely for the extraordinary circumstances attending Smith's execution and the good fortune which attended him on his subsequent trials. The report says that 'he was turned off in the usual manner', and that he was hanging for fifteen minutes before he was cut down, but that nevertheless he recovered. This is not quite as remarkable as it sounds. For one thing, the process of hanging malefactors was not very scientific, and death was by no means instantaneous, as it is to-day. Consequently hangmen could be bribed not to do their duty, and when they were so bribed, it was not very difficult to arrange for the apparently hanged offender to be brought back to life. It was not altogether unusual for persons who were presumably dead when taken to the dissecting table, to come to life, and to be fully restored. There is quite a literature on this gruesome topic, some of it faintly humorous, if the word can be allowed, most of it intensely dramatic, and certainly full of human interest. It will be observed in many of the reports in this book that the act of hanging is described as being 'turned off', the condemned men are described as 'sufferers', and the gallows becomes 'the fatal tree'.

Narrative of the Cases of DANIEL DAMAREE, GEORGE PURCHASE, and FRANCIS WILLIS, who were tried for High-Treason.

WHEN the whig ministry of queen Anne were turned out of, or, in the modern phrase, had resigned their places, the tory ministry who succeeded them encouraged a young divine named Henry Sacheverell to enflame the passions of the public by preaching against the settlement made at the revolution, and inculcating all those doctrines which were then held as the favourite tenets of what was called the high church party. Sacheverell was a man of abilities, and eminently possessed of those kind of talents which are calculated to inspire such sentiments as the preacher wishes his auditors to possess.

It is well known to the public in general that Dr Sacheverell's discourses tended to instigate the people against the house of Hanover, and to insinuate the right of the pretender to the throne of these realms. This caused such a general commotion that it became necessary to bring him to a trial in some way; and contrary to all former practice respecting a man of his rank, he was tried before the house of peers, and being convicted, was silenced for three years.

However, in consequence of his insinuations, the passions of the populace were so excited, that they almost adored him as a prophet; and some of them were led to commit those outrages which gave rise to the following trials.

Messieurs Bradbury and Burgess, two dissenting ministers, having made themselves conspicuous by preaching in behalf of the revolution settlement, and freedom of sentiment in matters of religion, they became the immediate objects of the resentment of the mob. What arose in consequence hereof will appear from the following abstract of the trials of the criminals in question.

On the 19th of April, 1710, Daniel Damaree was indicted for being concerned with a multitude of men, to the number of five hundred, armed with swords and clubs, to levy war against the queen.

27

A gentleman deposed, that 'going through the Temple, he saw some thousands of people, who had attended Dr Sacheverell from Westminster-Hall: that some of them said they would pull down Dr Burgess's meeting-house that night.' Others differed as to the time of doing it, but all agreed on the act, and the meeting-house was demolished on the following night.

Captain Orril swore that on the first of March, hearing that 'the mob had pulled down Dr Burgess's meeting-house, he resolved to go among them, to do what service he could to government, by making discoveries.'

The captain going to Mr Bradbury's meeting, found the people plundering it, who obliged him to pull off his hat. After this he went to Lincoln's-Inn-Fields, where he saw a bonfire made of some of the materials of Dr Burgess's meeting-house, and saw the prisoner, who twirled his hat, and said 'D—n it, I will lead you on: G—d d—n me, we will have all the meeting-houses down; high church and Sacheverell, huzza!'

Another evidence proved that the prisoner headed part of the mob, some of whom proposed to go to the meeting-house in Wild-street; but this was objected to by others, who recommended going to Drury-lane, saying 'that meeting-house was worth ten of that in Wild-street'.

Joseph Collier swore that he saw the prisoner carry a brass sconce from Dr Burgess's meeting-house, and throw it into the fire in Lincoln's-Inn-Fields, huzzaing, and crying 'High church and Sacheverell.' There was other evidence to prove the concern that the prisoner had in these illegal acts; and several persons appeared in his behalf; but as in their testimony they contradicted each other, the jury could not credit their evidence; but brought in a special verdict.

GEORGE PURCHASE was indicted for levying war against the queen, &c. in the same manner that Damaree had been. On this trial captain Orril deposed, that after seeing Dr Burgess's meeting-house demolished, and a fire made in Lincoln's-Inn-Fields with some of the materials thereof, he met a party of the guards, whom he directed to go to

Drury-lane, where a bonfire was made of the pews, and other utensils; and that there was a great mob, which was dispersed by the guards: that the prisoner was very active, pushing at the breasts of the horses with a drawn sword: that this evidence asked him what he meant, telling him that in opposing the guard he opposed the queen, and would have persuaded him to put up his sword, and go home; but instead of taking this advice, he replied, 'D—n you, who are you? for High-Church and Sacheverell or no? I am, G—d d—n them all,' meaning the guards, 'for I am as good a man as any of them all': that he then called to the mob 'Come on, come on boys; I'll lead you on, I am for High-Church and Sacheverell, and I'll lose my life in the cause.'

Captain Orril farther deposed, that after this the prisoner ran resolutely with his sword in his hand, and made a full pass at the officer who commanded the guards; and if one of the guards had not given a spring and beat down his sword, he would have run the officer through the left flank: that the prisoner now retired a little lower, and the guards had by this time dispersed the mob, having knocked down forty or fifty of them in the action.

Richard Russell, one of the guards, deposed, that they were ordered by the serjeant to march into Drury-lane, and to return their bayonets and draw their swords; that when they came to Drury-lane, there was a bonfire with a large mob about it; that near the fire the horse were all drawn up into one line, with their tails against the wall, that none of the mob might come behind: that the prisoner then stood in the middle of the lane, huzzaing, and came up, and would have thrust himself between the horses; but the guards beat him off with the flats of their swords.

The prisoner produced some witnesses; but as what they said did not contradict the testimony of the evidences against him, their depositions had no weight. The jury were satisfied with the proofs that had arisen; but having a doubt respecting the points of law, they brought in a special verdict.

At the same time and place Francis Willis was tried for assisting in demolishing the meeting-house of Mr Bradbury in Fetter-lane, and burning the materials at a bonfire in Holborn; but was acquitted for want of sufficient evidence against him.

The verdicts respecting Damaree and Purchase being left special, their cases were argued in the court of King's-Bench in Westminster-Hall, the following term, before the lord chief justice Parker and the other judges; when, though every artifice of the law was made use of in their behalf, they were adjudged to be guilty; in consequence of which they received sentence of death, and were executed at Tyburn, on the 15th of June, 1710.

From the fate of these unhappy men we may learn the extreme folly of the lower orders of people interesting themselves in religious and political disputes. These offenders were watermen to the queen; but their loyalty to their sovereign and a proper regard to themselves, equally called on them to discharge the duties of their station with punctuality, and to leave the management of the church and state to those to whom they immediately belonged.

It is well known that, towards the close of the reign of queen Anne, political disputes were carried to a very unusual height in this kingdom. The body of the people were divided into two great factions, known by the names of High Church and Low Church: but though the church was the word, religion was almost out of the question; and the principal object of dispute was of a political kind. The question was, whether the house of HANOVER, or the family of STUART should sway the sceptre of these kingdoms. But it is astonishing to think that, even at that period, any son of the church of England could be so deluded as to think that a catholic prince, of an obnoxious family, proscribed by the laws of the land, could be a proper sovereign for a protestant people. The supposition carries absurdity in the face of it; yet such was the violence of the passions of the people, that the pretender had nearly half as many friends in the kingdom as the rightful heir to the throne!

With regard to the malefactors in question, their offence was of the most atrocious nature. Every man has an equal right to worship God according to the dictates of his own conscience. It was therefore in a high degree criminal to demolish the meeting-houses of the dissenting ministers. We should have no more spleen against a man for differing from us in religious sentiments, than for being taller, or shorter, or of a different complection from ourselves. It was a wise saying of a celebrated writer, that 'I would no more quarrel with a man for his differing in sentiments from me, than I would for the colour of his eye-brows.'

The operations of the mind, being free by nature, ought to be allowed the most unlimited scope. A good protestant will not quarrel with a Roman catholic for the peculiarities of his worship: he will only pity him for those parts of it which he thinks absurd, and endeavour to regulate his own worship by what he deems a purer standard.

Upon the whole, the fate of these malefactors ought to teach us obedience to our superiors, love to our neighbours, and duty to our God. There can be no peace of mind expected by those who do not live in the discharge of their duty; while those who perform it may reasonably hope for the serene comforts of a good conscience in this world, and console themselves with the hope of immortal happiness in the next.

It will be observed that a 'Special Verdict' was returned in this case, and the term perhaps needs a little explanation. The usual verdicts returned by a jury are, of course, 'Guilty' or 'Not Guilty'. But the jury have always had the right to return a 'special verdict', though the judges have never had power to compel them to do so. A 'special verdict' must state the facts themselves, and all the facts must be found by the jury to enable the Court to give judgment. 'Special verdicts' are now always dealt with in the Court of Criminal Appeal. They are unusual, but an important case in the law of bigamy, the case of the King v. Wheat and Stocks (1912, 2 K.B. 118), is a comparatively recent illustration. A 'special verdict' was found by a jury to the effect that the two prisoners reasonably believed on reasonable grounds that they had been divorced, and so were free to marry. The judge thereupon entered a verdict of 'Guilty' and sent the matter to the Court of Criminal Appeal. After much argument by the Attorney General on behalf of the Crown, and by counsel for the prisoner, it was held that the judge was right, and that it was no defence to a charge of bigamy that the prisoners reasonably believed that they were free to marry, when in fact they were not. This finding was arrived at on the grounds that the jury had no basis for belief that the prisoners had, in fact, made adequate inquiries, and does not alter a previous ruling in which a reasonable belief that a first marriage had been dissolved by death had been held to be a good defence.

Engraved for The Malefactors Register

Execution of John Hamilton Esq.r by the Machine called **THE MAIDEN**, at Edinburgh.

The Case of RICHARD THORNHILL, Esq. who was tried for the Murder of Sir CHOLMONDE-LEY DEERING in a Duel, and found guilty of Manslaughter.

SIR CHOLMONDELEY DEERING and Mr Thornhill were intimate acquaintance, and had dined together, on the 7th of April, 1711, in company of several other gentlemen, at the Toy at Hampton-Court, where a quarrel arose which occasioned the unhappy catastrophe that afterwards happened.

During the quarrel Sir Cholmondeley struck Mr Thornhill, and a scuffle ensuing, the wainscot of the room broke down, and Thornhill falling, the other stamped on him, and beat out some of his teeth. The company now interposing, Sir Cholmondeley, convinced that he had acted improperly, declared that he was willing to ask pardon: but Mr Thornhill said that asking pardon was not a proper retaliation for the injury that he had received; adding, 'Sir Cholmondeley, you know where to find me.' Soon after this the company broke up, and the prisoners went home in different coaches, without any further steps being taken towards their reconciliation.

On the 9th of April Sir Cholmondeley went to the Coffee-house at Kensington, and asked for Mr Thornhill, who not being there, he went to his lodgings, and the servant shewed him to the dining-room, to which he ascended with a brace of pistols in his hands, and soon afterwards Mr Thornhill coming to him, asked him if he would drink tea, which he declined, but drank a glass of small beer.

After this the gentlemen ordered a hackney-coach, in which they went to Tothill-Fields, and there advanced towards each other in a resolute manner, and fired their pistols almost in the same moment.

Sir Cholmondeley being mortally wounded, fell to the ground; and Mr Thornhill, after lamenting the unhappy

B

33

catastrophe, was going away, when a person stopped him, told him he had been guilty of murder, and took him before a justice of the peace, who committed him to prison.

On the 18th of May, 1711, Richard Thornhill, Esq. was indicted at the Old-Bailey sessions for this murder. In the course of the trial the above-recited facts were proved, and a letter was produced, of which the following is a copy.

Sir,   April 8th, 1711

'I shall be able to go abroad to-morrow morning, and desire you will give me a meeting with your sword and pistols, which I insist on. The worthy gentleman who brings you this, will concert with you the time and place. I think Tothill-Fields will do well; Hyde-Park will not, at this time of the year, being full of company.

I am,

Your humble Servant,

RICHARD THORNHILL

Mr Thornhill's servant swore that he believed this letter to be his master's hand-writing; but Mr Thornhill hoped the jury would not pay any regard to this testimony, as the boy had acknowledged in court that he never saw him write.

Mr Thornhill called several witnesses to prove how ill he had been used by Sir Cholmondeley: that he had languished some time of the wounds he had received, during which he could take no other sustenance than liquids, and that his life was in imminent danger.

Several persons of distinction testified that Mr Thornhill was of a peaceable disposition, and that, on the contrary, the deceased was of a remarkably quarrelsome temper. On behalf of Mr Thornhill it was farther deposed, that Sir Cholmondeley being asked if he came by his hurt through unfair usage, he replied 'No: poor Thornhill! I am sorry for him: this misfortune was my own fault, and of my own seeking: I heartily forgive him, and desire you all to take notice of it, that it may be of some service to him; and that one misfortune may not occasion another.'

The jury acquitted Mr Thornhill of the murder, but

found him guilty of manslaughter, in consequence of which he was burnt in the hand.

Of all the vices which disgrace our age and nation that of duelling is one of the most ridiculous, absurd, and criminal. Ridiculous, as it is a compliance with a custom that would plead fashion in violation of the laws of our country: Absurd, as it produces no test by which to determine on the merits of the point in dispute; for the aggrieved is equally liable to fall with the aggressor; and criminal (criminal indeed in the highest degree!) as it arises from pre-determined murder on each side. Gentlemen talk of the dignity of honour, and the sacredness of character, without reflecting that there can be no honour in deliberate murder, no purity of character in a murderer!

The man who sends a challenge to another, does but say, in other words, 'I am a professed murderer. I mean to send you into the other world, with all your imperfections on your head.—But I am a man of honour—though I will not take a purse, I will cut a throat. I will do every thing in my power to deprive you of life, and to make your friends and relations wretched for life. If I fall by your hands, my friends will be equally miserable:—but no matter—the laws of honour demand that we should be murderers, and we are both too wise to obey the laws of our God.'

Horrid practice! disgraceful to our country, and equally contrary to all Divine and human institutions!—It is to be hoped the time will come when the legislature shall decree that every man who is base enough to send a challenge shall be doomed to suffer death as a murderer. Let no fear be entertained that this can derogate from our national character of genuine courage. Nothing is more true than the observation of the poet, that

> Cowards are cruel, but the brave
> Love mercy, and delight to save.

Particulars respecting the LORDS and other Persons, who were tried on Account of the Rebellion in the year 1715.

WHEN, in pursuance of the act of settlement, king George the First succeeded to the throne of these realms, the earl of Mar, a Scottish nobleman, who had been deeply concerned with queen Anne's tory ministry, was deprived of all the places he held under the government; in revenge for which he retired to Scotland, and meditated a scheme to dethrone the king, and overturn the constitution.

Being assured of the assistance of a number of the Highlanders, he communicated his plan to some noblemen in Scotland and the north of England, who joined with him in sending an invitation to the Pretender to invade these kingdoms: and they also dispatched three men to London, to endeavour to enlist soldiers for the Pretender's service.

The names of these men were Robert Whitty, Felix O'Hara, and Joseph Sullivan; and though the business in which they engaged was of the most dangerous nature, yet they continued it for some time; but were at length apprehended, brought to trial, and being convicted, were executed at Tyburn on the 28th of May, 1715.

ROBERT WHITTY was born in Ireland, and having enlisted for a soldier when young, served in an English regiment in Spain, where being wounded, he was brought to England, and received the bounty of Chelsea-College as an out-pensioner.

FELIX O'HARA, who was about 29 years of age, was likewise an Irishman, and having lived some time in Dublin as a waiter at a tavern, he saved some money, and entered into business for himself; but that not answering as he could have wished, he came to London.

JOSEPH SULLIVAN was a native of Munster in Ireland, and about the same age as O'Hara. He had for some time served in the Irish brigades, but obtaining his discharge, he came to England, and was thought a fit agent to engage in the business which cost him and his companions their lives.

These men denied, at the time of their trial, that they had been guilty of any crime; and even at the place of execution they attempted to defend their conduct. They all died professing the Roman catholic religion.

Hence let us learn to abhor the pernicious doctrines of that church which could encourage subjects in the wish to dethrone their lawful sovereign; and may we be taught the force of the instruction 'Fear God, and honour the king.'

We will now continue the narrative of which this is but the introduction. The earl of Mar had resolved to keep his proceedings an absolute secret; but it is almost impossible for transactions of this nature to remain so; and information of what had passed having been transmitted to court, the king went to the house on the 20th of July, 1715, and having sent for the commons, informed both houses of parliament that he had received authentic intelligence of an intention formed by the Pretender to invade his kingdoms; and that he was apprehensive he had but too many abettors in this country.

Wherefore, that the ends of public justice might be speedily obtained, the king requested that the habeas corpus act might be suspended till the rebellion should be at an end. Accordingly the legislature suspended the said act, in consequence of which several suspected persons were taken into custody. The militia was now raised in different parts of the kingdom, the guards were encamped in Hyde-Park; a number of ships were ordered to guard the coasts, and other proper steps taken for the public security.

The earl of Mar was by this time at the head of three thousand men, with whom he marched from town to town in Scotland, proclaiming the Pretender by the title of James the Third. Some of the soldiers in the castle of Edinburgh having been bribed to assist some of the earl of Mar's men in getting over the walls by means of rope-ladders, they were dispatched to surprize the castle: but the lord justice clerk was so much on his guard, that this scheme was frustrated, and some of the parties concerned in it suffered death.

Chagrined by this circumstance, and hearing that the French king was just then dead, many of the rebels were for abandoning their enterprize till the arrival of the Pretender: but this intention did not take place; for on the 6th of October, 1715, Thomas Foster Esq. member of parliament for Northumberland, set up the Pretender's standard in that county, and being joined by several noblemen and gentlemen, they made an attempt to seize Newcastle, but did not succeed. They were afterwards joined by a body of the Scotch at Kelso, and after marching to different places, they came to Preston in Lancashire.

In the mean time the generals Carpenter and Wills marched into the North, but finding the rebels gone southwards, they went to Preston, which place the rebels intended to defend against the king's forces, whom they for some time annoyed by firing from the windows of the houses; but at length the royal troops were victorious, after the loss of about 150 men.

It is uncertain how many of the rebels were killed; but the number of prisoners was about fifteen hundred, among whom were the earl of Derwentwater[1], lord Widdrington[1]; the earls of Nithisdale, Winton, and Carnwarth; viscount Kenmure, and lord Nairn. The common soldiers among the rebels were imprisoned at Liverpool, and other places in that neighbourhood; but the above-mentioned noblemen, with other persons above the common rank, to the number of near three hundred, were brought to London.

They arrived at Highgate on the 14th of November, where they were met by a party of the foot-guards, and their arms being tied back with cords, their horses were led, each by a grenadier; and in this ignominious manner they were conducted to the metropolis; when the noblemen were committed to the Tower, and the rest to Newgate.

In the mean time a number of the Scotch rebels had marched to Perth, where they proclaimed the Pretender; in consequence of which John Duke of Argyle, who had been commissioned to raise forces, marched against, and

[1]These two were English peers; the rest Scotch.

came up with them, at Sheriffmuir near Dumblane, on the very day of the other engagement: and the rebellion would have been crushed, but that some of the duke's troops ran away on the first fire, and got to Stirling, about seven miles from the field of battle: however, the duke obtained a partial victory, by forcing the enemies lines with his dragoons.

The earl of Mar retired to Perth on the following day, proposing to cross the Forth, with a view to join the rebels in England: but a fleet lying opposite Edinburgh, prevented this design from being carried into execution.

About this period Sir John M'Kenzie having fortified the town of Inverness for the Pretender, lord Lovat,[1] at the head of his tenants, drove him from that place; a circumstance of great importance to the royal cause, as a communication was thereby opened between the Highlands, and the south of Scotland: and the earl of Seaforth, and the marquis of Huntly laid down their arms, in consequence of the earl of Sutherland having armed his tenants in support of government.

The rebels now went into winter quarters at Perth, and the duke of Argyle at Stirling; and the Pretender having landed at Peterhead, with six attendants only, met his friends at Perth on the 22d of December, and on the ninth of the following month made a public entry into the palace of Scone, and assuming the dignity of a sovereign prince, issued a proclamation for his coronation, and another for the assembling the states.

But this farce continued only for a very short time; for general Cadogan arriving with six thousand Dutch forces to the aid of the duke of Argyle, about the end of January, the latter marched towards Perth, but the rebels fled as soon as they heard he was advancing. For a while they had expectation of aid from France, in the hope of which the Pretender and his adherents went to Dundee, and thence

---

[1]The famed lord Lovat who was beheaded on Tower-Hill, for being concerned in the rebellion of 1745. What an inconsistency in this man's character!

to Montrose; but after waiting a while, and no aid arriving, they began to despair; and as the king's troops pursued them, the common men dispersed to their own habitations, and the Pretender, with the earl of Mar, and some others of his principal adherents, embarked on board a ship in the harbour of Montrose, and were soon landed in France, after having narrowly escaped an English fleet which lay on the coast of Scotland, through the extreme darkness of the night in which they embarked.

The disturbances in the north being thus at an end, both houses of parliament combined to shew their loyalty to their sovereign, and regard to the public welfare. Mr Foster was expelled from the house of commons, who unanimously agreed to impeach the seven lords, which was accordingly done.

These unhappy noblemen were informed of what had passed; and earl Cowper, lord high chancellor, being appointed lord high steward on the occasion, all the lords pleaded guilty to the indictment, except the earl of Winton: but they offered such pleas in extenuation of their crimes, as they thought might induce the king to extend his royal mercy to them: and the earl of Derwentwater hinted that the proceeding of the house of commons in the impeachment was out of the ordinary course of law.

In consequence of their having pleaded guilty, proclamation was made for silence, and the lord high steward passed sentence of death on them, prefacing the solemn sentence with the following affecting speech:

'James Earl of Derwentwater, William lord Widdrington, William earl of Nithisdale, Robert earl of Carnwarth, William viscount Kenmure, William lord Nairn.

'You stand impeached by the commons of Great-Britain in parliament assembled, of high treason, in traitorously imagining, and compassing the death of his most sacred majesty, and in conspiring for that end to levy a bloody and destructive war against his majesty, in order to depose and murder him; and in levying war accordingly, and proclaiming a Pretender to his crown to be king of these realms.

'Which impeachment, though one of your lordships, in the introduction to his plea, supposes to be out of the ordinary and common course of the law and justice, is yet as much a course of proceeding according to the common law, as any other whatsoever.

'If you had been indicted, the indictment must have been removed and brought before the house of lords, (the parliament sitting). In that case you had ('tis true) been accused only by the grand-jury of one county; in the present, the whole body of the commons of Great-Britain, by their representatives, are your accusers.

'And this circumstance is very observable (to exclude all possible supposition of hardship, as to the method of proceeding against you) that however all great assemblies are apt to differ on other points, you were impeached by the unanimous opinion of the house of commons, not one contradicting.

'They found themselves, it seems, so much concerned in the preservation of his most truly sacred majesty, and the Protestant succession (the very life and soul of these kingdoms) that they could not omit the first opportunity of taking their proper part, in order to so signal and necessary an act of his majesty's justice.

'And thus the whole body politic of this free kingdom, has in a manner rose up in its own defence, for the punishment of those crimes, which, it was rightly apprehended, had a direct tendency to the everlasting dissolution of it.

'To this impeachment you have severally pleaded, and acknowledged yourselves guilty of the high treason therein contained.

'Your pleas are accompanied with some variety of matter to mitigate your offences, and to obtain mercy.

'Part of which, as some of the circumstances said to have attended your surrender (seeming to be offered rather as arguments only for mercy, than any thing in mitigation of your preceding guilt) is not proper for me to take notice of.

'But as to the other part which is meant to extenuate the crimes of which you are convicted, it is fit I should take this occasion to make some observations to your lordships upon

B*   *41*

it, to the end that the judgment to be given against you may clearly appear to be just and righteous, as well as legal; and that you may not remain under any fatal error in respect of a greater judicature, by reflecting with less horror and remorse on the guilt you have contracted, than it really deserves.

'It is alledged by some of your lordships, that you engaged in this rebellion without previous concert or deliberation, and without suitable preparations of men, horses, and arms.

'If this should be supposed true, on some of your lordships averring it, I desire you to consider, that as it exempts you from the circumstance of contriving this treason, so it very much aggravates your guilt in that part you have undoubtedly borne in the execution of it.

'For it shews, that your inclinations to rebel were so well known (which could only be from a continued series of your words and actions) that the contrivers of that horrid design depended upon you, and therein judged rightly; that your zeal to engage in this treason was so strong, as to carry you into it on the least warning, and the very first invitation: that you would not excuse yourselves by want of preparation, as you might have done; and that rather than not have share in the rebellion, you would plunge yourselves into it, almost naked and unprovided for such an enterprize: in short, that your men, horses, and arms, were not so well prepared as they might, and would have been on longer warning; but your minds were.

'It is alledged also as an extenuation of your crimes, that no cruel or harsh action (I suppose is meant no rapine or plunder, or worse) has been committed by you.

'This may, in part only, be true: but then your lordships will at the same time consider, that the laying waste a tract of land, bears but a little proportion in point of guilt, compared with that crime of which you stand convicted; an open attempt to destroy the best of kings, to ruin the whole fabrick, and rase the very foundations of a government, the best suited of any in the world, to perfect the happiness, and support the dignity of human nature. The former offence causes but a mischief that is soon recovered, and is usually pretty much confined; the latter, had it succeeded, must have brought a lasting and universal destruction on the whole kingdom.

'Besides, much of this was owing to accident; your march was so hasty, partly to avoid the king's troops, and partly from a vain hope to stir up insurrections in all the counties you passed through, that you had not time to spread devastation, without deviating from your main, and, as I have observed, much worse design.

'Farther: 'Tis very surprizing that any concerned in this rebellion, should lay their engaging in it on the government's doing a necessary and usual act in like cases, for its preservation; the giving orders to confine such as were most likely to join in that treason: 'tis hard to believe that any one should rebel, merely to avoid being restrained from rebelling; or that a gentle confinement would not much better have suited a crazy state of health, than the fatigues and inconveniences of such long and hasty marches in the depth of winter.

'Your lordships rising in arms therefore, has much more justified the prudence and fitness of those orders, than those orders will in any wise serve to mitigate your treason. Alas! happy had it been for all your lordships, had you fallen under so indulgent a restraint!

'When your lordships shall in good earnest apply yourselves to think impartially on your case, surely you will not yourselves believe that it is possible, in the nature of the thing, to be engaged, and continue so long engaged, in such a difficult and laborious enterprize, through rashness, surprize, or inadvertency; or that had the attack at Preston been less sudden (and consequently the rebels better prepared to receive it) your lordships had been reduced the sooner, and with less, if not without any bloodshed.

'No, my lords, these, and such like, are artful colourings proceeding from minds filled with expectation of continuing in this world, and not from such as are preparing for their defence before a tribunal, where the thoughts of the heart, and the true springs and causes of actions must be laid open.

'And now, my lords, having thus removed some false colours you have used; to assist you yet farther in that necessary work of thinking on your great offence as you ought, I proceed to touch upon several circumstances that seem greatly to aggravate your crime, and which will deserve your most serious consideration.

'The divine virtues ('tis one of your lordships own epithets) which all the world, as well as your lordships, acknowledge to be in his majesty, and which you now lay claim to, ought certainly to have with-held your hands from endeavouring to depose, to destroy, to murder, that most excellent prince; so the impeachment speaks, and so the law construes your actions: and this is not only true in the notion of law, but almost always so in deed and reason. 'Tis a trite, but very true remark, that there are but few hours between kings being reduced under the power of pretenders to their crown, and their graves. Had you succeeded, his majesty's case would, I fear, have hardly been an exception to that general rule, since 'tis highly improbable that flight should have saved any of that illustrious and valiant family.

''Tis a further aggravation of your crime, that his majesty, whom your lordships would have dethroned, affected not the crown by force, or by the arts of ambition, but succeeded peaceably and legally to it; and on the decease of her late majesty without issue, became undoubtedly the next in course of descent capable of succeeding to the crown, by the law and constitution of this kingdom, as it stood declared some years before the crown was expressly limited to the house of Hanover. This right was acknowledged, and the descent of the crown limited or confirmed accordingly, by the whole legislature in two successive reigns, and more than once in the latter, which your lordships accomplices are very far from allowing would bias the nation to that side.

'How could it then enter into the heart of man, to think that private persons might with a good conscience endeavour to subvert such a settlement by running to tumultuary arms, and by intoxicating the dregs of the people, with contradictory opinions, and groundless slanders; or that God's

44

providence would ever prosper such wicked, such ruinous attempts? especially if in the next place it be considered, that the most fertile inventions on the side of the rebellion, have not been able to assign the least shadow of a grievance as the cause of it: to such poor shifts have they been reduced on this head, that for want of better colours, it has been objected, in a solemn manner, by your lordship's associates, to his majesty's government, that his people do not enjoy the fruits of peace as our neighbours have done since the last war: thus they first rob us of our peace, and then upbraid us that we have it not. 'Tis a monstrous rebellion that can find no fault with the government it invades, but what is the effect of the rebellion itself.

'Your lordships will likewise do well to consider what an additional burden your treason has made necessary on the people of this kingdom, who wanted, and were about to enjoy some respite: to this end, 'tis well known, that all new, or increase of taxes, were the last year carefully avoided, and his majesty was contented to have no more forces than were just sufficient to attend his person, and shut the gates of a few garrisons.

'But what his majesty thus did for the ease and quiet of his people, you most ungratefully turned to his disadvantage, by taking encouragement from thence, to endanger his and his kingdoms safety, and to bring oppression on your fellow-subjects.

'Your lordships observe, I avoid expatiating on the miseries of a civil war, a very large and copious subject; I shall but barely suggest to you on that head, that whatever those calamities may happen to be in the present case, all who are, at any time, or in any place, partakers in the rebellion (especially persons of figure and distinction) are in some degree responsible for them; and therefore your lordships must not hold yourselves quite clear from the guilt of those barbarities which have been lately committed, by such as are engaged in the same treason with you, and not yet perfectly reduced, in burning the habitations of their countrymen, and thereby exposing many thousands to cold and hunger in this rigorous season.

45

'I must be so just to such of your lordships, as profess the religion of the church of Rome, that you had one temptation, and that a great one, to engage you in this treason, which the others had not; in that, 'twas evident, success on your part must for ever have established Popery in this kingdom, and that probably you could never have again so fair an opportunity.

'But then, good God! how must those Protestants be covered with confusion, who entered into the same measures, without so much as capitulating for their religion (that ever I could find from any examination I have seen or heard) or so much as requiring, much less obtaining a frail promise, that it should be preserved, or even tolerated.

'It is my duty to exhort your lordships thus to think of the aggravations as well as the mitigations (if there be any) of your offences: and if I could have the least hopes, that the prejudices of habit and education would not be too strong for the most earnest and charitable entreaties, I would beg you not to rely any longer on those directors of your consciences, by whose conduct you have, very probably, been led into this miserable condition; but that your lordships would be assisted by some of those pious and learned divines of the church of England, who have constantly borne that infallible mark of sincere Christians, universal charity.

'And now, my lords, nothing remains, but that I pronounce upon you (and sorry I am that it falls to my lot to do it) that terrible sentence of the law, which must be the same that is usually given against the meanest offender in the like kind.

'The most ignominious and painful parts of it are usually remitted by the grace of the crown to persons of your quality; but the law, in this case, being deaf to all distinctions of persons, requires I should pronounce, and accordingly it is adjudged by this court;

'That you, James Earl of Derwentwater, William Lord Widdrington, William Earl of Nithisdale, Robert Earl of Carnwarth, William Viscount Kenmure, and William Lord Nairn, and every one of you, return to the prison of the

Tower from whence you came; from thence you must be
drawn to the place of execution; when you come there, you
must be hanged by the neck, but not till you be dead; for
you must be cut down alive, then your bowels must be
taken out, and burnt before your faces; then your heads
must be severed from your bodies, and your bodies divided
each into four quarters; and these must be at the king's
disposal. And God Almighty be merciful to your souls.'

After sentence thus passed, the lords were remanded back
to the Tower, and on the 18th of February orders were
sent to the lieutenant of the Tower and sheriffs for their
execution; and great solicitations were made in favour of
them, which did not only reach the court, but came down to
the two houses of parliament, and petitions were delivered
in both, which being backed by some, occasioned debates:
that in the house of commons arose no higher than to
occasion a motion for adjournment, thereby to prevent any
further interposition there; but the matter in the house of
peers was carried on with more success, where their petitions were delivered and spoke to, and it was carried by
nine or ten voices, that the same should be received and
read. And the question was put, whether the king had power
to reprieve in case of impeachment? which being carried in
the affirmative, a motion was made to address his majesty
to desire him to grant a reprieve to the lords under sentence;
but the movers thereof only obtained this clause, viz. 'To
reprieve such of the condemned lords as deserve his mercy;
and that the time of the respite should be left to his majesty's
discretion.'

To which address his majesty replied,

'That on this, and other occasions, he would do what he
thought most consistent with the dignity of his crown, and
the safety of his people.'

The great parties they had made, as was said, by the
means of money, and also the rash expressions too common
in the mouths of many of their friends, as if the government
did not dare to execute them, did not a little contribute to
the hastening their execution: for on the same day the

address was presented, the 23rd of February, it was resolved in council, that the earl of Derwentwater, and the lord Kenmure should be beheaded; and the earl of Nithisdale apprehending he should be included in the warrant, made his escape the evening before, in a woman's riding-hood, supposed to have been conveyed to him by his mother on a visit.

In the morning of the 24th of February three detachments of the life guards went from Whitehall to Tower-Hill, and having taken their stations round the scaffold, the two lords were brought from the Tower at ten o'clock, and being received by the sheriffs at the bar, were conducted to the Transport-Office on Tower-Hill; and at the expiration of about an hour, the earl of Derwentwater sent word that he was ready; on which Sir John Fryer, one of the sheriffs, walked before him to the scaffold, and when there, told him he might have what time he pleased to prepare himself for death.

His lordship desired to read a paper which he had written, the substance of which was, that he was sorry for having pleaded guilty; that he acknowledged no king but James the Third, for whom he had an inviolable affection, and that these kingdoms would never be happy till the antient constitution was restored; and he wished his death might contribute to that desirable end. His lordship professed to die a Roman catholic, and in the postscript to his speech, said, 'If that prince, who now governs, had given me life, I should have thought myself obliged never more to have taken up arms against him.'

Sir John Fryer desiring to have the paper, he said he had sent a copy of it to his friends, and then delivered it. He then read some prayers out of two small books, and kneeled down to try how the block would fit his neck. This being done, he had again recourse to his devotions, and having told the executioner that he forgave him, and likewise forgave all his enemies, he directed him to strike when he should repeat the words 'sweet Jesus' the third time.

He then kneeled down, and said 'sweet Jesus! receive my spirit; sweet Jesus! be merciful to me; sweet Jesus'—and appeared to be proceeding in his prayer, when his head was struck off at one blow; and the executioner taking it up, exhibited it at the four corners of the scaffold, saying, 'Behold the head of a traitor:—God save king George.'

The body was now wrapped up in black bays, and being carried to a coach, was delivered to the friends of the deceased: and the scaffold having been cleared, fresh bays put on the block, and straw-dust strewed, that none of the blood might appear, lord Kenmure was conducted to the scaffold.

His lordship, who was a Protestant, was attended by two clergymen; but he declined saying much, telling one of them that he had prudential reasons for not delivering his sentiments; which were supposed to arise from his regard to lord Carnwarth, who was his brother in law, and was then interceding for the royal mercy; as his talking in the way that lord Derwentwater had done, might be supposed to injure his lordship with those most likely to serve him.

Lord Kenmure having finished his devotions, declared that he forgave the executioner, to whom he made a present of eight guineas. He was attended by a surgeon, who drew his finger over that part of the neck where the blow was to be struck; and being executed as lord Derwentwater had been, his body was delivered to the care of an undertaker.

George earl of Winton, not having pleaded guilty with the other lords, was brought to his trial on the 15th of March, when the principal matter urged in his favour was, that he had surrendered at Preston in consequence of a promise from general Wills to grant him his life: in answer to which it was sworn, that no promise of mercy was made, but that the rebels surrendered at discretion.

The earl of Winton having left his house, with fourteen or fifteen of his servants, well mounted and armed;—his joining the earl Carnwarth and lord Kenmure; his proceeding with the rebels through the various stages of their march, and his surrendering with the rest, were circumstances fully proved: notwithstanding which his council moved in arrest of judgment: but the plea on which this motion was founded being thought insufficient, his peers unanimously found him guilty; and then the lord high steward pronounced sentence on him, after having addressed him in the following forcible terms:

'George Earl of Winton, I have acquainted you, that your peers have found you guilty; that is, in the terms of the law, convicted you of the high treason whereof you stand impeached; after your lordship has moved in arrest of judgment, and their lordships have disallowed that motion, their next step is to proceed to judgment.

'The melancholy part I am to bear, in pronouncing that judgment upon you, since it is his majesty's pleasure to appoint me to that office, I dutifully submit to it; far, very far, from taking any satisfaction in it.

'Till conviction, your lordship has been spoke to without the least prejudice, or supposition of your guilt; but now it must be taken for granted, that your lordship is guilty of the high treason whereof you stand impeached.

'My lord, this your crime is the greatest known to the law of this kingdom, or of any other country whatsoever, and it is of the blackest and most odious species of that crime; a conspiracy and attempt, manifested by an open rebellion, to depose and murder that sacred person, who sustains, and is the majesty of the whole; and from whom, as from a fountain of warmth and glory, are dispersed all the honours, all the dignity of the state; indeed the lasting and operative life and vigour of the laws, which plainly subsist by a due administration of the executive power.

'So that attempting this precious life, is really striking at the most noble part, the seat of life, and spring of all motion in this government; and may therefore properly be called a design to murder not only the king, but also the body politick of this kingdom.

'And this is most evidently true in your lordship's case, considering that success in your treason must infallibly have established Popery, and that never fails to bring with it a civil as well as ecclesiastick tyranny: which is quite another sort of constitution than that of this kingdom, and cannot take place till the present is annihilated.

'This your crime (so I must call it) is the more aggravated, in that where it proceeds so far as to take arms openly, and to make an offensive war against lawful authority, 'tis generally (as in your case) complicated with the horrid and crying sin of murdering many, who are not only innocent, but meritorious: and if pity be due (as I admit it is in some degree) to such as suffer for their own crimes; it must be admitted a much greater share of compassion is owing to them, who have lost their lives merely by the crimes of other men.

'As many as have so done in the late rebellion, so many murders have they to answer for, who promoted it; and your lordship in examining your conscience, will be under a great delusion, if you look on those who fell at Preston, Dumblain, or elsewhere, on the side of the laws, and defence of settled order and government, as slain in lawful war, even judging of this matter by the law of nations.

'Alas! my lord, your crime of high treason is yet made redder, by shedding a great deal of the best blood in the kingdom; I include in this expression the brave common soldiers, as well as those gallant and heroic officers, who continued faithful to death, in defence of the laws: for sure but little blood can be better than that, which is shed while it is warm, in the cause of the true religion, and the liberties of its native country.

'I believe it, notwithstanding the unfair arts and industry used, to stir up a pernicious excess of commiseration toward such as have fallen by the sword of justice (few, if compared with the numbers of good subjects, murdered from doors and windows at Preston only) the life of one honest loyal subject is more precious in the eye of God, and all considering men, than the lives of many rebels and parricides.

'This puts me in mind to observe to your lordship, that there is another malignity in your lordship's crime (open rebellion) which consists in this, that it is always sure of doing hurt to a government, in one respect, though it be defeated; (I will not say, it does so on the whole matter).

'For if the offence is too notorious to be let pass unobserved, by any connivance; then is government reduced to this dilemma: if it be not punished, the state is endangered by suffering examples to appear, that it may be attacked with impunity; if it be punished, they who are publickly or privately favourers of the treason (and perhaps some out of mere folly) raise undeserved clamours of cruelty against those in power; or the lowest their malice flies, is to make unseasonable, unlimited, and injudicious encomiums, upon mercy and forgiveness (things rightly used, certainly of the greatest excellence).

'And this proceeding, it must be admitted, does harm, with silly and undistinguishing people. So that the rebels have the satisfaction of thinking they hurt the government a little even by their fall.

'The only, but true consolation, every wise government has, in such a case (after it has tempered justice with mercy, in such proportion as sound discretion directs, having always a care of the public safety above all things) is this; that such like seeds of unreasonable discontents, take root on very shallow soil only; and that therefore, after they have made a weak shoot, they soon wither and come to nothing.

'It is well your lordship has given an opportunity of doing the government right, on the subject of your surrender at Preston.

'How confidently had it been given out by the faction, that the surrender was made on assurances, at least hopes, insinuated of pardon. Whereas the truth appears to be, that fear was the only motive to it: the evil day was deferred; and the rebels rightly depended, fewer would die at last by the measures they elected, than if they had stood an assault. They were awed by the experienced courage, discipline, and steadiness of the king's troops, and by the superior genius and spirit of his majesty's commanders, over those of the rebels: so that in truth, they were never flattered with any other terms, than to surrender as rebels and traitors; their lives only to be spared till his majesty's pleasure should be known.

'It was indeed a debt due to those brave commanders and soldiers (to whom their king and country owe more than can be well expressed) that their victory should be vindicated to the present and future ages, from untrue detraction, and kept from being sullied by the tongues of rebels and their accomplices, when their arms could no longer hinder it.

"Tis hard to leave this subject without shortly observing, that this engine which sets the world on fire, a lying tongue, has been of prodigious use to the party of the rebels, not only since, and during the rebellion, but before, while it was forming, and the rebels preparing for it.

'False facts, false hopes, and false characters, have been the greater half of the scheme they set out with, and yet seem to depend upon.

'It has been rightly observed, your lordship's answer does not so much as insist, with any clearness, on that which only could excuse your being taken in open rebellion; that is, you was forced into it, remained so under a force, and would have escaped from it, but could not.

'If you had so insisted, it has been clearly proved that that had not been true; for your lordship was active and forward in many instances, and so considerable in military capacity among your fellow-soldiers, as to command a squadron. These, and other particulars, have been observed by the managers of the house of commons, and therefore I shall not pursue them further, but conclude this introduction to the sentence, by exhorting your lordship with perfect charity, and much earnestness, to consider that now the time is come, when the veil of partiality should be taken from your eyes (it must be so when you come to die) and that your lordship should henceforward think with clearness and indifference (if possible) which must produce in you a hearty detestation of the high crime you have committed; and, being a Protestant, be very likely to make you a sincere penitent, for your having engaged in a design that must have destroyed the holy religion you profess, had it taken effect.

'Nothing now remains, but that I pronounce upon you that sentence which the law ordains, and which sufficiently shews, what thoughts our ancestors had of the crime of which your lordship is now convicted, viz. "That you George Earl of Winton, &c." '

Soon after the passing this sentence the earls of Winton

and Nithisdale found means to escape out of the Tower; and Messrs Foster and M'Intosh escaped from Newgate: but it was supposed that motives of mercy and tenderness in the prince of Wales, afterwards George the second, favoured the escape of all these gentlemen.

This rebellion occasioned the untimely death of many other persons. Five were executed at Manchester, six at Wigan, and eleven at Preston; but a considerable number were brought to London, and being arraigned in the court of exchequer, most of them pleaded guilty, and suffered the utmost rigour of the law.

We are fortunate in possessing a contemporary account of Derwentwater's trial and execution in *The Diary of Dudley Ryder* (Methuen and Co. Ltd., 1939), which covers the years 1715–16, when Ryder, who eventually became Attorney-General and Chief Justice of the King's Bench, was a young student at the Middle Temple.

Speaking of Derwentwater's capture at Preston he says:

'Mr Owen told us with relation to our victory at Preston that the surrender of the rebels was gained by General Wills's bullying and swearing rather than anything else. After the first attack when Wills had retired and invested the town, Derwentwater comes out with a trumpet and was brought into Wills's tent and told him that they were willing to stop the effusion of blood and therefore offered to surrender the town in twelve day's time if they had no relief. Upon this Wills swore a great oath and pulls his watch out of this pocket, and swore that if they did not surrender within twelve hours time he would cut every man of them in pieces, and swore he would not give them a moment's time longer. This he confirmed by the most bitter oaths, curses and execrations in the world, that Lord Derwentwater was perfectly terrified so that his very lips trembled. . . . In short, he swore so violently and with such a terrible air . . . that before the twelve hours expired they surrendered.'

Here is his diary for Thursday, 9th February:

'Mr Porter came to call me to go to Westminster Hall to hear the sentence passed on the six impeached lords that pleaded guilty. We bought two tickets at a crown apiece and got into the gallery, where we had a full view of the whole assembly which was the largest I ever saw in my life, the Lords and Commons being there, and a greater number of spectators than both together. I thought it one of the noblest sights my eyes ever beheld. The Lords came to their places, which was on the bottom, in their robes, which was a very magnificent sight, and after them the Lord High Steward, who was my Lord Chancellor Cowper, came in attended by twelve maces. He first took his place upon the woolpacks where he usually sits as Chancellor, and then the Commission to make him High Steward was read. After which he had a white wand delivered to him, and he went to the Chair placed under the throne and sat down and then he commenced High Steward. Then the Crier spoke aloud that the lieutenant of the Tower should bring his prisoners to the Bar, and the Lord High Steward after they were come, spoke to them and told them they were impeached of High Treason and the articles of impeachment were read aloud by the Crier, and then their several answers were read also. Then the order of the day for giving speeches was read, and the Lord High Steward asked the prisoners whether they had anything to offer in arrest of judgment why sentence should not pass upon them. Upon which they each of them made speeches. Lord Derwentwater began first and so the rest. Being behind them I could not hear much of what was said, but in general they pleaded for mercy and offered nothing in arrest of judgment. When this was done, the Lord High Steward told them and the House of Lords he thought he was obliged to make such observations upon the pleas and answers of the impeached lords as might vindicate the justice of the sentence that was to be passed upon them. My Lord spoke his speech with a great deal of temperance and with an excellent delivery and voice, and at last pronounced the sentence in a most solemn and tender manner.'

The sentence which is here set out was described by the Lord High Steward as 'that terrible sentence of the law', but he added, 'the most painful and ignominious parts of it are usually remitted by the grace of the crown to persons of your quality.' The horrible parts of this dreadful sentence were usually mitigated in practice, and in the case of Lord Derwentwater we have again the diary of Dudley Ryder. His entry for Friday, 24th February, 1716, reads:

'So went to Tower Hill and got a convenient place to see the execution. The whole hill was full of people that I never saw so large a collection of people in my life, and a vast circle was made by the Horse Guards round about the scaffolds and a great many foot guards in the middle. At length Lord Derwentwater and Kenmure came in two hackney coaches from the Tower to the transport office over against the scaffolds. I saw them both. Lord Derwentwater looked with a melancholy aspect, but Lord Kenmure looked very bold and unconcerned. Lord Derwentwater was executed first. After he was brought upon the stage and was saluted by several officers and others that were there, he prayed and spoke to them and told them, as I am informed, that since he was to die he was sorry that he pleaded guilty, for he was an innocent man, for he knew no King but King James the Third. He was a papist and therefore had no priest along with him. He seemed to behave himself very well and make his exit decently enough, though with but a melancholy and pious aspect. Sir John Fryer, one of the Sheriffs of London, attended both of them upon the scaffold. The executioner struck off his head with one blow, and then held it in his hand and showed it to the people and said "Here is the head of a traitor." "God Bless King George." His head and body were wrapped in a black cloth and put into the coach in which he came and carried back to the Tower.'

Then Ryder describes the beheading of Lord Kenmure 'who looked with all the courage and resolution of an old Roman', and adds an interesting passage about his emotions when witnessing this dreadful scene. He says:

'It is very moving and affecting to see a man that was but this moment in perfect health and strength sent the next into another world. Few that die in their bed have so easy an end of life. But then what must be the thoughts of a man in that condition, that could count every moment before his death and reflect to the very last, it is impossible to conceive, because one cannot put one-self into that form and temper of mind which these circumstances will necessarily put a man into. The pain of dying is nothing. It is but like a flash of lightning, begun and ended in the compass of a thought. Life itself is attended in every one with much more grievous pains. Why then are we afraid to die? Is it the loss of the pleasures of life, of all the agreeable things in which we delighted? That cannot be all. No, the strange uncertain dark prospect that is before us terrifies us and makes afraid to be we know not what and go we know not where.'

This case illustrates the tendency of the eighteenth century to be extremely severe in the punishments decreed but to mitigate the punishments actually imposed.

Case of JOHN HAMILTON, Esq. who was tried in Scotland for Murder, and beheaded.

THIS offender was born in the county of Clydesdale, and was related to the ducal family of Hamilton. His parents, to whom he was an only son, sent him to Glasgow to study the law; but the young gentleman's disposition leading him to the profession of arms, his friends exerted their interest to procure a commission, but the intervention of the crime of which we are about to relate the particulars, prevented their generous intention taking effect.

Young Hamilton soon becoming connected with some abandoned young gentlemen at Edinburgh, he lost considerable sums at gaming; and going to his parents for more, they supplied him for the present, but said they would not advance him any farther sums while he continued his dissipated course of life.

Being possessed of this money, Hamilton went to a village near Glasgow, to meet his companions at a public-house kept by Thomas Arkle. Having drank and gamed for several successive days and nights, Hamilton's companions left him while he was asleep, leaving him to discharge the bill, which exceeding his ability, a quarrel ensued between him and Arkle, and while they contended, Arkle stripped Hamilton's sword from the scabbard. The latter immediately ran away, but finding he had no scabbard to his sword, he instantly went back to the house, when Arkle calling him several scandalous names, he stabbed him so that he instantly expired.

The daughter of Arkle being present, attempted to seize Hamilton; in doing which she tore off the skirt of his coat, which was left on the floor, together with his sword, on his effecting a second escape. This daughter of Arkle was almost blind; but her keeping the sword and the skirt of the coat, proved the means of bringing Hamilton to justice.

The murderer having gone to Leith, embarked on board a ship, and landed in Holland, where he continued two years; but his parents dying in the interval, he returned to

57

Scotland, when he was taken into custody on account of the murder.

On his trial he pleaded that he was intoxicated at the time the fact was committed, to which he was instigated by the extreme ill usage he had received from Arkle. The jury, not allowing the force of these arguments, found him guilty, and he was sentenced to be beheaded by the MAIDEN, to give a description of which instrument may be grateful to our readers.

The town of Halifax in Yorkshire having been antiently famous for the manufacture of woollen cloths, a law was made for the protection of the property of the manufacturers, by which it was ordained that persons convicted of stealing cloth from the tenter-grounds, should be executed immediately after being convicted before two justices of the peace.[1]

The machine by which persons thus convicted were executed, was constructed in the following manner: 'Two strong wooden beams were fixed on a scaffold, and between them, in a transverse form, ran another beam, to the lower side of which was fixed a sharp instrument in the form of a chopping-knife, with a large quantity of lead on the upper part. The criminal put his neck between the two side-beams, and the cross-beam being drawn by a pulley, was suffered to fall down; and the head was severed from the body in a moment.'

The earl of Morton, regent of Scotland, returning from the court of Queen Elizabeth in the year 1574, saw this machine at Halifax, and had a model taken of it, with a view to the execution of such of the Scottish nobility as should oppose his measures; but it happened that his lordship was the first who suffered by this mode of execution; whence it was called the MAIDEN.

After this many persons of rank in Scotland were executed by this machine; but Mr Hamilton, of whom we are

[1]Whatever necessity there might appear for enacting the law in question, we cannot but lament that any Englishman should suffer without the formality of a trial by jury; a practice that is the boast of this country, and the envy of others.

now writing, was the last who yielded his life in this manner; and the instrument of death is now kept in a room adjacent to the council-chamber of Edinburgh.

After Mr Hamilton received sentence of death, his friends made great interest to procure a pardon; but their endeavours proving ineffectual, he suffered death, by the mode abovementioned, on the 30th of June, 1716.

At the place of execution he owned that he had killed Arkle, but presumed to think he was justified on the principle of self-defence.

Mr Hamilton's case will teach us to reflect on the sad consequences of keeping bad company, and an attachment to gaming. But for these vices, he might have lived happy in himself, and a credit to the worthy family from which he was descended. The youth who will devote those hours to the gaming-table, which he ought to employ in the honest advancement of his fortune, can expect only to be reduced to beggary at the best: but in a thousand instances, as well as the present, the consequences have been much more fatal.

Hence let young gentlemen learn to shun the gaming-table as they would a pestilence; to proceed in the plain path of honour and integrity, and to know that there can be no true happiness in a departure from the line of virtue!

This case is interesting only for the fact that Hamilton was the last person to be beheaded in Scotland by the machine known as The Maiden. The Halifax gibbet to which the case makes reference was in use in Yorkshire until 1650. Macaulay makes reference to its use in Scotland as 'The rude old guillotine of Scotland called The Maiden.'

Circumstances respecting the Trial and Execution of JOHN PRICE, otherwise JACK KETCH, who was hanged for Murder; with some particulars of his life.

JOHN PRICE was indicted at the Old Bailey on the 24th of April, 1718, for the murder of Elizabeth, the wife of William White, on the 13th of the preceding month.

In the course of the evidence it appeared that Price met the deceased near ten at night in Moorfields, and attempted to ravish her; but the poor woman (who was the wife of a watchman, and sold gingerbread in the streets,) doing all in her power to resist his villainous attacks, he beat her so cruelly that streams of blood issued from her eyes and mouth, broke one of her arms, beat out some of her teeth, bruised her head in a most dreadful manner, forced one of her eyes from the socket, and otherwise so ill-treated her that the language of decency cannot describe it.

Some persons, hearing the cries of the unhappy creature, repaired to the spot, took Price into custody, and lodged him in the watch-house; and conveyed the woman to a house where a surgeon and nurse were sent for to attend her. Being unable to speak, she answered the nurse's questions by signs, and in that manner described what had happened to her. She died after having languished four days.

The prisoner, on his trial, denied being guilty of the fact; and said that as he was crossing Moorfields he found something lying in his way; that he kicked at it, but discovering that it was a woman, he lifted her up, but she could not stand on her legs: and he said that he was taken into custody while he was thus employed. This defence, however, could not be credited, from what some former evidences had sworn; and the jury did not hesitate to find him guilty.

After sentence of death was passed on him he abandoned himself to the drinking of spirituous liquors[1] to such a

---

[1] Since the fate of this man we have had a law to prevent the carrying spirituous liquors into prisons.

degree as rendered him totally incapable of all the exercises of devotion. He obstinately denied the fact till the day of his execution, when he confessed that he had been guilty of it; but said that the crime was perpetrated when he was in a state of intoxication. He was executed in Bunhill-Fields on the 31st of May, 1718, and, in his last moments, begged the prayers of the multitude, and hoped they would take warning by his untimely end. He was afterwards hung in chains near Holloway.

This offender was born in the parish of St Martin in the Fields, and while he was very young his father was blown up at the demolishing of Tangier. His mother being left in circumstances of distress, was not able to give him a proper education; but she put him apprentice to a dealer in rags. Having served about two years, his master died, and he soon afterwards ran away from his mistress, and got employment in loading waggons with rags for other dealers. After this he went to sea, and served on board several ships in the royal navy for the space of about eighteen years; but at length he was paid off, and discharged from the service.

The place of public executioner becoming vacant by death, he accepted of it, and might have continued in it but for his own extravagance; for spending more money than his income, he ran in debt; and one day, as he was returning from an execution at Tyburn, he was arrested in Holborn for a trifling sum. However, he discharged this debt, and the costs, partly with a small sum of money he had in his pocket, and partly by the produce of three suits of cloaths, which he had taken from the bodies of poor wretches who had been that day executed.

Soon after this two other writs were taken out against him, when having no money, nor being able to procure bail, he was obliged to go to the Marshalsea Prison, where he continued till after the following sessions at the Old Bailey, when William Marvel was appointed executioner in his stead. Having continued some time longer in the Marshalsea, he and a fellow-prisoner broke a hole in the wall, through which they made their escape: and soon after this

Price committed the horrid murder for which his life paid
the forfeit.

One would imagine that the dreadful scenes of calamity
to which this man had been witness, if they had not taught
him humanity, would at least have given him wisdom
enough not to have perpetrated a crime that must necessarily
bring him to a similarly fatal end to what he had so often
seen of others: but perhaps his profession tended rather to
harden his mind than otherwise.

The murder of which Price was guilty appears to have
been one of the most barbarous and unprovoked we ever
remember to have read of: and his pretence that he was
drunk when he perpetrated it was no sort of excuse; since
drunkenness itself is a crime, and one which frequently
leads to the commission of others.

The lesson to be learnt from the fate of this man is to
moderate our passions of every kind; and to live by the rules
of temperance and sobriety. We are told, from the best
authority, that 'hands that shed innocent blood are an
abomination to the Lord.'

'Jack Ketch' was the name applied by the public to every hangman,
but there was a real Jack Ketch who attained to the dignity of an
entry in the *Dictionary of National Biography*. He published a
pamphlet to vindicate his conduct at the execution of Lord Russell
in 1683, John Evelyn in the Diary having referred to the execution
as being done in a 'butcherly manner'. Ketch was also the executioner
at the death of Monmouth in 1685, and on the scaffold Monmouth
spoke to him about the manner of Russell's execution. This appears
to have unnerved Ketch altogether, so that, according to Macaulay,
he was finally compelled to use a knife to sever the head. He also
took part in the dreadful punishments of Titus Oates and his col-
leagues. There are many books and pamphlets about hangmen in
general, and Jack Ketch in particular. On formal occasions he was
referred to as 'John Ketch, Esq.,' and this title was claimed by all the
hangmen who followed Brandon, the executioner of Charles the
First, because Brandon had been granted a coat of arms.

Singular Case of CATHERINE JONES, who was tried for Bigamy, and acquitted.

CATHERINE JONES was indicted at the Old Bailey, on the 5th of September, 1719, for marrying Constantine Boone during the life of her former husband, John Rowland.

Proof was made that she was married to Rowland, in the year 1713, at a house in the Mint, Southwark, and that six years afterwards, while her husband was abroad, she was again married, in the same house, to Constantine Boone; but Rowland, soon returning to England, caused his wife to be indicted for this crime.

The prisoner did not hesitate to acknowledge the double marriage, but insisted that the latter was illegal, as Boone was an hermaphrodite, and had been shewn as such at Southwark and Bartholomew fairs, and at other places.

To prove this a person swore that he knew Boone when a child, that his (or *her*) mother dressed *it* in girls apparel, and caused it to be instructed in needle-work, till it had attained the age of twelve years, when it *turned man, and went to sea*.

These last words were those of the deposition; and the fact was confirmed by Boone, who appeared in court, acknowledged being an hermaphrodite, and having been publickly shewn in that character.

Other witnesses deposed that the female sex prevailed over that of the male in the party in question; on which the jury acquitted the prisoner.

It is impossible to describe how much this affair was the subject of the public conversation at, and long after, the time that it happened: and it would be idle to make any serious remarks on it. We can only express our astonishment that an hermaphrodite should think of such a glaring absurdity as the taking a wife!

Particulars respecting WILLIAM SPIGGOT, and THOMAS PHILLIPS, who were hanged for robbing on the Highway.

AT the sessions held at the Old-Bailey in the month of January 1720, William Spiggot and Thomas Phillips were indicted for committing several robberies on the highway; but they refused to plead unless the effects taken from them when they were apprehended were returned: but this being directly contrary to an act of the 4th and 5th year of king William and queen Mary, entitled, 'An act for encouraging the apprehending of highwaymen,' the court informed them that their demand could not be complied with.

Still however, they refused to plead, and no arguments could convince them of the absurdity of such an obstinate proceedure: on which the court ordered that the judgment ordained by law in such cases should be read, which is to the following purpose:

'That the prisoner shall be sent to the prison from whence he came, and put into a mean room, stopped from the light, and shall there be laid on the bare ground, without any litter, straw or other covering, and without any garment about him, except something to hide his privy members. He shall lie upon his back, his head shall be covered, and his feet shall be bare. One of his arms shall be drawn with a cord to one side of the room, and the other arm to the other side; and his legs shall be served in the like manner. Then there shall be laid upon his body as much iron or stone as he can bear, and more. And the first day after he shall have three morsels of barley bread, without any drink; and the second day, he shall be allowed to drink as much as he can, at three times, of the water that is next the prison-door, except running water, without any bread; and this shall be his diet till he dies: and he, against whom this judgment shall be given, forfeits his goods to the King.'[1]

[1] By an act passed in 1772 it is determined that persons refusing to plead shall be deemed guilty, as if convicted by a jury: an alteration that does honour to modern times.

The reading of this sentence producing no effect, they were ordered back to Newgate, there to be pressed to death: but when they came into the press-room, Phillips begged to be taken back to plead, a favour that was granted, though it might have been denied to him: but Spiggot was put under the press, where he continued half an hour with three hundred and fifty pounds weight on his body, but, on the addition of fifty pounds more, he likewise begged to plead.

In consequence hereof they were brought back and again indicted, when the evidence being clear and positive against them, they were convicted, and received sentence of death, in consequence of which they were executed at Tyburn on the 8th of February, 1720.

WILLIAM SPIGGOT, who was about twenty-seven years of age when he suffered, was a native of Hereford, but coming to London, he apprenticed himself to a cabinet-maker. He was a married man, and had three children living at the time of his fatal exit. He and Phillips were hanged for robbing Charles Sybbald on Finchley Common, and were convicted principally on the evidence of Joseph Lindsey, a clergyman of abandoned character, who had been of their party. One Burroughs, a lunatic, who had escaped from Bedlam, was likewise concerned with them, but afterwards publicly spoke of the affair, which occasioned their being taken into custody: and when it was known that Burroughs was disordered in his mind, he was sent back to Bedlam.

THOMAS PHILLIPS, aged thirty-three years, was a native of Bristol, totally uneducated, and being sent to sea when very young, he served under Lord Torrington, when he attacked and took the Spanish fleet in the Mediterranean Sea, near the harbour of Cadiz.

Phillips returning to England, became acquainted with Spiggot and Lindsey, in company with whom he committed a great number of robberies on the highway. Phillips once boasted that he and Spiggot robbed above a hundred passengers one night, whom they obliged to come out of different waggons, and having bound them, placed them

c

by each other on the side of the road: but this story is too absurd to be believed.

While under sentence of death Phillips behaved in the most hardened and abandoned manner; he paid no regard to anything that the minister said to him, and swore or sung songs while the other prisoners were engaged in acts of devotion; and towards the close of his life, when his companions became more serious, he grew still more wicked; and yet, when at the place of execution, he said, 'he did not fear to die, for he was in no doubt of going to Heaven.'

The lesson of instruction to be drawn from the fate of these malefactors will be compromised in a few words. As the law now stands, no other criminal can ever undergo the punishment that Spiggot sustained; and we hope no other will ever behave in so hardened a manner as Phillips did. It is horrid to think of a man's jesting of sacred matters at any time; but particularly so when he knows himself to be on the verge of eternity. The character of Lindsey ought to be held in universal contempt. The clergyman who could desert the duties of his sacred function to join with highwaymen, and then become an evidence to convict them, must be an object of detestation to every honest man!

Narrative of the Case of BARBARA SPENCER, who was hanged for High-Treason.

IN the month of May, 1721, Barbara Spencer, Alice Hall, and Elizabeth Bray, were indicted at the Old Bailey, for high-treason, in counterfeiting the current coin of the kingdom; when Hall and Bray were acquitted, as being only agents to the other, and Spencer being found guilty, was sentenced to be burnt.[1]

The account that Barbara Spencer gave of herself was in substance as follows. That she was born in the parish of St Giles without Cripplegate, and being naturally of a violent temper, her mother was too indulgent to restrain her in a proper manner. At length her mother finding her quite unmanageable at home, put her apprentice to a mantua-maker, who having known her from a child, treated her with great kindness.

Barbara had served about two years, when on a dispute with her mistress she went home to her mother, with whom she had not long resided before she insisted on having a maid kept, to which the old woman consented. A quarrel soon happening between Barbara and the maid, the mother interposed; on which the daughter left her for a time, but soon returned again.

Not long after this it happened that some malefactors were to be executed at Tyburn, and Barbara insisted on going to see the execution. This was prudently opposed by her mother, who struggling to keep her at home, struck her; but the daughter getting out of the house, went to a female acquaintance, who accompanied her to Tyburn, and from thence to a house near St Giles's Pound, where Barbara made a vow that she would never again return to her mother.

In this fatal resolution she was encouraged by the company present, who persuaded her to believe that she might live in an easy manner, if she would but follow their way of

[1] Women convicted of high, or petit-treason, are always thus sentenced; but they are first tied to a stake, and strangled before they are burnt.

life. To this she readily agreed; and as they were coiners, they employed her in uttering counterfeit money, for which she was detected, tried, fined and imprisoned.

Not taking warning by what had happened, she returned to her old connections, commenced coiner herself, and was at length apprehended for the crime for which she suffered.

While under sentence of death she behaved in the most indecent and turbulent manner; nor could she be convinced that she had been guilty of any crime in making a few shillings. She was for some time very impatient under the idea of her approaching dissolution, and was particularly shocked at the thought of being burnt; but at the place of execution she seemed willing to exercise herself in devotion; but was much interrupted by the mob throwing stones and dirt at her.

She was strangled and burnt at Tyburn on the 5th of July, 1721.

The unhappy fate of this woman seems to have been occasioned by the violence of her temper, and a want of duty to her mother. Hence let all young people learn to keep their passions in subjection, and to remember the injunction in the fifth commandment; 'Honour thy father and thy mother, that thy days may be long in the land which the Lord thy God giveth thee:' for surely no crime is more likely to lead to destruction than that of disobedience to parents. It is the inlet to every other vice, and the source of a thousand calamities.

> Let children that would fear the Lord
>   Hear what their teachers say;
> With rev'rence meet their parents word,
>   And with delight obey.

> For those who worship God, and give
>   Their parents honour due,
> Here on this earth they long shall live,
>   And live hereafter too.

It will be observed that the offence for which Barbara Spencer suffered death is described as high treason. In 1721, this offence covered the usual political offences and also the counterfeiting of the current coin of the realm. Petit treason, for which the penalty was also death, included the murder by the wife of her husband, or of conspiring to murder, most commonly by poisoning.

It will be seen that the footnote explains that women at this time were strangled before they were burnt. It was not always so, and Dr Radzinowicz has collected some of the contemporary accounts of the burning of women, in his *History of the English Criminal Law.* One of his sources was the *Annals of Newgate* (1776) written by the Rev. Villette, the Ordinary of the prison. (We should now describe the Ordinary as the Chaplain of the prison, and his duty was to prepare the criminals for their execution.) Villette said of the execution of Barbara Spencer that 'she was very desirous of praying, and complained of the dirt and stones thrown by the mob behind her, which prevented her thinking sedately on futurity. One time she was quite beat down by them.' In 1790 burning as a punishment was abolished.

Account of RICHARD PARVIN, EDWARD EL-LIOT, ROBERT KINGSHELL, HENRY MARSHALL, EDWARD PINK, JOHN PINK, and JAMES ANSEL, commonly called the *Waltham Blacks,* who were hanged for Murder.

THE actions of these offenders became so much the object of public notice, that it was deemed proper to frame a particular act of parliament in order to bring them to justice. Having blacked their faces they went in the daytime, to the Parks of the nobility and gentry, whence they repeatedly stole deer, and at length murdered the bishop of Winchester's keeper on Waltham-Chace; and from the name of the place, and their blacking their faces, they obtained the name of the *Waltham Blacks*.

The following is the substance of the act of parliament on which they were convicted: 'Any person appearing in any forest, chace, park, &c. or in any high road, open heath, common, or down, with offensive weapons, and having his face blacked, or otherwise disguised, or unlawfully and wilfully hunting, wounding, killing, or stealing any red or fallow deer, or unlawfully robbing any warren, &c. or stealing any fish out of any river or pond, or (whether armed and disguised or not) breaking down the head or mound of any fish-pond, whereby the fish may be lost or destroyed; or unlawfully, and maliciously killing, maiming, or wounding any cattle, or cutting down, or otherwise destroying any trees planted in any avenue, or growing in any garden, orchard, or plantation, for ornament, shelter, or profit; or setting fire to any house, barn, or outhouse, hovel, cock, mow, or stack of corn, straw, hay, or wood; or maliciously shooting at any person, in any dwelling-house or other place; or knowingly sending any letter without any name, or signed with a fictitious name, demanding money, venison, or other valuable thing, or forcibly rescuing any person, being in custody for any of the offences before-mentioned, or procuring any person by gift, or promise of

70

money, or other reward, to join in any such unlawful act, or concealing or succouring such offenders, when by order of council, &c. required to surrender,—shall suffer death.'

The offence of deer-stealing was formerly only a misdemeanor at common law; but the act of parliament abovementioned has been rendered perpetual by a subsequent statute: it therefore behoves people to be cautious that they do not endanger their lives, while they think they are committing what they may deem an inferior offence. We will now give such particulars as we have been able to obtain respecting the malefactors in question.

RICHARD PARVIN was heretofore the master of a public-house in Portsmouth, which he had kept with reputation for a considerable time, till he was imprudent enough to engage with the gang of ruffians who practised the robbing noblemens and gentlemens parks through the country. The reader is already apprized that it was the custom of these fellows to go disguised. Now a servant-maid of Parvin's having left his house during his absence, had repaired to an alehouse in the country; and Parvin calling there on his return from one of his dishonest expeditions, the girl discovered him; in consequence of which he was committed to Winchester Gaol, by the mayor of Portsmouth, till his removal to London for trial.

EDWARD ELLIOT was an apprentice to a taylor at Guildford, and was very young when he engaged with the gang, whose orders he implicitly obeyed, till the following circumstance occasioned his leaving them. Having met with two countrymen who refused to enter into the society, they dug holes in the ground, and placed the unhappy men in them, up to their chins, and had they not been relieved by persons who accidentally saw them, they must have perished. Shocked by this deed, Elliot left them, and for some time served a lady as a footman; but on the day the keeper was murdered he casually met them in the fields, and, on their promise that no harm should attend him, he unhappily consented to bear them company.

Having provided themselves with pistols, and blacked their faces with gunpowder, they proceeded to their lawless depredations; and while the rest of the gang were killing of deer, Elliot went in search of a fawn; but while he was looking for it, the keeper and his assistants came up, and took him into custody. His associates were near enough to see what happened; and immediately coming to his assistance, a violent affray ensued, in which the keeper was shot by Henry Marshall, so that he died on the spot, and Elliot made his escape; but he was soon afterwards taken into custody, and lodged in the gaol of Guildford.

ROBERT KINGSHELL, who was a native of Farnham in Surrey, was placed by his parents with a shoemaker; but being too idle to follow his profession, he was guilty of many acts of irregularity, before he associated himself with the Waltham Blacks, with whom he afterwards suffered. While he was in bed on the night preceding the fatal murder, one of the gang awaked him, by knocking at his window; on which he arose, and went with him to join the rest of the deer-stealers.

HENRY MARSHALL was a man distinguished for his strength and agility: we have no account of the place of his birth, or the manner of his education; but it is reasonable to think that the latter was of the inferior kind, since he appears to have been chiefly distinguished by his skill in the vulgar science of bruising. He was once the occasion of apprehending a highwayman, who had robbed a coach, by giving him a single blow which broke his arm. He seems to have been one of the most daring of the Waltham Blacks, and was the man who shot the chace-keeper, as above-mentioned.

EDWARD PINK and JOHN PINK were brothers, who spent the former part of their lives as carters, at Portsmouth, and had maintained the character of honest men till they became weak enough to join the desperate gang of deer-stealers.

It now remains to speak only of JAMES ANSEL, who likewise lived at Portsmouth. We are not informed in what way he had originally supported himself; but for some years before he joined the desperate gang above-mentioned he was a highwayman; and had been concerned with the

Waltham Blacks about two years before the commission of the murder which cost them their lives.

By a vigilant exertion of the civil power, all the above-mentioned offenders were taken into custody, and it being thought prudent to bring them to trial in London, they were removed thither under a strong guard, and lodged in Newgate.

On the 13th of November, 1723, they were brought to their trial in the court of King's Bench, and being convicted on the clearest evidence, were found guilty, and sentenced to die; and it was immediately ordered that they should suffer on the fourth of the next month. One circumstance was very remarkable on this occasion :—the judge had no sooner pronounced the sentence, than Henry Marshall, the man who had shot the keeper, was immediately deprived of the use of his tongue; nor did he recover his speech till the day before his death.

After passing the solemn sentence the convicts behaved in a manner equally devout and resigned, were regular in their devotions, and prepared themselves for eternity with every mark of unfeigned contrition. They received the sacrament before they left Newgate, acknowledged the justice of the sentence against them, and said they had been guilty of many crimes besides that for which they were to suffer.

At the place of execution they were so dejected as to be unable to address the populace; but they again confessed their sins, and recommended their souls to God, beseeching his mercy, through the merits of Christ, with the utmost fervency of devotion.

These malefactors were hanged at Tyburn, on the 4th of December, 1723.

A very short, though important lesson, may be learnt from the fate of these unhappy men. Idleness must have been the great source of their lawless depredations, which at length ended in murder. No man, however successful in the profession, can expect to get as much profit by deer-stealing, as by following his lawful business. The truth is, that, in almost every instance, it costs a man more pains

c*   73

to be a rogue than to be honest. Exclusive of the duties of religion, young persons cannot learn a more important maxim than that in the scripture; 'the hand of the diligent maketh rich.'

In this place it may not be improper to make a single remark on the game laws. These are supposed to be, possibly not without reason, severe: it is contended that those animals which are wild by nature are equally the property of every man. Perhaps this is the truth: but persons in the lower ranks of life should remember, that when laws are once enacted, THEY MUST BE OBEYED. Safety lies in acquiescence with, not in opposition to, legal institutions.

This case is not particularly interesting in itself, but it is included in order to draw attention to an Act of Parliament passed in 1722 called the Waltham Black Act, which reveals the nature of the criminal law in the eighteenth century as nothing else can. It was passed to deal with the offenders at Waltham in the first instance, but applied to the whole country and was made so comprehensive that it is impossible to compute with accuracy the number of offences it created, all of which were punishable by death without benefit of clergy. It was estimated that three hundred and fifty offences were made capital, and it is difficult to think of a criminal act that did not come within its provisions, particularly when the judges had given it the widest possible construction. It was passed originally for a period of three years, but it lasted till 1823. For a hundred years, therefore, this statute, which displayed the doctrine of Retribution in its most severe form, was the law of England, and was responsible for suffering and death on a most horrible scale. An analysis of the provisions of the Act would be out of place here, but its nature may be rather strikingly illustrated by saying that if a man simply appeared in a forest where deer 'have been or usually shall be kept' with his face blacked or otherwise disguised, although he had otherwise committed no crime, he was guilty of an offence for which, if he was convicted, he could be sentenced to death. It is to be observed that the Editors in their concluding sentences seem to be troubled about the severity of this Act, but they could not refrain from their customary homily to the lower ranks of life.

Particular Account of the Life and Trial of JONATHAN WILD; including genuine Memoirs of his numerous Accomplices.

WOOLVERHAMPTON in Staffordshire gave birth to Jonathan Wild about the year 1682. He was the eldest son of his parents, who at a proper age put him to a day school, which he continued to attend till he had gained a sufficient knowledge in reading, writing, and accounts, to qualify him for business. His father intended to bring him up to his own trade; but changed that design, and at about the age of fifteen apprenticed him for seven years to a bucklemaker in Birmingham. Upon the expiration of his apprenticeship he returned to Woolverhampton, where he married a young woman of good character, and gained a tolerable livelihood by following his business as a journeyman.

He had been married about two years, in which time his wife had bore to him a son, when he formed the resolution of visiting London, and very soon after deserted his wife and child, and set out for the metropolis, where he got into employment, and maintained himself by his trade. Being of an extravagant disposition, many months had not elapsed after his arrival in London when he was arrested and thrown into Wood street Compter, where he remained a prisoner for debt upwards of four years. In a pamphlet which he published, and which we shall more particularly mention hereafter, he says, that during his imprisonment 'it was impossible but he must in some measure be let into the secrets of the criminals there under confinement; and particularly Mr Hitchen's management.'

During his residence in the Compter Wild assiduously cultivated the acquaintance of the criminals who were his fellow-prisoners, and attended to their accounts of the exploits in which they had been engaged with singular satisfaction. In this prison was a woman named Mary Milliner, who had long been considered as one of the most notorious pickpockets and abandoned prostitutes on the town. After having escaped the punishment due to the

variety of felonies of which she had been guilty she was put
under confinement for debt. A strict intimacy was contracted between Wild and this woman; but whether a
criminal intercourse subsisted between them while they
remained in the Compter we cannot affirm; but, considering
the character of the parties, there will appear but little
reason to suppose they adhered to the rules of chastity.
They had no sooner obtained their freedom than they lived
under the denomination of man and wife. By their iniquitous practices they soon obtained a sum of money, which
enabled them to open a little public-house in Cock-Alley,
facing Cripplegate-Church.

Milliner being personally acquainted with most of the
notorious characters by whom London and its environs
were infested, and perfectly conversant as to the manner of
their proceedings, she was considered by Wild as a most
useful companion; and indeed she very materially contri-
buted towards rendering him one of the most accomplished
characters in the arts of villainy.

Wild industriously penetrated into the secrets of felons
of every denomination, who resorted in great numbers to
his house, in order to dispose of their booties; and they
looked upon him with a kind of awe; for, being acquainted
with their proceedings, they were conscious that their
lives were continually in his power.

Wild was at little difficulty to dispose of the articles
brought to him by thieves, at something less than the real
value; for at this period no law existed for the punishment
of the receivers of stolen goods: but the evil encreasing to
so enormous a degree, it was deemed expedient by the
legislature to frame a law for its suppression. An act
therefore was passed consigning such as should be convicted
of receiving goods, knowing them to have been stolen, to
transportation for the space of fourteen years.

Wild's practices were considerably interrupted by the
above-mentioned law; to obviate the intention of which,
however, he suggested the following plan: he called a
meeting of all the thieves whom he knew, and observed
to them, that if they carried their booties to such of the

pawnbrokers who were known to be not much troubled with scruples of conscience, they would scarcely advance on the property one fourth of its real value; and that if they were offered to strangers either for sale, or by way of deposit, it was a chance of ten to one but the parties were rendered amenable to the laws. He observed that the most industrious thieves were now scarcely able to obtain a livelihood; and that they must either submit to be half-starved, or be in great and continual danger of Tyburn. He informed them that he had devised a plan for removing the inconveniences under which they laboured, recommending them to follow his advice, and to behave towards him with honor. He then proposed that when they had gained any booty they should deliver it to him, instead of carrying it to the pawnbroker, saying he would restore the goods to the owners, by which means greater sums would be raised than by depositing them with the pawnbrokers, while the thieves would be perfectly secure from detection.

This proposal was received with general approbation, and it was resolved to carry it into immediate execution. All the stolen effects were to be given into the possession of Wild, who soon appointed convenient places wherein they were to be deposited, judging that it would be imprudent to have them left at his own house.

The infamous plan being thus concerted, it was the business of Wild to apply to persons who had been robbed, pretending to be greatly concerned at their misfortunes, saying that some suspected property had been stopped by a very honest man, a broker, with whom he was acquainted, and that if their goods happened to be in the hands of his friend, restitution should be made. But he failed not to plead that the broker might be rewarded for his trouble and disinterestedness, and to use every argument in his power for exacting a promise that no disagreeable consequences should ensue to his friend, who had imprudently neglected to apprehend the supposed thieves.

Happy in the prospect of regaining their property without the trouble and expence necessarily attending prosecutions, people generally approved the conduct of Wild, and sometimes rewarded him even with one half of the real value of the goods restored. Persons who had been robbed, however, were not always satisfied with Wild's declaration; and sometimes they questioned him particularly as to the manner of their goods being discovered. On these occasions he pretended to be offended that his honor should be disputed, saying that his motive was to afford all the service in his power to the injured party, whose goods he imagined might possible be those stopped by his friend; but since his good intentions were received in so ungracious a manner, and himself interrogated respecting the robbers, he had nothing further to say on the subject, but must take his leave; adding that his name was Jonathan Wild, and that he was every day to be found at his house in Cock-Alley, Cripplegate. This affectation of resentment seldom failed to possess the people who had been robbed with a more favourable opinion of his principles; and the suspicion of his character being removed, he had an opportunity of advancing his demands.

Wild received no gratuity from the owners of stolen goods, but deducted his profit from the money which was to be paid the broker: thus did he amass considerable sums without danger of prosecution; for his offences came under the description of no law then existing. For several years he preserved a tolerably fair character, so consummate was the art he employed in the management of all his schemes.

Wild's business greatly encreasing and his name becoming exceedingly popular, he altered his mode of proceeding. Instead of applying to persons who had been robbed, he opened an office, to which great numbers resorted in hopes of recovering their effects. He made a great parade in his business, and assumed a consequence that enabled him more effectually to impose on the public. When persons came to his office they were informed that they must each pay a crown in consideration of receiving his advice. This ceremony being dispatched, he entered in his book, the names and places of abode of the parties, with all the particulars which they could communicate respecting the robberies, and the rewards that would be given, provided the goods were recovered; and they were then desired to call again in a few days, when he hoped he should be able to give them some agreeable intelligence.

Upon calling to know the success of his enquiries, he informed them that he had received some information concerning their goods, but that the agent he had employed to trace them had informed him that the robbers pretended they could raise more money by pawning the property than by returning it for the proposed reward; saying, however, that if he could by any means procure an interview with the villains he doubted not of being able to settle matters agreeable to the terms already proposed; but, at the same time, artfully insinuating that the most safe, expeditious and prudent method would be to make some addition to the reward.

Wild, at length, became eminent in his profession, which proved highly lucrative. When he had discovered the utmost sum that it was likely people would give for the recovery of their property, he requested them to call again, and in the mean time he caused the goods to be ready for delivery. He derived considerable advantages from examining persons who had been robbed; for he thence became acquainted with the particulars which the thieves had omitted to communicate to him, and was enabled to detect them if they concealed any part of their booties. Being in possession of the secrets of all the notorious robbers, they were under the necessity of complying with whatever terms he thought proper to exact; for they were conscious that by opposing his inclination they should involve themselves in the most imminent danger of being sacrificed to the injured laws of their country.

Through the infamous practices of this man articles which had been before considered as of no use but to the owners, now became matters claiming a particular attention from the thieves by whom the metropolis and its environs were interested. Pocket-books, books of accounts, watches, rings, trinkets, and a variety of articles of but small intrinsic worth, were now esteemed very profitable booty. Books of accounts and other writings being of great importance to the owners, produced very handsome rewards; and the same may be said of pocket-books, for they generally contained memorandums, and sometimes bank-notes and other articles on which money could be readily procured.

Wild accumulated money so fast that he considered himself as a man of consequence, and to support his imaginary dignity he dressed in laced clothes, and wore a sword. He first exercised his martial instrument on the person of his accomplice and reputed wife, Mary Milliner. Having on some occasion provoked him, he, with an oath, declared he would 'mark her for a bitch,' and instantly drawing his sword struck at her, and cut off one of her ears. This event was the cause of a separation; but in acknowledgment of the great services she had rendered him, by introducing him to so lucrative a profession, he allowed a weekly stipend till her decease.

Before Wild had brought the plan of his office to perfection he for some time acted as an assistant to Charles Hitchen, the city-marshal. These celebrated co-partners in villainy, under the pretext of reforming the manners of the dissolute part of the public, paraded the streets from Temple-bar to the Minories, searching houses of ill-fame, and apprehending disorderly and suspected persons: but such as complimented these *public* reformers with *private* douceurs were allowed to practice every species of wickedness with impunity. Hitchen and Wild, however, became jealous of each other, and an open rupture taking place, they parted, each pursuing the business of thief-taking on his own account.[1]

In 1718 the marshal attacked Wild in a pamphlet, called, *The Regulator; or a Discovery of Thieves, Thief-takers, &c.* which was answered by his antagonist; and from each of these curious performances we shall here introduce some extracts.

[1] In the year 1715 Wild removed from his house in Cock-Alley, to a Mrs Seagoe's in the Old Bailey, where he pursued his business with the usual success notwithstanding the efforts of Hitchen (his rival in iniquity) to suppress his proceedings.

Abstract of the City Marshal's *Account of* Jonathan Wild, &c.

If these should hold their peace, the stones in the street would cry out of such abominable practices, as are committed and carried on in this city and places adjacent, by thieves and robbers, and—thief-takers.

One thief-taker brought to justice, is more for the advantage of the city, than a hundred thieves; and in order thereto, I shall here take notice of only one of the aforesaid felonious practices, taking it for granted, that all the rest are of the same management; to wit, a gentlewoman, as she was passing along in the evening in a coach, on the South-side of St Paul's Church-yard, was there, in a most audacious and barbarous manner, robbed to a considerable value, by three of the most notorious rogues, William Matthews, Christopher Matthews, and Obadiah Lemon (who agreed to make himself an evidence) that ever this kingdom was plagued with; which being discovered and sought after, in order to bring them to justice for so doing, the Thief-taker hearing of the same, and fearing that he might by this means lose three of the most profitable customers which belonged to his felonious shop, immediately summoned the three aforesaid offenders to a friendly conference, where it was unanimously agreed that the only way to save them, at this critical juncture, was, for one of them to make himself an evidence, &c. 'Well then,' saith the Thief-taker, 'in order to blind the justice, and that he may take the information, is to induce him to believe that we are doing something for the good of the public: therefore, you must put into the information a numerous train of offenders which have been concerned with you, either in robberies, or buying, or receiving of your stolen goods; and at the same time you must be sure to promise him, the said justice, that you will convict them all: and, that there may be a perfect harmony between us, you shall hear me, your Counsellor, your Thief-taker, and Factor, promise as faithfully that I will apprehend, take, and bring them to justice for the same. But, by the bye, I must give you this caution, to leave out the sixty dozen of handkerchiefs that were taken by Mr

Ridley, from a dyer's servant, whom they sent on a sham errand, for which handkerchiefs I received thirty guineas from the owner, but gave Oakey, Lemon, and Mr Johnson but ten guineas. That you do not put such and such robberies into the information, because I was employed by the persons that you robbed, to get their goods again, and, they not bidding money enough for the same, they were not returned to the right owner. Therefore, you know such must be left out, otherwise I shall bring my own neck into the noose, and put it in the power of every little prig, as well as others, to pull the cord at their pleasure; and upon such terms, who the devil would be your factor?'

Let us now see what is the consequence of this *skittish* and felonious information; but deceiving the magistrate, and letting the three aforesaid notorious offenders escape the hand of justice, and hanging up a couple of shim sham thieves (Hugh Oakley and Henry Chickley) which he got little or nothing by, in their room: and likewise to give the Thief-taker an opportunity to rob or extort a sum of money out of all the rest in the information, by making up and compounding the felonies with them, which, by a modest computation, cannot amount to less than a hundred pounds, or more, &c.

Then is it not high time for the citizens of London, and the places adjacent, to bestir themselves, when the greatest offenders have found a way, with the assistance of their friend the Thief-taker, to escape the hand of justice? This will give them encouragement, and make them desperate, as well as frequent in their robberies, and, what the citizens and others must dearly pay for, if not timely prevented, by putting a stop to the same.

In short, the thief, the gaol, the justice, and the king's evidence, all of them seem to be influenced and managed by him, and, at this rate, none will be brought to the gallows, but such as he thinks fit, &c.

Now, if enquiry were to be made, by what means he arrived to this pitch of preferment he is now at, you will find that he hath been a great proficient in all matters and things, that he hath hitherto engaged in.

I. Who, when in a private station, and followed the trade of buckle-making, knew how to plate a crown-piece as well as any that followed the employment.

II. When he became an evidence, did the business skittishly, and as effectually, as any of those he now sets up.

III. When he was a twang, and followed the tail of his wife, Mary Milliner, a common night-walker, no sooner had she picked a pocket, and given him the signal by a hem! or otherwise, but he had impudence and courage enough to attack the cull, untill the buttock had made her escape.

IV. When king of the gipsies, Jonathan Wild did execute the hidden and dark part of a stroller to all intents and purposes, untill, in Holborn, by order of the justice, his *skittish* and *baboonish* majesty was set in the stocks for the same.

V. Now King among the thieves, and Lying-master-general of England, Captain-general of the army of plunderers, and Ambassador Extraordinary from the Prince of the Air, hath taken up his residence in an apartment fitted up on purpose for him in the Palace of the Queen of Hell, where continual attendance is given for receiving and buying stolen goods; as likewise, to *pay them back* again, provided the right owners will offer money enough for the same; but if not, then doth his excellency fly off, and give you to understand, that the goods he hath heard of, are not yours, and that he cannot assist you, and that you may be gone about your business, for——he will take a sum of money of the thief, or dispose of the goods some other way. Certainly, such a monster of iniquity as this is not to be found in any part of the habitable world, save only in this kingdom, and this infatuated city, and places adjacent, those places of general corruption.

VI. There being one thing more, which he earnestly desires, and solicits to be employed in finding out, and setting up evidences against the false coiners, and, then you need not doubt but in a little time you will have as many coiners, as you have thieves. O! London! London! so much famed for thy good order; by what means is it now come to pass, that thou art become a receptacle for a den of thieves and robbers, and all sorts of villainous persons and practices?

It may be proper to examine a little into the trade of punishing wickedness and vice, the same being become one of the most mysterious, profitable, and flourishing trades now in the kingdom—and the open, but unwarrantable and pernicious practice of the regulator (Jonathan Wild).

And, in order thereto, I shall here take a view of him in the public streets, which he so much boasteth of, and fain would persuade you, that he doth so much good to the public, by stopping the whores, and other persons viciously inclined, and forcibly entering the houses of bawdry, and taking them out from thence, and committing them to gaols. And now pray, what's the consequence of all this? woeful experience plainly shews, that, by the ill acquaintance, and conversation they meet with there, they learn to be thieves, and find the way to the Thief-takers houses, set up by them on purpose to harbour and train up one brood of thieves under another, and so screen and save them from the gallows, to the end that they may live by the reversion of them. And now it is the general complaint, that people are afraid, when it is dark, to come to their houses, for fear that their hats and wigs should be snatched from off their heads, or their swords taken from their sides, or, that they may be blinded, knocked down, cut or stabbed; nay, the coaches cannot secure them, but, they are likewise assaulted, cut and robbed in the public streets.—And, how can you suppose it to be otherwise, when there are so many public offices, public and private houses, public inns and public shops, set up on purpose to harbour thieves and robbers, and carry on the basest designs with them.—

Jonathan Wild's *Account of himself and the* City Marshal.

When two of a profession are at variance, the world is let into many important discoveries; and, whether it be among thief-takers, lawyers, or clergymen, an expectation naturally arises of some Billingsgate treatment.—For the satisfaction of the world in this particular, I shall, like a true cock of the game, answer Mr Hitchen at his own weapons.—

—Says my old master in iniquity, 'One thief-taker brought to justice, is more for the advantage of the city, than a hundred thieves:' Not to justify the practice of thief-taking, I acquiesce with him in this, if the *oldest* offenders are to be *first* prosecuted, and then I'll leave the world to judge,——Who will first deserve an exemplary punishment.

This looks as if Jonathan was not the original thief-taker, but, that he borrowed some hints from the marshal, and afterwards improved them.

The information he mentioned, in respect to the setting up an evidence, is entirely groundless, the person accused being perfectly ignorant of it; and there are enough to prove that the evidence voluntarily appeared before my lord mayor: and, as for not returning of goods for want of a reward sufficient to the value, I shall shew what flagrant crimes the city marshall has been guilty of, of this nature.—

Jonathan does not here deny the charge of not returning the goods, and therefore we may venture to take it for fact.

Says this author,—'He knew how to plate a crown piece as well as any that followed that employment.' Now, if he could prove this assertion, or any thing like it, it is very rational to suppose, that he would bring the thief-taker to condign punishment, being his implacable enemy.—

That setting up evidences against false coiners is the way to have as many coiners as thieves, is such a piece of nonsense, absurdity, and contradiction, that it is not to be paralleled.

And it is a notable piece of inconsistency to say, that taking whores out of bawdy-houses, and sending them to workhouses, makes them thieves. By this way of arguing, the houses of correction, instead of deterring iniquity, increase thefts, and robberies, and the reformers of manners are the promoters of wickedness.—But it is no wonder that the marshal, throughout his treatise, expresses a great deal of uneasiness at the informers, for those persons very much lessen his interest in suppressing houses of lewdness, the keepers whereof have been generally pensioners to him.—— I can produce persons who will make it appear, that several houses of ill fame are supported by quarterly payments to him. Besides, there being frequently sums of money extorted from libertines for connivance at their lewdness, and sometimes from persons intirely innocent, and unacquainted with the character of those houses. And he has of late been so audacious, as to examine taverns of the best reputation, and insist upon yearly compositions from them, though the only payment he has met with, has been a salute with a crab-tree cudgel, and a decent toss in a blanket.

He has shewn such an excellence in the flash or cant dialect, that every body must allow him a master, and that experience only must have compleated him.—His dialogue demonstrates his great knowledge in the intrigues of pickpockets, house-breakers, and highwaymen; and a man would swear by his apt description, that he had been an actor in all. The boys in the ken swearing and grinning like so many hell-cats, and the man in the silver-buttoned coat, and knotted wig, with a sword by his side, is an exact scene of a city-officer, and his company of pick-pockets at an alehouse between Moorfields and Islington, where they used to rendezvous daily, the boys giving an account of their day's work, and the master dispensing further instructions.

I need not mention his being nearer the pillory than ever a certain person was to the stocks.—And, however a certain diminutive person may resemble a baboon, it is evident to all that know the gigantic city marshal, that he wants nothing but a cloven foot to personate, in all respects, his father Beelzebub.

We shall now proceed to give some further account of the hero of this narrative. When the thieves with whom he was in league faithfully related to him the particulars of the robberies they had committed, and entrusted to him the disposal of their booties, he assured them that they might safely rely on him for protection against the vengeance of the law: and, indeed, it must be acknowledged that in cases of this nature he would persevere in his endeavours to surmount very great difficulties rather than wilfully falsify his word.

Wild's artful behaviour, and the punctuality with which he discharged his engagements, obtained him a great share of confidence among thieves of every denomination; in so much that if he caused it to be intimated to them that he was desirous of seeing them, and that they should not be molested, they would attend him with the utmost willingness, without entertaining the most distant apprehension of danger, although conscious that he had informations against them, and that their lives were absolutely in his power: but if they presumed to reject his proposals, or proved otherwise refractory, he would address them to the following effect: 'I have given you my word that you should come and go in safety, and so you shall: but take care of yourself, for if ever you see me again, you see an enemy.'

The great influence that Wild obtained over the thieves will not be thought a very extraordinary matter if it is considered that when he promised to use his endeavours for rescuing them from impending fate he was always desirous, and generally able, to succeed. Such as complied with his measures he would never interrupt; but, on the contrary, afford them every encouragement for prosecuting their iniquitous practices; and if apprehended by any other person he seldom failed of procuring their discharge. His most usual method (in desperate cases, and when matters could not be managed with more ease and expedition) was to procure them to be admitted evidences, under pretext that it was in their power to make discoveries of high importance to the public. When they were in prison he frequently attended them, and communicated to them from his own memorandums such particulars as he judged it would be prudent for them to relate to the court. When his accomplices were apprehended and he was not able to prevent their being brought to trial, he contrived stratagems (in which his invention was amazingly fertile) for keeping the principal witnesses out of court; so that the delinquents were generally dismissed in defect of evidence.

Jonathan was ever a most implacable enemy to those thieves who were hardy enough to reject his terms, and dispose of their stolen effects for their own separate advantage. He was industrious to an extreme in his endeavours to surrender them into the hands of justice; and being acquainted with all their usual places of resort, it was scarcely possible for them to escape his vigilance.

By subjecting those who incurred his displeasure to the punishment of the law he obtained the rewards offered for pursuing them to conviction; greatly extended his ascendency over the other thieves, who considered him with a kind of awe; and, at the same time, established his character as being a man of great public utility.

It was the practice of Wild to give instructions to the thieves whom he employed as to the manner in which they should conduct themselves; and if they followed his directions, it was seldom that they failed of success. But if they neglected a strict observance of his rules, or were, through inadvertency or ignorance, guilty of any kind of mismanagement or error in the prosecution of the schemes he had suggested, it was to be understood almost as an absolute certainty that he would procure them to be convicted at the next sessions, deeming them to be unqualified for the profession of roguery.

He was frequently asked, how it was possible that he could carry on the business of restoring stolen effects, and yet not be in league with the robbers; and his replies were always to this purpose: 'My acquaintance among thieves is very extensive, and when I receive information of a robbery I make enquiry after the suspected parties, and leave word at proper places that if the goods are left where I appoint the reward shall be paid, and no questions asked. Surely no imputation of guilt can fall upon me; for I hold no interviews with the robbers, nor are the goods given into my possession.'

We shall now proceed to a relation of the most remarkable exploits of the hero of these pages; and our account must necessarily include many particulars relating to other notorious characters.

A lady of fortune being on a visit in Piccadilly, her servants, leaving her sedan at the door, went to refresh themselves at a neighbouring public-house. Upon their return the vehicle was not to be found; in consequence of which the men immediately went to Wild, and having informed him of their loss, and complimented him with the usual fee, they were desired to call upon him again in a few days. Upon their second application Wild extorted from them a considerable reward, and then directed them to attend the Chapel in Lincoln's-Inn-Fields on the following morning during the time of prayers. The men went according to the appointment, and under the Piazzas of the Chapel perceived the chair, which upon examination they found to contain the velvet seat, curtains, and other furniture, and that it had received no kind of damage.

A young gentleman named Knap accompanied his mother to Sadler's-Wells on Saturday, March 31, 1716. On their return they were attacked about ten at night near the wall of Gray's-Inn-Gardens by five villains. The young gentleman was immediately knocked down, and his mother being exceedingly alarmed, called for assistance; upon which a pistol was discharged at her, and she instantly fell down dead. A considerable reward was offered by proclamation in the Gazette for the discovery of the perpetrator of this horrid crime; and Wild was remarkably assiduous in his endeavours to apprehend the offenders. From a description given of some of the villains Wild immediately judged the gang to be composed of William White, Thomas Thurland, John Chapman, alias Edward Darvel, Timothy Dun, and Isaac Rag.

In the evening of Sunday, April 8, Wild received intelligence that some of the above-named men were drinking with their prostitutes at a house kept by John Weatherly in Newtoner's Lane. He went to Weatherly's, accompanied by his man Abraham, and seized White, whom he brought away about midnight in a hackney coach, and lodged him in the Round-house.

White being secured, information was given to Wild that a man named James Aires was then at the Bell Inn, Smithfield, in company with a woman of the town. Having an information against Aires, Wild, accompanied by his assistants, repaired to the inn, under the gateway of which they met Thurland, whose person had been mistaken by the informer for that of Aires. Thurland was provided with two brace of pistols, but being suddenly seized, he was deprived of all opportunity of making use of those weapons, and taken into custody.

They went, on the following night to a house in White Horse Alley, Drury-Lane, where they apprehended Chapman, alias Darvel. Soon after the murder of Mrs Knap, Chapman and others stopped the coach of Thomas Middlethwaite, Esq., but that gentleman escaped being robbed by discharging a blunderbuss and wounding Chapman in the arm, on which the villains retired.

In a short time after this Wild apprehended Isaac Rag at a house which he frequented in St Giles's, in consequence of an information charging him with a burglary. Being taken before a magistrate, in the course of his examination Rag impeached twenty-two accomplices, charging them with being house-breakers, footpads, and receivers of stolen effects; and in consequence hereof he was admitted an evidence for the crown.

Rag was convicted of a misdemeanor in January, 1714–15, and sentenced to stand three times in the pillory. He had concealed himself in the dust-hole belonging to the house of Thomas Powell, where being discovered, he was searched, and a pistol, some matches, and a number of pick-lock keys were found in his possession. His intention was evidently to commit a burglary, but as he did not enter the house, he was indicted for a misdemeanor in entering the yard with intent to steal. He was indicted in October, 1715 for a burglary in the house of Elizabeth Stanwell on the 24th of August: but he was acquitted of this charge.

White, Thurland, and Chapman were arraigned on the 18th of May, 1716, at the sessions house in the Old Bailey, on an indictment for assaulting John Knap, Gent. putting him in fear, and taking from him a hat and wig, on the 31st of March, 1716. They were also indicted for the murder of Mary Knap, widow; White by discharging a pistol loaded with powder and bullets, and thereby giving her a wound, of which she immediately died, May [March] 31, 1716. They were a second time indicted for assaulting and robbing John Gough. White was a fourth time indicted with James Russel for a burglary in the house of George Barclay. And Chapman was a fourth time indicted for a burglary in the house of Henry Cross. These three offenders were executed at Tyburn on the 8th of June, 1716.

Wild was indefatigable in his endeavours to apprehend Timothy Dun, who had hitherto escaped the hands of justice by removing to a new lodging, where he concealed himself in the most cautious manner. Wild, however, did not despair of discovering this offender, whom he supposed must either perish through want of the necessaries of life, or obtain the means of subsistence by returning to his felonious practices; and so confident was he of success that he made a wager of ten guineas that he would have him in custody before the expiration of an appointed time.

Dun's confinement, at length, became exceedingly irksome to him, and he sent his wife to make enquiries respecting him of Wild, in order to discover whether he was still in danger of being apprehended. Upon her departure from Wild's, he ordered one of his people to follow her home. She took water at Black-Friars, and landed at the Falcon, but suspecting the man was employed to trace her, she again took water and crossed to White-Friars; observing that she was still followed, she ordered the waterman to proceed to Lambeth, and having landed there, it being nearly dark, she imagined she had escaped the observation of Wild's man, and therefore walked immediately home. The man traced her to Maid-Lane, near the Bank-side, Southwark, and perceiving her enter a house, he marked the wall with chalk, and then returned to his employer with an account of the discovery he had made.

Wild, accompanied by his man Abraham, one Riddlesden, and another man, went on the following morning to the house where the woman had been seen to enter. Dun hearing a noise, and thence suspecting that he was discovered, got through a back window on the second floor upon the roof of a pantry, the bottom of which was about eight feet from the ground. Abraham discharged a pistol, and wounded Dun in the arm, in consequence of which he fell from the pantry into the yard: after his fall Riddlesden discharged a pistol and wounded him in the face with small shot. Dun was secured and carried to Newgate, and being tried at the ensuing sessions, he was soon after executed at Tyburn.

Riddlesden was bred to the law, but he entirely neglected that business, and abandoned himself to every species of wickedness. His irregular course of life having greatly embarrassed his circumstances, he broke into the Chapel at Whitehall, and stole the communion plate. He was convicted of this offence, and received sentence of death, but through the exertion of powerful interest a pardon was obtained on condition of transporting himself for the term of seven years. He went to America, but soon returned to England, and had the address to ingratiate himself into the favour of a young lady, daughter to an opulent merchant at Newcastle upon Tyne. Before he could get his wife's fortune, which was considerable, into his hands, he was discovered and committed to Newgate. His wife followed him, and was brought to bed in the prison. Her friends, however, being apprized of her unhappy situation, caused her to return home. He contracted an intimacy with the widow of Richard Revel, one of the turnkeys of Newgate; and being permitted to transport himself again, the woman went with him to Philadelphia, under the character of his wife.

In consequence of a disagreement between them, Mrs Revel returned, and took a public-house in Golden-Lane: but what became of Riddlesden we have not been able to learn.

A thief of most infamous character, named Arnold Powel, being confined in Newgate on a charge of having robbed a house in the neighbourhood of Golden-square of property to a great amount, he was visited by Jonathan, who informed him that in consideration of a sum of money he would save his life, adding that if the proposal was rejected he should inevitably die at Tyburn for the offence on account of which he was then imprisoned. The prisoner, however, not believing that it was in Wild's power to do him any injury, bid him defiance. Powell was brought to trial; but through a defect of evidence he was acquitted. Having gained intelligence that Powell had committed a burglary in the house of Mr Eastlick, near Fleet-ditch, he caused that gentleman to prosecute the robber. Upon receiving information that a bill was found for the burglary, Powell sent for Wild, and a compromise was effected according to the terms which Wild himself proposed, in consequence of which Powell was assured that his life should be preserved.

Upon the approach of the sessions Wild informed the prosecutor that the first and second days would be employed in other trials, and as he was willing Mr Eastlick should avoid attending with his witnesses longer than was necessary, he would give timely notice when Powell would be arraigned. But he contrived to have the prisoner put to the bar, and no persons appearing to prosecute, he was ordered to be taken away: but after some time he was again set to the bar, then ordered away, and afterwards put up a third time, proclamation being made each time for the prosecutor to appear. At length the jury were charged with the prisoner, and as no accusation was adduced against him, he was necessarily dismissed; and the court ordered Mr Eastlick's recognizances to be estreated.

Powell was ordered to remain in custody till the next sessions, there being another indictment against him; and Mr Eastlick represented the behaviour of Wild to the court, who justly reprimanded him with great severity.

Powell put himself into a salivation in order to avoid being brought to trial the next sessions, but notwithstanding this stratagem he was arraigned and convicted; and executed on the 20th of March, 1716–17.

At this time Wild had quitted his apartments at Mrs Seagoe's, and hired a house adjoining to the Cooper's Arms on the opposite side of the Old Bailey. The unexampled villainies of this man were now become an object of so much consequence as to excite the particular attention of the legislature. In the year 1718 an act was passed deeming every person guilty of a capital offence who should accept a reward in consideration of restoring stolen effects without prosecuting the thief.

It was the general opinion that the above law would effectually suppress the iniquitous practices of Wild; but after some interruptions to his proceedings he devised means for evading the law, which were for several years attended with success.

He now declined the custom of receiving money from the persons who applied to him, but upon the second or third time of calling informed them that all he had been able to learn respecting their business was, that if a sum of money was left at an appointed place their property would be restored the same day.

Sometimes as the person robbed was returning from Wild's house he was accosted in the street by a man who delivered the stolen effects, at the same time producing a note expressing the sum that was to be paid for them.

In cases wherein he supposed danger was to be apprehended he advised people to advertise that whoever would bring the stolen goods to Jonathan Wild should be rewarded, and no questions asked them.

In the two first instances it could not be proved that he either saw the thief, received the goods, or accepted a reward; and in the latter case he acted agreeable to the directions of the injured party, and there appeared no reason to criminate him as being in confederacy with the felons.

When he was asked what would satisfy him for his trouble, he told the persons who had recovered their property that what he had done was without any interested view, but merely from a principle of doing good; that therefore he made no claim: but if he accepted a present he should not consider it as being his due, but as an instance of generosity which he should acknowledge accordingly.

Our adventurer's business encreased exceedingly, and he opened an office in Newtoner's-Lane, to the management of which he appointed his man Abraham. This Israelite proved a remarkably industrious and faithful servant to Jonathan, who intrusted him with matters of the greatest importance.

By too strict an application to business Wild much impaired his health, so that he judged it prudent to retire into the country for a short time. He hired a lodging at Dulwich, leaving both offices under the direction of Abraham.

A lady had her pocket picked of bank-notes to the amount of seven thousand pounds. She related the particulars of her robbery to Abraham, who in a few days apprehended three pickpockets, and conducted them to Jonathan's lodgings at Dulwich. Upon their delivering up all the notes, Wild dismissed them. When the lady applied to Abraham he restored her property, and she generously made him a present of four hundred pounds, which he delivered to his employer.

These three pickpockets were afterwards apprehended for some other offences, and transported. One of them carefully concealed a bank note for a thousand pounds in the lining of his coat. On his arrival at Maryland he procured cash for the note, and having purchased his freedom, went to New-York, where he assumed the character of a gentleman.

Wild's business would not permit him to remain long at Dulwich; and being under great inconvenience from the want of Abraham's assistance, he did not keep open the office in Newtoner's-Lane for more than three months.

About a week after the return of Wild from Dulwich a mercer in Lombard-street ordered a porter to carry to a particular inn a box containing goods to the amount of two hundred pounds. In his way the porter was observed by three thieves, one of whom, being more genteelly dressed than his companions, accosted the man in the following manner: 'If you are willing to earn six-pence, my friend, step to the tavern at the end of the street, and ask for the roquelaur I left at the bar; but lest the waiter should scruple giving it you, take my gold watch as a token. Pitch your burden upon this bulk and I will take care of it till your return; but be sure you make haste.' The man went to the tavern, and having delivered his message, was informed that the thing he enquired for had not been left there; upon which the porter said, 'Since you scruple to trust me, look at this gold watch, which the gentleman gave me to produce as a token.' What was called a gold watch being examined proved to be only pewter lacquered. In consequence of this discovery the porter hastened back to where he had left the box, but neither that nor the sharpers were to be found.

The porter was, with reason, apprehensive that he should incur his master's displeasure if he related what had happened; and in order to excuse his folly he determined upon the following stratagem: he rolled himself in the mud, and then went home, saying he had been knocked down and robbed of the goods.

The proprietor of the goods applied to Wild, and related to him the story he had been told by his servant. Wild told him he had been deceived as to the manner in which the trunk was lost, and that he should be convinced of it if he would send for his servant. A messenger was dispatched for the porter, and upon his arrival, Abraham conducted him into a room separated from the office only by a slight partition. 'Your master (said Abraham) has just been here concerning the box you lost; and he desired that you might be sent for in order to communicate the particulars of the robbery. What kind of people were the thieves, and in what manner did they take the box away?' In reply the man said, 'Why, two or three fellows knocked me down, and then carried off the box.' Hereupon Abraham told him that 'If they knocked him down there was but little chance of the property being recovered, since that offence rendered them liable to be hanged. But (continued he) let me prevail upon you to speak the truth; for if you persist in a refusal, be assured we shall discover it by some other means. Pray do you recollect nothing about a token? Were you not to fetch a roquelaur from a tavern, and did not you produce a gold watch as a token to induce the waiter to deliver it?' Astonished at Abraham's words, the porter declared 'he believed he was a witch,' and immediately acknowledged in what manner he had lost the box.

Engraved for The Malefactor's Register.

The New SESSIONS-HOUSE, in the Old Bailey

The New Goal of NEWGATE.

One of the villains concerned in the above transaction lived in the house formerly inhabited by Wild in Cock-Alley, near Cripplegate. To this place Jonathan and Abraham repaired, and when they were at the door, they overheard a dispute between the man and his wife, during which the former declared that he would set out for Holland the next day. Upon this they forced open the door, and Wild, saying he was under a necessity of preventing his intended voyage, took him into custody, and conducted him to the Compter.

On the following day the goods being returned to the owner, Wild received a handsome reward; and he contrived to procure the discharge of the thief.

On the 23rd or 24th of January, 1718–19, Margaret Dodwell and Alice Wright went to Wild's house, and desired to have a private interview with him. Observing one of the women to be with child, he imagined she might want a father to her expected issue; for it was a part of his business to procure persons to stand in the place of the real fathers of children born in consequence of illicit commerce. Being shewn into another room, Dodwell spoke in the following manner: 'I do not come, Mr Wild, to inform you that I have met with any loss, but that I wish to find something. If you will follow my advice you may acquire a thousand pounds, or perhaps many thousands.' Jonathan here expressed the utmost willingness to engage in an enterprize so highly lucrative, and the woman proceeded thus : 'My plan is this; you must procure two or three stout resolute fellows, who will undertake to rob a house in Wormwood-street, near Bishopsgate. This house is kept by a cane-chair maker, named John Cooke, who has a lodger, an ancient maiden lady, immensely rich; and she keeps her money in a box in her apartment: she is now gone into the country to fetch more. One of the men must find an opportunity of getting into the shop in the evening, and conceal himself in a saw-pit there; he may let his companions in when the family are retired to rest. But it will be particularly necessary to secure two stout apprentices and a boy, who lay in the garret. I wish, however, that no murder may be committed.' Upon this Wright said, 'Phoo! phoo! when people engage in matters of this sort they must manage as well as they can, and so as to provide for their own safety.' Dodwell now resumed her discourse to Jonathan: 'The boys being secured no kind of difficulty will attend getting possession of the old lady's money, she being from home, and her room under that where the boys sleep. In the room facing that of the old lady, Cooke and his wife lay: he is a man of remarkable courage, great caution, therefore, must be observed respecting him; and indeed I think it would be as well to knock him on the head; for then his drawers may be rifled, and he is never without money. A woman and a child lay under the room belonging to the old lady, but I hope no violence will be offered to them.'

Having heard the above proposal Wild took the women into custody, and lodged them in Newgate. It is not to be supposed that his conduct in this affair proceeded from a principle of virtue or justice, but that he declined engaging in the iniquitous scheme from an apprehension that their design was to draw him into a snare.

Dodwell had lived five months in Mr Cooke's house, and though she paid no rent, he was too generous to turn her out, or in any manner to oppress her. Wild prosecuted Dodwell and Wright for a misdemeanor, and being found guilty, they were sentenced each to suffer six months imprisonment.

Wild had inserted in his book a gold watch, a quantity of fine lace and other property of considerable value which John Butler had stolen from a house at Newington-Green: but as Butler, instead of coming to account as usual, had declined his felonious practices, and lived on the produce of his booty, Wild, highly enraged at being excluded his share, determined to pursue every possible means for subjecting him to the power of justice.

Being informed that he lodged at a public-house in Bishopsgate-street, Wild went to the house early one morning, when Butler, hearing him ascending the stairs, jumped out of the window of his room, and climbing over the wall of the yard, got into the street. Wild broke open the door of the room; but was exceedingly disappointed and mortified to find that the man in whom he was in pursuit had escaped. In the mean time Butler ran into a house, the door of which stood open, and descending to the kitchen, where some women were washing, told them he was pursued by a bailiff, and they advised him to conceal himself in the coal-hole.

Jonathan coming out of the ale-house, and seeing a shop on the opposite side of the way open, he enquired of the master, who was a dyer, whether a man had not taken refuge in his house. The dyer answered in the negative, saying he had not left his shop more than a minute since it had been opened. Wild requested to search the house, and the dyer readily complied. Wild asked the women if they knew whether a man had taken shelter in the house, which they denied; but informing them that the man he sought for was a thief, they said he would find him in the coal-hole.

Having procured a candle, Wild and his attendants searched the place without effect, and they examined every part of the house with no better success. He observed that the villain must have escaped into the street; on which the dyer said, that could not be the case; that if he had entered, he must still be in the house, for he had not quitted the shop, and it was impossible that a man could pass to the street without his knowledge; and he advised Wild to search the cellar again. They now all went together into the cellar, and after some time spent in searching, the dyer turned up a large vessel, used in his business, and Butler appeared. Wild asked him in what manner he had disposed of the goods he stole from Newington-green, upbraided him as being guilty of ingratitude, and declared that he should certainly be hanged.

Butler, however, knowing the means by which an accommodation might be effected, directed Wild to go to his lodging and look behind the head of the bed, where he would find what would recompence him for his time and trouble. Wild went to the place, and found what perfectly satisfied him; but as Butler had been apprehended in a public manner, the other was under the necessity of taking him before a magistrate, who committed him for trial. He was tried the ensuing sessions at the Old Bailey; but by the artful management of Wild, instead of being condemned to die, he was only sentenced to transportation.

Being at an inn in Smithfield Wild observed a large trunk in the yard, he imagining that it contained property of value, and hastened home, and instructed one of the thieves he employed to carry it off. The man he employed in this matter was named Jeremiah Rann, and he was reckoned one of the most dexterous thieves in London. Having dressed himself so as exactly to resemble a porter, he carried away the trunk without being observed.

Mr Jarvis, a whip-maker by trade, and the proprietor of the trunk, had no sooner discovered his loss than he applied to Wild, who returned him the goods, in consideration of receiving ten guineas. Some time after a disagreement took place between Jonathan and Rann, and the former apprehended the latter, who was tried and condemned to die. The day preceding that on which Rann was executed, he sent for Mr Jarvis, and related to him all the particulars relative to the trunk. Mr Jarvis threatened Wild with a prosecution, but all apprehensions on that score were soon dissipated by the decease of Mr Jarvis.

Wild being much embarrassed in endeavouring to find out some method by which he might safely dispose of the property that was not claimed by the respective proprietors, resolved in his mind a variety of schemes; but, at length, he adopted that which follows: he purchased a sloop, in order to transport the goods to Holland and Flanders, and gave the command of the vessel to a notorious thief named Roger Johnson.

Ostend was the port where this vessel principally traded, but when the goods were not disposed of there Johnson navigated her to Bruges, Ghent, Brussels, and other places. He brought home lace, wine, brandy, &c. and these commodities were landed in the night, without causing any increase in the business of the revenue officers. This trade was continued about two years, when two pieces of lace being lost, Johnson deducted the value of them from the mate's pay. Violently irritated by this conduct, the mate lodged an information against Johnson, for running a great quantity of various kinds of goods. In consequence of this the vessel was exchequered, Johnson cast in damages to the amount of £700 and the commercial proceedings were entirely ruined.

A disagreement had for some time subsisted between Johnson and Thomas Edwards, who kept a house of resort for thieves in Long-lane, concerning the division of some booty. Meeting one day in the Strand, they charged each other with felony, and were both taken into custody. Wild bailed Johnson, and Edwards was not prosecuted. The latter had no sooner recovered his liberty than he gave information against Wild, whose private warehouses being searched, a great quantity of stolen goods was there found. Wild arrested Edwards in the name of Johnson, to whom he pretended the goods belonged, and he was taken to the Marshalsea, but the next day he procured bail. Edwards, determined to wreak revenge upon Johnson, for some time industriously sought for him in vain; but meeting him accidentally in Whitechapel-road he gave him into the custody of a peace-officer, who conducted him to an adjacent ale-house. Johnson sent for Wild, who immediately attended, accompanied by his man Quilt Arnold. Wild promoted a riot, during which Johnson availed himself of an opportunity of effecting an escape.

Information being made against Wild for the rescue of Johnson, he judged it prudent to abscond, and he remained concealed for three weeks, at the end of which time, supposing all danger to be over, he returned to his house. Learning that Wild had returned, Mr Jones, high-constable of Holborn division, went to his house in the Old Bailey on the 15th of February, 1725, and apprehended him and Quilt Arnold, and took them before Sir John Fryer, who committed them to Newgate on a charge of having assisted in the escape of Johnson.

On Wednesday the 24th of the same month Wild moved to be either admitted to bail, or discharged, or brought to trial that sessions. On the following Friday a warrant of detainer was produced against him in court, and to it was affixed the following articles of information:

I. That for many years past he had been a confederate with great numbers of highwaymen, pick-pockets, house-breakers, shop-lifters, and other thieves.

II. That he had formed a kind of corporation of thieves, of which he was the head or director, and that notwithstanding his pretended services, in detecting and prosecuting offenders, he procured such only to be hanged as concealed their booty, or refused to share it with him.

III. That he had divided the town and country into so many districts, and appointed distinct gangs for each, who regularly accounted with him for their robberies. That he had also a particular set to steal at churches in time of divine service: and likewise other moving detachments to attend at court, on birth-days, balls, &c. and at both houses of parliament, circuits, and country fairs.

IV. That the persons employed by him were for the most part felons convict, who had returned from transportation before the time, for which they were transported, was expired; and that he made choice of them to be his agents, because they could not be legal evidences against him, and because he had it in his power to take from them what part of the stolen goods he thought fit, and otherwise use them ill, or hang them as he pleased.

V. That he had from time to time supplied such convicted felons with money and cloaths, and lodged them in his own house, the better to conceal them: particularly some, against whom there are now informations for counterfeiting and diminishing broad pieces and guineas.

VI. That he had not only been a receiver of stolen goods, as well as of writings of all kinds, for near fifteen years past, but had frequently been a confederate, and robbed along with the above-mentioned convicted felons.

VII. That, in order to carry on these vile practices, to gain some credit with the ignorant multitude, he usually carried a short silver staff, as a badge of authority from the government, which he used to produce, when he himself was concerned in robbing.

VIII. That he had, under his care and direction, several warehouses for receiving and concealing stolen goods; and also a ship for carrying off jewels, watches, and other valuable goods, to Holland, where he had a superannuated thief for his factor.

IX. That he kept in pay several artists to make alterations, and transform watches, seals, snuff-boxes, rings, and other valuable things, that they might not be known, several of which he used to present to such persons as he thought might be of service to him.

X. That he seldom or never helped the owners to the notes and papers they had lost, unless he found them able exactly to specify and describe them, and then often insisted on more than half the value.

XI. And lastly, it appears that he has often sold human blood, by procuring false evidence to swear persons into facts they were not guilty of; sometimes to prevent them from being evidences against himself, and at other times for the sake of the great reward given by the government.

The information of Mr Jones was also read in court, setting forth that two persons would be produced to accuse the prisoner of capital offences. The men alluded to in the above affidavit were John Follard and Thomas Butler, who had been convicted: but it being deemed expedient to grant them a pardon on condition of their appearing in support of a prosecution against Wild, they pleaded to the same, and were remanded to Newgate till the next sessions.

Saturday the 10th of April Wild by council moved that his trial might be postponed till the ensuing sessions, and an affidavit made by the prisoner was read in court, purporting that till the preceding evening he was entirely ignorant of a bill having been found against him; that he knew not what offence was charged against him; and was unable to procure two material witnesses, one of them living near Brentford, and the other in Somersetshire. This was opposed by the council for the crown, who urged that it would be improper to defer the trial on so frivolous a pretext as that made by the prisoner; that the affidavit expressed an ignorance of what offence he was charged with, and yet declared that two nameless persons were material witnesses.

The prisoner informed the court that his witnesses were —— Hays, at the Packhorse, on Turnham-green, and —— Wilson, a clothier at Frome; adding that he had heard it slightly intimated that he was indicted for a felony committed upon a person named Stetham. Wild's council moved that the names of Hays and Wilson might be inserted in the affidavit, and that it should be again sworn to by the prisoner. The council for the prosecution observed that justice would not be denied the prisoner, though it could not be reasonably expected that he would be allowed any extraordinary favours or indulgencies. Follard and Butler were, at length, bound each in the penalty of £500 to appear at the ensuing sessions, when it was agreed that Wild's fate should be determined.

Saturday, May the 15th, 1725, Jonathan Wild was indicted for privately stealing in the house of Catherine Stetham, in the parish of St Andrew, Holborn, fifty yards of lace, the property of the said Catherine, on the 22nd of January, 1724–5. He was a second time indicted for feloniously receiving of the said Catherine on the 10th of March ten guineas on account, and under pretence of restoring the said lace, without apprehending and prosecuting the felon who stole the property.

Before his trial came on Wild distributed among the jurymen, and other persons who were walking on the leads before the court, a great number of printed papers, under the title of, 'A List of Persons discovered, apprehended, and convicted of several Robberies on the High-Way; and also for Burglary and House-Breaking; and also for returning from Transportation; by Jonathan Wild.' This list contained the names of thirty-five for robbing on the highway; twenty-two for house-breaking; and ten for returning from transportation. To the list was annexed the following,

'Note, several others have been also convicted for the like crimes, but, remembering not the persons names who had been robbed, I omit the criminals names.

'Please to observe, that several others have been also convicted for shop-lifting, picking of pockets, &c. by the female sex, which are capital crimes, and which are too tedious to be inserted here, and the prosecutors not willing of being exposed.

'In regard therefore of the numbers above convicted, some, that have yet escaped justice are endeavouring to take away the life of the said   JONATHAN WILD.'

The prisoner being put to the bar, he requested that the witnesses might be examined apart, which was complied with. Henry Kelley deposed that by the prisoner's direction he went, in company with Margaret Murphy, to the prosecutor's shop under pretence of buying some lace; that he stole a tin box, and gave it to Murphy in order to deliver to Wild, who waited in the street for the purpose of receiving their booty, and rescuing them if they should be taken into custody; that they returned together to Wild's house, where the box being opened was found to contain eleven pieces of lace; that Wild said he could afford to give no more than five guineas, as he should not be able to get more than ten guineas for returning the goods to the owner; that he received, as his share, three guineas and a crown, and that Murphy had what remained of the five guineas.

Margaret Murphy[1] was next sworn, and her evidence corresponded in every particular with that of the former witness.

Catherine Stetham, the elder, deposed that between three and four in the afternoon of the 22d of January, a man and a woman came to her house pretending that they wanted to purchase some lace; that she shewed them two or three parcels, to the quality and price of which they objected; and that in about three hours after they had left the shop, she missed a tin-box containing a quantity of lace, the value of which she estimated at £50.

[1] She was executed on the 27th of March, 1728, for stealing plate.

The prisoner's council observed that it was their opinion he could not be legally convicted because the indictment positively expressed that *he stole* the lace *in* the house, whereas it had been proved in evidence that he was at a considerable distance when the fact was committed. They admitted that he might be liable to conviction as an accessary before the fact, or guilty of receiving the property, knowing it to be stolen, but conceived that he could not be deemed guilty of a capital felony unless the indictment declared (as the act directs) that he did *assist, command,* or *hire.*

Lord Raymond presided when Wild was tried, and in summing up the evidence his Lordship observed, that the guilt of the prisoner was a point beyond all dispute; but that as a similar case was not to be found in the law books it became his duty to act with great caution; he was not perfectly satisfied that the construction urged by the council for the crown could be put upon the indictment; and as the life of a fellow-creature was at stake, recommended the prisoner to the mercy of the jury, who brought in their verdict NOT GUILTY.

Wild was indicted a second time for an offence committed during his confinement in Newgate. The indictment being opened by the council for the crown, the following clause in an act passed in the 4th year of Geo. I. was ordered to be read.

'And whereas, there are divers persons, who have secret acquaintance with felons, and who make it their business to help persons to their stolen goods, and by that means gain money from them, which is divided between them and the felons, whereby they greatly encourage such offenders. Be it enacted, by the authority aforesaid, that wherever any person taketh money or reward, directly or indirectly, under pretence, or upon account of helping any person or persons to any stolen goods or chattels, every such person so taking money or reward as aforesaid (unless such person do apprehend, or cause to be apprehended, such felon, who stole the same, and give evidence against him) shall be guilty of felony, according to the nature of the felony committed in stealing such goods, and in such and the same

manner, as if such offender had stolen such goods and
chattels, in the manner, and with such circumstances as the
same was stolen.'

Catherine Stetham deposed to the following effect;
'A box of lace being stolen out of my shop, on the 22d of
January, I went in the evening of the same day to the
prisoner's house, in order to employ him in recovering my
goods; but not finding him at home I advertised them,
offering a reward of fifteen guineas, and saying no questions should be asked. The advertisement proved ineffectual: I therefore went again to the prisoner's house, and
by his desire gave the best description that I was able of the
persons I suspected to be the robbers; and promising to
make enquiry after my property, he desired me to call
again in two or three days. I attended him a second time,
when he informed me that he had learnt something concerning my goods, and expected more particular information
in a short time. During this conversation we were joined by
a man, who said he had reason to suspect that one Kelley,
who had been tried for circulating gilt shillings, was concerned in stealing the lace. I went to the prisoner again on
the day he was apprehended, and informed him that though
I had advertised a reward of no more than fifteen, I would
give twenty or twenty-five guineas, rather than not recover
my property; upon which he desired me not to be in too
great a hurry, and said the people who had the lace were
gone out of town, but that he would contrive to foment a
disagreement between them, by which means he should be
enabled to recover the goods on more easy terms. He sent
me word, on the 10th of March, that if I would attend him
in Newgate, and bring ten guineas with me, the goods
should be returned. I went to the prisoner, who desired
a person to call a porter, and then gave me a letter, saying
it was the direction he had received where to apply for the
lace. I told him I could not read, and gave the letter to the
man he had sent for, who appeared to be a ticket-porter.
The prisoner then told me I must give the porter ten
guineas that he might pay the people who had my goods,
otherwise they would not return them. I gave the money,

and the man went out of the prison; but in a short time he returned with a box sealed up: though it was not the box I lost, I opened it, and found all my lace, excepting one piece. I asked the prisoner what satisfaction he expected; and he answered, Not a farthing; I have no interested views in matters of this kind, but act from a principle of serving people under misfortunes. I hope I shall be soon able to recover the other piece of lace, and to return you the ten guineas, and perhaps cause the thief to be apprehended. For the service I can render you, I shall only expect your prayers. I have many enemies, and know not what will be the consequence of this imprisonment.'

The prisoner's council argued that as Murphy had deposed that Wild, Kelley, and herself were concerned in the felony, the former could by no means be considered as coming within the description of the act on which the indictment was founded; for the act in question was not meant to operate against the actual perpetrators of felony, but to subject such persons to punishment as held a correspondence with felons.

The council for the crown observed that from the evidence adduced no doubt could remain of the prisoner's coming under the meaning of the act, since it had been proved that he had engaged in combinations with felons, and had not discovered them.

The judge recapitulated the arguments inforced on each side, and was of opinion that the case of the prisoner was clearly within the meaning of the act; for it was plain that he had maintained a secret correspondence with felons, and received money for restoring stolen goods to the owners, which money was divided between him and the felons, whom he did not prosecute. The jury pronounced him guilty, and he was executed at Tyburn, on Monday the 24th of May, 1725.

While he was under sentence of death he frequently declared that he thought the service he had rendered the public in returning stolen goods to the owners, and apprehending felons, was so great as justly to intitle him to the royal mercy. He said that had he considered his case as being desperate he should have taken timely measures for inducing some powerful friends, at Woolverhampton, to intercede in his favour; and that he thought it not unreasonable to entertain hopes of obtaining a pardon through the interest of some of the dukes, earls and other persons of high distinction who had recovered their property through his means. It was observed to him that he had trained up a great number of thieves, and must be conscious that he had not inforced the execution of the law from any principle of virtue, but had sacrificed the lives of a great number of his accomplices in order to provide for his own safety, and to gratify his desire of revenge against those who had incurred his displeasure.

He was observed to be in an unsettled state of mind, and being asked whether he knew the cause thereof, he said he attributed his disorder to the many wounds he had received in apprehending felons, and particularly mentioned two fractures of his skull, and his throat being cut by Blueskin.

He declined attending divine service in the chapel, excusing himself on account of his infirmities, and saying that there were many people highly exasperated against him, and therefore he could not expect but that his devotions would be interrupted by their insulting behaviour. He said he had fasted four days, which had greatly encreased his weakness. He asked the Ordinary the meaning of the words, 'Cursed is every one that hangeth on a tree,' and what was the state of the soul immediately after its departure from the body? He was advised to direct his attention to matters of more importance, and sincerely to repent of the crimes he had committed.

By his desire the Ordinary administered the sacrament to him, and during the ceremony he appeared to be somewhat attentive and devout. The evening preceding the day on which he suffered he enquired of the Ordinary whether self-murder could be deemed a crime, since many of the Greeks and Romans who had put a period to their own lives were so honourably mentioned by historians? He was informed that the most wise and learned heathens accounted those guilty of the greatest cowardice who had not fortitude sufficient to maintain themselves in the station to which they had been appointed by the providence of Heaven; and that the christian doctrine condemned the practice of suicide in the most express terms.

He pretended to be convinced that self-murder was a most impious crime: but about two in the morning he endeavoured to put an end to his life by drinking laudanum; but on account of the largeness of the dose and his having fasted for a considerable time, no other effect was produced than drowsiness a kind of stupefaction. The situation of Wild being observed by two of his fellow-prisoners, they advised him to rouse his spirits that he might be able to attend to the devotional exercises, and taking him by the arms they obliged him to walk, which he could not have done alone, being much afflicted with the gout. The exercise revived him a little, but he presently became exceedingly pale, then grew very faint; a profuse sweating ensued, and soon afterwards his stomach discharged the greatest part of the laudanum.

Though he was now somewhat recovered he was nearly in a state of insensibility, and in this situation he was put into the cart and conveyed to Tyburn.

In his way to the place of execution the populace treated this offender with remarkable severity, incessantly pelting him with stones, dirt, &c. and execrating him as the most consummate villain that had ever disgraced human nature.

Upon his arrival at Tyburn he appeared to be much recovered from the effects of the laudanum; and the executioner informed him that a reasonable time would be allowed him for preparing himself for the important change that he must soon experience. He continued sitting some time in the cart; but the populace were, at length, so enraged at the indulgence shewn him, that they outrageously called to the executioner to perform the duties of his office, violently threatening him with instant death if he presumed any longer to delay. He judged it prudent to comply with their demands, and when he began to prepare for the execution the popular clamour ceased.

About two o'clock on the following morning the remains

of Wild were interred in St Pancras Church-yard: but a few nights afterwards the body was taken up (for the use of the surgeons, as it was supposed). At midnight a hearse and six was waiting at the end of Fig-lane, where the coffin was found the next day.

Wild had, by the woman he married at Woolverhampton, a son about 19 years old, who came to London a short time before the execution of his father. He was a youth of so violent and ungovernable a disposition that it was judged prudent to confine him while his father was conveyed to Tyburn, lest he should create a tumult and prove the cause of mischief among the populace. Soon after the death of his father he accepted a sum of money to become a servant in one of our plantations.

Besides the woman to whom he was married at Woolver-hampton, five others lived with him under the pretended sanction of matrimony; the first was Mary Milliner; the second Judith Nun, who bore to him a daughter; the third Sarah Grigson, alias Perrin; the fourth Elizabeth Man, who cohabited with him about five years; the fifth, whose real name is uncertain, married some time after the death of Wild.

History cannot furnish an instance of such complicated villainy as was shewn in the character of Jonathan Wild, who possessed abilities, which had they been properly cultivated, and directed into a right course, would have rendered him a respectable and an useful member of society; but it is to be lamented that the profligate turn of mind that distinguished him in the early part of life, disposed him to adopt the maxims of the abandoned people with whom he became acquainted.

During his apprenticeship Wild was observed to be fond of reading, but as his finances would not admit of his buying books, his studies were confined to such as casually fell in his way; and they unfortunately happened to contain those abominable doctrines to which thousands have owed the ruin of both their bodies and souls. In short, at an early period of life he imbibed the principles of Deism and Atheism, and the sentiments he thus early contracted he strictly adhered to nearly till the period of his dissolution.

Voluminous writings were formerly beyond the purchase of persons in the inferior classes of life: but the great encouragement that has of late years been given to the publication of weekly numbers has so liberally diffused the streams of knowledge, that but few even of the lower ranks of mankind, can be sensible of any impediment to the gratification of the desire of literary acquirements.

Wild trained up and instructed his dependants in the practice of villainy, and when they became the objects of his displeasure he laboured with unremitting assiduity to procure their deaths. Thus his temporal and private interest sought gratification at the expence of every religious and moral obligation. We must conceive it to be impossible for a man acknowledging the existence of an Almighty Being to employ his attention upon devising the means of corrupting his fellow creatures, and cutting them off 'even in the blossom of their sins;' but the Atheist having nothing after this world either to hope or fear, is only careful to secure himself from detection, and the success of one iniquitous scheme naturally induces him to engage in others, and the latter actions are generally attended with circumstances of more aggravated guilt than the former.

There is a principle implanted in our nature that will exert itself when we are approaching to a state of dissolution, and impress our minds with a full confidence in the existence of an eternal God, who will reward or punish us according to our deserts or demerits. Thus it happened to the miserable subject of these pages, who when he had relinquished the hope of surviving the sentence of the law, anxiously enquired into the meaning of several texts of scripture, and concerning the intermediate state of the soul. The horrors of his guilt rushed upon his conscience with such force that reflection became intolerable, and instead of repenting of his enormous crimes, he employed his last moments that were enlightened by reason (the distinguishing characteristic of humanity) in meditating the means of self-murder!

A full Account of the Life and Transactions of the famous RICHARD TURPIN, who was hanged for Horse-stealing.

THE transactions of this malefactor made a greater noise in the world at the time they happened than those of almost any other offender whose life we have recorded: and we shall therefore be the more particular in our account of him.

He was the son of John Turpin, a farmer at Hempstead in Essex, and having received a common school education, was apprenticed to a butcher in Whitechapel; but was distinguished from his early youth for the impropriety of his behaviour, and the brutality of his manners.

On the expiration of his apprenticeship he married a young woman of East-Ham in Essex, named Palmer: but he had not been long married before he took to the practice of stealing his neighbours cattle, which he used to kill and cut up for sale.

Having stolen two oxen belonging to Mr Giles of Plaistow, he drove them to his own house; but two of Giles's servants suspecting who was the robber, went to Turpin's, where they saw two beasts of such size as had been lost; but as the hides were stripped from them, it was impossible to say that they were the same: but learning that Turpin used to dispose of his hides at Waltham-Abbey, they went thither, and saw the hides of the individual beasts that had been stolen.

No doubt now remaining who was the robber, a warrant was procured for the apprehension of Turpin; but learning that the peace-officers were in search of him, he made his escape from the back-window of his house, at the very moment that the others were entering at the door.

Having retreated to a place of security, he found means to inform his wife where he was concealed; on which she furnished him with money, with which he travelled into the hundreds of Essex, where he joined a gang of smugglers, with whom he was for some time successful; till a set of the Custom-house officers, by one successful stroke, deprived him of all his ill-acquired gains.

Thrown out of this kind of business, he connected himself with a gang of deer-stealers, the principal part of whose depredations were committed on Epping-Forest, and the parks in its neighbourhood: but this business not succeeding to the expectation of the robbers, they determined to commence house-breakers.

Their plan was to fix on houses that they presumed contained any valuable property; and, while one of them knocked at the door, the others were to rush in, and seize whatever they might deem worthy of their notice.

Their first attack of this kind was at the house of Mr Strype, an old man who kept a chandler's shop at Watford, whom they robbed of all the money in his possession, but did not offer him any personal abuse.

Turpin now acquainted his associates that there was an old woman at Loughton, who was in possession of seven or eight hundred pounds; whereupon they agreed to rob her; and when they came to the door, one of them knocked, and the rest forcing their way into the house, tied handkerchiefs over the eyes of the old woman and her maid.

This being done, Turpin demanded what money was in the house; and the owner hesitating to tell him, he threatened to set her on the fire if she did not make an immediate discovery. Still, however, she declined to give the desired information; on which the villains actually placed her on the fire, where she sat till the tormenting pains compelled her to discover her hidden treasure; so that the robbers possessed themselves of above four hundred pounds, and decamped with the booty.

Some little time after this they agreed to rob the house of a farmer near Barking; and knocking at the door, the people declined to open it; on which they broke it open; and having bound the farmer, his wife, his son-in-law, and the servant-maid, they robbed the house of above seven hundred pounds; which delighted Turpin so much, that he exclaimed, 'Aye, this will do, if it would always be so!' and the robbers retired with their prize, which amounted to above eighty pounds for each of them.

This desperate gang, now flushed with success, determined

to attack the house of Mr Mason, the keeper of Epping-Forest; and the time was fixed when the plan was to be carried into execution: but Turpin having gone to London, to spend his share of the former booty, intoxicated himself to such a degree that he totally forgot the appointment.

Nevertheless, the rest of the gang resolved that the absence of their companion should not frustrate the proposed design; and having taken a solemn oath to break every article of furniture in Mason's house, they set out on their expedition.

Having gained admission, they beat and kicked the unhappy man with great severity. Finding an old man sitting by the fire-side, they permitted him to remain uninjured; and Mr Mason's daughter escaped their fury, by running out of the house, and taking shelter in a hog-stie.

After ransacking the lower part of the house, and doing much mischief, they went up stairs, where they broke every thing that fell in their way, and among the rest a China punch-bowl, from which dropped one hundred and twenty guineas, which they made prey of, and effected their escape. They now went to London in search of Turpin, with whom they shared the booty, though he had not taken an active part in the execution of the villainy.

On the 11th of January, 1735, Turpin and five of his companions went to the house of Mr Saunders, a rich farmer at Charlton in Kent, between seven and eight in the evening, and having knocked at the door, asked if Mr Saunders was at home. Being answered in the affirmative, they rushed into the house, and found Mr Saunders, with his wife and friends, playing at cards in the parlour. They told the company that they should remain uninjured if they made no disturbance. Having made prize of a silver snuff-box which lay on the table, a part of the gang stood guard over the rest of the company, while the others attended Mr Saunders through the house, and breaking open his escrutores and closets, stole above a hundred pounds, exclusive of plate.

During these transactions the servant-maid ran up stairs, barred the door of her room, and called out 'Thieves,' with a view of alarming the neighbourhood: but the robbers broke open the door of her room, secured her, and then robbed the house of all the valuable property they had not before taken. Finding some minced-pies, and some bottles of wine, they sat down to regale themselves: and meeting with a bottle of brandy, they compelled each of the company to drink a glass of it.

Mrs Saunders fainting through terror, they administered some drops in water to her, and recovered her to the use of her senses. Having staid in the house a considerable time, they packed up their booty and departed, having first declared that if any of the family gave the least alarm within two hours, or advertised the marks of the stolen plate, they would return and murder them at a future time.

Retiring to a public-house at Woolwich, where they had concerted the robbery, they crossed the Thames to an empty house in Ratcliffe-Highway, where they deposited the stolen effects till they found a purchaser for them.

The division of the plunder having taken place, they, on the 18th of the same month, went to the house of Mr Sheldon, near Croydon in Surrey, where they arrived about seven in the evening. Having got into the yard, they perceived a light in the stable, and going into it, found the coachman attending his horses. Having immediately bound him, they quitted the stable, and meeting Mr Sheldon in the yard, they seized him, and compelling him to conduct them into the house, they stole eleven guineas, with the jewels, plate, and other things of value, to a large amount. Having committed this robbery, they returned Mr Sheldon two guineas, and apologized for their conduct.

This being done, they hastened to the Black Horse in the Broad-way Westminster, where they concerted the robbery of Mr Lawrence of Edgware, near Stanmore in Middlesex, for which place they set out on the 4th of February, and arrived at a public-house in that village about five o'clock in the evening. From this place they went to Mr Lawrence's house, where they arrived about seven o'clock, just as he had discharged some people who had worked for him.

Having quitted their horses at the outer-gate, one of the robbers going forwards, found a boy who had just returned from folding his sheep: the rest of the gang following, a pistol was presented, and instant destruction threatened if he made any noise. They then took off his garters, and tied his hands, and told him to direct them to the door, and, when they knocked, to answer, and bid the servants open it, in which case they would not hurt him: but when the boy came to the door he was so terrified that he could not speak; on which one of the gang knocked, and a man-servant, imagining it was one of the neighbours, opened the door, whereupon they all rushed in, armed with pistols.

Having seized Mr Lawrence and his servant, they threw a cloth over their faces, and taking the boy into another room, demanded what firearms were in the house; to which he replied only an old gun, which they broke in pieces. They then bound Mr Lawrence and his man, and made them sit by the boy; and Turpin searching the gentleman, took from him a guinea, a Portugal piece, and some silver: but not being satisfied with this booty, they forced him to conduct them up stairs, where they broke open a closet, and stole some money and plate: but that not being sufficient to satisfy them, they threatened to murder Mr Lawrence, each of them destining him to a different death, as the savageness of his own nature prompted him. At length one of them took a kettle of water from the fire, and threw it over him; but it providentially happened not to be hot enough to scald him.

In the interim the maid-servant, who was churning butter in the dairy, hearing a noise in the house, apprehended some mischief; on which she blew out her candle, to screen herself: but being found in the course of their search, one of the miscreants compelled her to go up stairs, where he gratified his brutal passion by force. They then robbed the house of all the valuable effects they could find, locked the family into the parlour, threw the key into the garden, and took their ill-gotten plunder to London.

The particulars of this atrocious robbery being represented to the king, a proclamation was issued for the apprehension of the offenders, promising a pardon to any one of them who would impeach his accomplices; and a reward of fifty pounds was offered, to be paid on conviction. This, however, had no effect: the robbers continued their depredations as before, and, flushed with the success they had met with, seemed to bid defiance to the laws.

On the 7th of February six of them assembled at the White-Bear Inn in Drury-Lane, where they agreed to rob the house of Mr Francis, a farmer near Marybone. Arriving at the place, they found a servant in the cow-house, whom they bound fast, and threatened to murder him if he was not perfectly silent. This being done, they led him into the stable, where finding another of the servants, they bound him in the same manner.

In the interim Mr Francis happening to come home, they presented their pistols to his breast, and threatened instant destruction to him, if he made the least noise or opposition.

Having bound the master in the stable with his servants, they rushed into the house, tied Mrs Francis, her daughter, and the maid-servant, and beat them in a most cruel manner. One of the thieves stood as a sentry while the rest rifled the house, in which they found a silver tankard, a medal of Charles the First, a gold watch, several gold rings, a considerable sum of money, and a variety of valuable linen and other effects, which they conveyed to London.

Hereupon a reward of an hundred pounds was offered for the apprehension of the offenders; in consequence of which two of them were taken into custody, tried, convicted on the evidence of an accomplice, and hanged in chains: and the whole gang being dispersed, Turpin went into the country, to renew his depredations on the public.

On a journey towards Cambridge he met a man genteelly dressed, and well mounted; and expecting a good booty, he presented a pistol to the supposed gentleman, and demanded his money. The party thus stopped happened to be one King, a famous highwayman, who knew Turpin; and when the latter threatened instant destruction if he did not deliver his money, King burst into a fit of laughter, and said, 'What dog eat dog?—Come, come, brother Turpin;

if you don't know me, I know you, and shall be glad of your company.'

These brethren in iniquity soon struck the bargain, and immediately entering on business, committed a number of robberies; till at length they were so well known that no public-house would receive them as guests. Thus situated, they fixed on a spot between the King's-Oak and the Loughton Road, on Epping-Forest, where they made a cave which was large enough to receive them and their horses.

This cave was enclosed within a sort of thicket of bushes and brambles, through which they could look and see passengers on the road, while themselves remained unobserved.

From this station they used to issue, and robbed such a number of persons, that at length the very pedlars who travelled the road carried fire-arms for their defence: and while they were in this retreat Turpin's wife used to supply them with necessaries, and frequently remained in the cave during the night.

Having taken a ride as far as Bungay in Suffolk, they observed two young women receive fourteen pounds for corn, on which Turpin resolved to rob them of the money. King objected, saying it was pity to rob such pretty girls: but Turpin was obstinate, and obtained the booty.

Upon their return home on the following day, they stopped a Mr Bradele of London, who was riding in his chariot with his children. The gentleman, seeing only one robber, was preparing to make resistance, when King called to Turpin to hold the horses. They took from the gentleman his watch, money, and an old mourning ring; but returned the latter, as he declared that its intrinsic value was trifling, yet he was very unwilling to part from it.

Finding that they readily parted with the ring, he asked them what he must give for the watch: on which King said to Turpin, 'What say ye Jack?—Here seems to be a good honest fellow; shall we let him have the watch?'—Turpin replied, 'Do as you please:' on which King said to the gentleman, 'You must pay six guineas for it: We never sell

for more, though the watch should be worth six and thirty.'
The gentleman promised that the money should be left at
the Dial in Birchin-Lane, where they might receive it, and
no questions would be asked.

Not long after this Turpin was guilty of murder, which
arose from the following circumstance. A reward of an
hundred pounds having been offered for apprehending him,
the servant of a gentleman named Thompson went out with
a higler, to try if they could take this notorious offender.
Turpin seeing them approach near his dwelling, Mr Thompson's man having a gun, he mistook them for poachers;
on which he said there were no hares near that thicket:
'No (said Thompson's servant) but I have found a Turpin;'
and presenting his gun, required him to surrender.

Hereupon Turpin spoke to him, as in a friendly manner,
and gradually retreated at the same time, till having seized
his own gun, he shot him dead on the spot, and the higler
ran off with the utmost precipitation.

This transaction making a great noise in the neighbourhood, Turpin went farther into the country in search of his
old companion, King; and in the mean time sent a letter to
his wife, to meet him at a public-house at Hertford. The
woman attended according to this direction; and her
husband coming into the house soon after she arrived, a
butcher to whom he owed five pounds happened to see him;
on which he said, 'Come, Dick, I know you have money
now; and if you will pay me it will be of great service.'

Turpin told him that his wife was in the next room; that
she had money, and that he should be paid immediately:
but while the butcher was hinting to some of his acquaintance, that the person present was Turpin, and that they
might take him into custody after he had received his debt,
the highwayman made his escape through a window, and
rode off with great expedition.

Turpin having found King, and a man named Potter,
who had lately connected himself with them, they set off
towards London in the dusk of the evening; but when they
came near the Green Man on Epping-Forest, they overtook
a Mr Major, who riding on a very fine horse, and Turpin's

beast being jaded, he obliged the rider to dismount, and exchange horses.

The robbers now pursued their journey towards London, and Mr Major going to the Green Man, gave an account of the affair; on which it was conjectured that Turpin had been the robber, and that the horse which he had exchanged must have been stolen.

It was on a Saturday evening that this robbery was committed; but Mr Major being advised to print hand-bills immediately, notice was given to the landlord of the Green Man, that such a horse as Mr Major had lost, had been left at the Red-Lion in Whitechapel. The landlord going thither, determined to wait till some person came for it; and, at about eleven at night, King's brother came to pay for the horse and take him away; on which he was immediately seized, and conducted into the house.

Being asked what right he had to the horse, he said he had bought it: but the landlord examining a whip which he had in his hand, found a button at the end of the handle half broken off, and the name of Major on the remaining half. Hereupon he was given into custody of a constable: but as it was not supposed that he was the actual robber, he was told that he should have his liberty, if he would discover his employer.

Hereupon he said that a stout man, in a white duffil coat, was waiting for the horse in Red-Lion Street; on which the company going thither, saw King, who drew a pistol, and attempted to fire it, but it flashed in the pan: he then endeavoured to pull out another pistol, but he could not, as it got entangled in his pocket.

At this time Turpin was watching at a small distance; and riding towards the spot, King cried out 'Shoot him, or we are taken:' on which Turpin fired, and shot his companion, who called out 'Dick, you have killed me;' which the other hearing, rode off at full speed.

King lived a week after this affair, and gave information that Turpin might be found at a house near Hackney-Marsh; and on enquiry it was discovered that Turpin had been there on the night that he rode off, lamenting that he had killed King, who was the most faithful associate he had ever had in his life.

For a considerable time did Turpin skulk about the forest, having been deprived of his retreat in the cave since he shot the servant of Mr Thompson. On the examination of this cave there were found two shirts, two pair of stockings, a piece of ham, and part of a bottle of wine.

Some vain attempts were made to take this notorious offender into custody; and among the rest the huntsman of a gentleman in the neighbourhood went in search of him with bloodhounds. Turpin perceiving them, got into a tree, under which the hounds passed, to his inexpressible terror, so that he determined to make a retreat into Yorkshire.

Going first to Long-Sutton in Lincolnshire, he stole some horses; for which he was taken into custody; but he escaped from the constable as he was conducting him before a magistrate, and hastened to Welton in Yorkshire, where he went by the name of John Palmer, and assumed the character of a gentleman.

He now frequently went into Lincolnshire, where he stole horses, which he brought into Yorkshire, and either sold or exchanged them.

He often accompanied the neighbouring gentlemen on their parties of hunting and shooting; and one evening, on a return from an expedition of the latter kind, he wantonly shot a cock belonging to his landlord. On this Mr Hall, a neighbour, said, 'You have done wrong in shooting your landlord's cock;' to which Turpin replied, that if he would stay while he loaded his gun he would shoot him also.

Irritated by this insult, Mr Hall informed the landlord of what had passed; and application being made to some magistrates, a warrant was granted for the apprehension of the offender, who being taken into custody, and carried before a bench of justices then assembled at the quarter sessions at Beverley, they demanded security for his good behaviour, which he being unable or unwilling to give, was committed to Bridewell.

On enquiry it appeared that he made frequent journies into Lincolnshire, and on his return he always abounded in money, and was likewise in possession of several horses; so that it was conjectured that he was a horse-stealer and highwayman.

On this the magistrates went to him on the following day, and demanded who he was, where he had lived, and what was his employment. He replied in substance, 'that about two years ago he had lived at Long-Sutton in Lincolnshire, and was by trade a butcher; but that having contracted several debts for sheep that proved rotten, he was obliged to abscond, and come to live in Yorkshire.'

The magistrates not being satisfied with this tale, commissioned the clerk of the peace to write into Lincoln-shire, to make the necessary enquiries respecting the supposed John Palmer. The letter was carried by a special messenger, who brought an answer from a magistrate in the neighbourhood, importing that John Palmer was well known, though he had never carried on trade there: that he had been accused of sheep-stealing, for which he had been in custody, but had made his escape from the peace-officers; and that there were several informations lodged against him for horse-stealing.

Hereupon the magistrates thought it prudent to remove him to York Castle, where he had not been more than a month, when two persons from Lincolnshire came and claimed a mare and foal, and likewise a horse, which he had stolen in that county.

After he had been about four months in prison he wrote the following letter to his brother in Essex.

'Dear Brother,   York, Feb. 6, 1739

'I Am sorry to acquaint you that I am now under con-finement in York Castle, for horse-stealing. If I could procure an evidence from London to give me a character, that would go a great way towards my being acquitted. I had not been long in this country before my being appre-hended, so that it would pass off the readier. For Heaven's sake, dear brother, do not neglect me; you will know what I mean, when I say——

'I am Yours,

'JOHN PALMER'

This letter being returned, unopened, to the Post-Office in Essex, because the brother would not pay the postage of it, was accidentally seen by Mr Smith, a schoolmaster, who having taught Turpin to write, immediately knew his hand, on which he carried the letter to a magistrate, who broke it open; by which it was discovered that the supposed John Palmer was the real Richard Turpin.

Hereupon the magistrates of Essex dispatched Mr Smith to York, who immediately selected him from all the other prisoners in the castle. This Mr Smith and another gentleman afterwards proved his identity on his trial.

On the rumour that the noted Turpin was a prisoner in York Castle, persons flocked from all parts of the country to take a view of him, and debates ran very high whether he was the real person or not. Among others who visited him was a young fellow who pretended to know the famous Turpin, and having regarded him a considerable time with looks of great attention, he told the keeper he would bet him half a guinea that he was not Turpin; on which the prisoner, whispering the keeper, said 'Lay him the wager, and I'll go your halves.'

When this notorious malefactor was brought to trial he was convicted on two indictments, and received sentence of death.

After conviction he wrote to his father, imploring him to intercede with a gentleman and lady of rank, to make interest that his sentence might be remitted; and that he might be transported. The father did what was in his power; but the notoriety of his character was such, that no persons would exert themselves in his favour.

This man lived in the most gay and thoughtless manner after conviction, regardless of all considerations of futurity, and affecting to make a jest of the dreadful fate that awaited him.

Not many days before his execution he purchased a new fustian frock and a pair of pumps, in order to wear them at the time of his death: and, on the day before, he hired five poor men, at ten shillings each, to follow the cart as mourners; and he gave hatbands and gloves to several other persons;

and he also left a ring, and some other articles, to a married woman in Lincolnshire, with whom he had been acquainted.

On the morning of his death he was put into a cart, and being followed by his mourners, as above-mentioned, he was drawn to the place of execution, in his way to which he bowed to the spectators with an air of the most astonishing indifference and intrepidity.

When he came to the fatal tree, he ascended the ladder; when his right leg trembling, he stamped it down with an air of assumed courage, as if he was ashamed to be observed to discover any signs of fear. Having conversed with the executioner about half an hour, he threw himself off the ladder and expired in a few minutes.

He suffered at York, on the tenth of April, 1739.

The spectators of the execution seemed to be much affected at the fate of this man, who was distinguished by the comeliness of his appearance. The corpse was brought to the Blue Boar, in Castle-Gate, York, where it remained till the next morning, when it was interred in the Church-yard of St George's parish, with an inscription on the coffin, with the initials of his name, and his age. The grave was made remarkably deep, and the people who acted as mourners took such measures as they thought would secure the body; yet about three o'clock on the following morning, some people were observed in the churchyard, who carried it off, and the populace having an intimation whither it was conveyed, found it in a garden belonging to one of the surgeons of the city.

Hereupon they took the body, laid it on a board, and having carried it through the streets, in a kind of triumphal manner, and then filled the coffin with unslackened lime, buried it in the grave where it had been before deposited.

We see in the case of his malefactor, what slight circumstances may lead to the conviction of the most notorious offender. The shooting of a cock, in the meer wantonness of his heart, occasioned Turpin's being taken into custody: the scrutiny into his character followed of course; and he was brought to condign punishment by an accident that would have been laughed at by any man of unblemished reputation.

His brother refusing to pay the postage of his letter, was another circumstance apparently trivial; yet this produced that sort of evidence which most materially affected him, by the schoolmaster's proving that he was the identical Turpin, who had been so notorious for his enormous offences in the southern counties.

It is not impossible but that he might have been pardoned, or transported, after a simple conviction for horse-stealing: but the notoriety of his character drew down certain destruction on his head.

Hence then, the young, the thoughtless, and all those whose dispositions may tempt them to acts of dishonesty, should learn the high value of an unblemished reputation: should consider that a good character is above all price, and that it ought to be preserved as a more precious jewel than could be purchased by all the riches of the eastern world!

In a word, the laws of the great Creator are, in every instance, so compatible with, and so productive of, the interest and happiness of mankind, that one would think no man could violate them, who did not wilfully seek his own destruction!

This rather ordinary criminal seems to have made a bigger noise in the world than his exploits warrant. Many romances have gathered about his name but they are, for the most part, quite legendary. He figures in William Harrison Ainsworth's first novel *Rookwood*, where an account is given of Turpin's ride to York on Black Bess.

A Particular Account of JAMES HALL, who was hanged for Petit-Treason, in the Murder of his Master.

THIS malefactor, according to the account given by himself, was descended of honest parents, of Wells in Hampshire, who gave him such an education as might qualify him for any ordinary rank of life.

Being unwilling to remain in the country, he came to London, and lived some time with a corn-chandler; and after a continuation in this service, he married, and had several children; but not living happily with his wife, articles of separation were executed between them. After this he married another woman, by whom he had one child, and who visited him after his being in custody for the murder.

At the sessions held at the Old Bailey, in August, 1741, he was indicted for the murder of John Penny, gentleman, and pleading guilty, received sentence of death.

Mr Penny had chambers in Clements Inn; and Hall had lived with him seven years before he committed the murder: nor had he formed any design of being guilty of the horrid deed till within about a month of its perpetration: but having kept more company than his circumstances could afford, he had involved himself in difficulties, which made him resolve to murder and rob his master.

On the 7th of June, 1741, he intoxicated himself with liquor, and then determined to carry his design into execution. Mr Penny coming home between eleven and twelve at night, Hall assisted in undressing him in the dining-room; and while he was walking towards the bed, the villain followed him with a stick which he had concealed for the purpose, and struck him one blow with such force that he never spoke afterwards; and continued his blows on the head till he was apparently dead.

Willing, however, to be certain of compleating the horrid tragedy, and to avoid detection, he went into the dining-room, and stripping himself naked, he took a small fruit knife belonging to his master, and returning to the chamber, cut his throat with it, holding his neck over the chamber-pot. Mr Penny bled very freely; for when the blood was mixed with a small quantity of water, it almost filled the pot five times; and three of the pots thus mixed the murderer threw into the sink, and two in the coal-hole. He then took his master's waistcoat, which was lined with duffil, and bound it round his neck, to suck up the remainder of the blood.

This being done, he took the body on his shoulders, carried it to the necessary, and threw it in head foremost; and flying back immediately to the chambers, under the most dreadful apprehensions of mind, he took his master's coat, bloody shirt, the stick that he had knocked him down with, and some rags that he had used in wiping up the blood, and running a second time naked to the necessary-house, threw them in at a hole on the opposite side of it.

The body being thus disposed of, he stole about thirty-six guineas from his master's pocket, and writing-desk; and such was the confusion of his mind, that he likewise took some franks, sealing-wax, and other articles for which he had no use: and then he employed the remainder of the night in washing and rubbing the rooms with cloths; but finding it no easy matter to get out the blood, he sent for the laundress in the morning to wash them again, telling her that his master's nose had bled over night.

On the following day the guilty wretch strolled from place to place, unable to find rest for a moment any where; and all his thoughts being engaged in concealing the murder, which he hoped was effectually done, from the place in which he had secreted the body.

On the Friday following he went to Mr Wooton, his master's nephew, on a pretence of enquiring for Mr Penny, who he said had quitted the chambers two days before, and gone somewhere by water; so that he was afraid some accident had happened to him.

Mr Wooton was so particular in his enquiries after his uncle, that Hall was exceedingly terrified at his questions, and knew not what answer to make to them. After this the criminal went twice every day to Mr Wooton, to enquire

Dodd delin.   J.Dodge sculp.

The manner of **BURNING** a **WOMAN** convicted of Treason.

after his master, for ten days; but lived all the while in a
torment of mind that is not to be described.

So wretched was he, that finding it impossible to sleep
in the chambers, he got his wife to come and be with him:
and they lay in Mr Penny's bed: but still sleep was a stranger
to him.

At length Mr Wooton had Hall taken into custody, on
a violent suspicion that he had murdered his uncle. On his
first examination before a magistrate, he steadily avowed his
innocence: but being committed to Newgate he attempted
an escape: this, however, was prevented; and a few days
afterwards he confessed his guilt before some relations of the
deceased.

We have already mentioned that he pleaded guilty on his
trial; and have now to add that, after sentence was passed
on him, he was exceedingly contrite and penitent, and
confessed his guilt in letters to his friends.

On the day before his death he received the sacrament,
with all apparent signs of that penitence which was necessary to prepare him for the dreadful scene that lay before him.

He was hanged at the end of Catherine Street in the
Strand, on the 15th of September, 1741, and his body afterwards hung in chains at Shepherd's Bush, three miles
beyond Tyburn Turnpike, on the road to Acton.

The following is a letter which this malefactor wrote to
his wife, the night preceding his execution.

'My Dear,   Twelve o'clock Sunday night
'I am very sorry we could not have the liberty of a little
time by ourselves, when you came to take your leave of me;
if we had, I should have thought of many more things to
have said to you than I did; but then I fear it would have
caused more grief at our parting. I am greatly concerned
that I am obliged to leave you and my child, and much more
in such a manner, as to give the world room to reflect upon
you on my account; though none but the ignorant will, but
rather pity your misfortunes, as being fully satisfied of
your innocency in all respects relating to the crime for which
I am in a few hours to suffer.

I now heartily wish, not only for my own sake, but the injured persons, yours, and my child's, that I was as innocent as you are, but freely own I am not, nor possibly can be in this world; yet I humbly hope, and fully trust, through God's great mercy, and the merits of my blessed Saviour Jesus Christ, to be happy in the next.

After I parted with you, I received the holy sacrament comfortably, which Mr Broughton was so good as to administer to me, who has also several times before taken a great deal of pains to instruct me, and so has some others of his acquaintance, by whose assistance, and my own endeavours, I hope God will pardon all my sins for Christ's sake, and admit me into his heavenly kingdom.

My dear, some of my latest prayers will be to God to direct and prosper you and my child in all good ways, so long as he pleases to let you live here on earth; that afterwards he may receive you both to his mercies to all eternity. I hope I shall willingly submit to my fate, and die in peace with all men. This is now all the comfort I can give you in this world, who living was, and dying hope to remain,

'Your loving and most affectionate husband,

'JAMES HALL'

To all we have said on the subject of murder, little need be added on this occasion. Those who fail to be struck by a recital of this horrid tale, must have less humanity than we hope falls to the share of any of our readers.

Instead, therefore, of making any remarks on this particular case, we will suppose it to be a sufficient comment on itself; and conclude with a prayer that we may all be delivered even from the temptation of spilling innocent blood!

Petit treason in English Law was the murder by an inferior of a superior to whom allegiance was owed in a natural, civil or spiritual relation. (Blackstone sets out the classes of persons who were superiors and inferiors in law.) Hall was hanged for murdering his master.

It was provided by the Offences against the Person Act of 1861 that every offence which before 1st July, 1828, would have amounted to petit treason should be deemed to be murder only and no greater offence.

It will be observed in the report of the case that Hall 'took the body on his shoulders, carried it to the necessary, and threw it in head foremost'. The necessary was a privy. It was usually referred to as a necessary house, necessary vault, or necessary place, but the words are now rarely used save in dialect speech.

A Narrative of the very singular Case of ROBERT FULLER, who was convicted on the Black Act, for shooting Francis Bailey; but recommended to Mercy.

AT the sessions held at the Old Bailey in the month of May, 1744, Robert Fuller, of Harefield in Middlesex, was indicted for shooting at Francis Bailey with a gun loaded with powder and small stones, and demanding his money, with intent to rob him.

Mr Bailey deposed, that, as he was returning from Uxbridge market, he saw a man near Harefield, sitting on a stile, having a gun in his hand: that he jumped off the stile, seized the horse's bridle, clapped the gun to Mr Bailey's body, and threatened to shoot him. Mr Bailey said, 'That will do you no good, nor me neither:' he then put his hand repeatedly into Bailey's pocket; but the latter would not submit to be robbed, and rode off: immediately on which Fuller shot at him, and wounded him in the right arm, so as to break the bone in splinters; and many stones, and bits of the bone, were afterwards taken out of the arm: nor did the prosecutor recover of the wound till after languishing near twenty weeks.

The prisoner, however, had not an opportunity of robbing Mr Bailey, as his horse took fright, and ran away at the report of the gun.

The substance of Mr Bailey's farther deposition was, that this happened about seven o'clock in the evening, on the 24th of February, but that, as it was a clear star-light night, he had a full view of the prisoner, whom he had known before.

Bailey was now asked, if he had ever been examined before any justice of the peace in relation to the fact; to which he answered in the negative. He was then asked, if he had never charged the crime on any other person except the prisoner, which he steadily denied the having done.

In contradiction to which, a commitment was produced,

in which Thomas Bowry was charged with assaulting Francis Bailey, with an intent to rob: and this Bowry was continued in custody, on the affidavit of Mr Mellish, a surgeon, that Mr Bailey was so ill of the wounds he had received, that he could not come to London without danger of his life: but Bowry was discharged at the gaol-delivery at the end of the sessions for June, 1743.

The copy of Bowry's commitment was now read, and authenticated by Richard Akerman, clerk of the papers to his father, the then keeper of Newgate.

On this contradictory evidence, the characters of both parties were enquired into, when that of the prosecutor appeared to be very fair, that of the prisoner rather doubtful.

Upon considering the whole matter, the jury gave a verdict that he was guilty; but on account of the circumstance abovementioned, relating to the commitment of Bowry for the same offence, on Bailey's oath, they recommended the prisoner to the court, as a proper object of the royal clemency.

This affair is one of that intricate nature, which must remain involved in mystery. It is impossible for us to say whether the prosecutor was, or was not, mistaken in the man against whom he swore; but we see that he had sworn the same fact, with equal positiveness, against Bowry: and this circumstance evinces the great propriety of the jury recommending the convict to mercy, where there is even but a bare probability remaining of his innocence. In doubtful cases we should always incline to the side of mercy; and it ought to be remembered, to the credit of the court at the Old Bailey, that this rule is constantly attended to; and it is a known fact, that persons charged with capital offences have been frequently heard to declare, that they would rather take their trials at the Old Bailey, than in any other court in the kingdom.

On this occasion it may not be improper to make a remark on the immense power that is lodged in the breasts of our judges who go the circuits. A great deal of this power is discretionary: it remains with them to reprieve the convict, or to leave him for execution: an awful trust! which makes the possessor of it accountable to God and his own conscience. We have no idea but that all the present judges exert their power in the mildest manner: but times have been, when magistrates have wantonly sported with their authority, to the destruction of the innocent, and the eternal disgrace of themselves.

This circumstance should hold forth a lesson of caution, never to trust the authority of a judge but with a man distinguished equally by his knowledge, integrity, and humanity.

This man was charged under the Waltham Black Act (see pp. 69–73). It is a very strange case where the prosecutor had made the very same charge against another person. This fact induced the jury to recommend him to mercy. The proper verdict, one would have thought, was 'Not Guilty', and certainly in our day the judge would have directed the jury to bring that verdict in, when the facts were brought out, for it is one of the cardinal principles of the administration of the law to-day that the prosecution must prove the charge beyond all reasonable doubt. The Editors refer to the power vested in the judges, and they add: 'it remains with them to reprieve the convict or to leave him for execution: an awful truth which makes the possessor of it accountable to God and his own conscience'. This power of postponing sentence of death when exercised by the judge who tried the prisoner, was considered by the Privy Council at which the King attended, and the King's decision almost invariably followed the advice tendered to him. This is illustrated by the case of Dr Dodd at p. 234 of this volume.

Narrative of the Case of Miss MARY BLANDY, who was executed for the murder of her Father; with some particulars respecting CAPTAIN CRANSTOUN.

MARY BLANDY was the only daughter of Mr Francis Blandy, an eminent attorney at Henley upon Thames, and town-clerk of that place. She had been educated with the utmost tenderness, and every possible care was taken to impress her mind with sentiments of virtue and religion. Her person had nothing in it remarkably engaging; but she was of a sprightly and affable disposition, polite in manners, and engaging in conversation; and was uncommonly distinguished by her good sense.

She had read the best authors in the English language, and had a memory remarkably retentive of the knowledge she had acquired. In a word, she excelled most of her sex in those accomplishments which are calculated to grace and dignify the female mind.

The father being reputed to be rich, a number of young gentlemen courted his acquaintance, with a view to make an interest with his daughter: but of all the visitors, none were more agreeable, both to father and daughter, than the gentlemen of the army: and the former was never better pleased than when he had some of them at his table.

Miss Blandy was about twenty-six years of age, when she became acquainted with captain William Henry Cranstoun, who was then about forty-six. He was the son of lord Cranstoun, of an ancient Scotch family, which had made great alliances, by intermarriages with the nobility of Scotland. Being a younger brother, his uncle lord Mark Ker procured him a commission in the army, which, with the interest of £1,500 was all he had for his support.

Cranstoun married a Miss Murray in Scotland in the year 1745, and received a handsome fortune with her: but he was defective in the great article of prudence. His wife was delivered of a son within a year after the marriage; and about this period he received orders to join his regiment in England, and was sent on a recruiting party to Henley, which gave rise to the unhappy connexion which ended so fatally.

It may seem extraordinary, and is, perhaps, a proof of Cranstoun's art, that he could ingratiate himself into the affections of Miss Blandy; for his person was diminutive; he was so marked with the small-pox, that his face was in seams, and he squinted very much: but he possessed that faculty of small-talk, which is but too prevalent with many of the fair sex.

Mr Blandy, who was acquainted with lord Mark Ker, was fond of being deemed a man of taste, and so open to flattery, that it is not to be wondered at, that a man of Cranstoun's artifice ingratiated himself into his favour, and obtained permission to pay his addresses to the daughter.

Cranstoun, apprehending that Miss Blandy might discover that he had a wife in Scotland, informed her that he was involved in a disagreeable law-suit in that country, with a young lady who claimed him as a husband; and so sure was he of the interest he had obtained in Miss Blandy's affections, that he had the confidence to ask her if she loved him well enough to wait the issue of the affair. She told him, that if her father and mother approved of her staying for him, she had no objection.

This must be allowed to have been a very extraordinary declaration of love, and as extraordinary a reply.

Cranstoun endeavoured to conduct the amour with all possible secrecy; notwithstanding which, it came to the knowledge of lord Mark Ker, who wrote to Mr Blandy, informing him that the captain had a wife and children in Scotland, and conjuring him to preserve his daughter from ruin.

Alarmed by this intelligence, Mr Blandy informed his daughter of it; but she did not seem equally affected, as Cranstoun's former declaration had prepared her to expect some such news: and, when the old gentleman taxed Cranstoun with it, he declared it was only an affair of gallantry, of which he should have no difficulty to free himself.

Mrs Blandy appears to have been under as great a degree of infatuation as her daughter; for she forbore all farther enquiry, on the captain's bare assurance that the report of his marriage was false. Cranstoun, however, could not be equally easy. He saw the necessity of devising some scheme to get his first marriage annulled, or of bidding adieu to all the gratifications he could promise himself by a second.

After revolving various schemes in his mind, he at length wrote to his wife, requesting her to disown him for a husband. The substance of this letter was, that, 'having no other way of rising to preferment but in the army, he had but little ground to expect advancement there, while it was known he was incumbered with a wife and family; but, could he once pass for a single man, he had not the least doubt of being quickly preferred: which would procure him a sufficiency to maintain her as well as himself, in a genteeler manner than now he was able to do. All therefore (adds he) I have to request of you, is, that you will transcribe the inclosed copy of a letter, wherein you disown me for a husband; put your maiden name to it, and send it by the post: all the use I shall make of it will be to procure my advancement, which will necessarily include your own benefit. In full assurance that you will comply with my request, I remain

'Your most affectionate husband,

'W. H. CRANSTOUN'

Mrs Cranstoun, ill as she had been treated by her husband, and little hope as she had of more generous usage, was, after repeated letters had passed, induced to give up her claim; and at length sent him the requested paper, signed Murray, which was her maiden name.

The villainous captain, being possessed of this letter, made some copies of it, which he sent to his wife's relations, and his own: the consequence of which was that they withdrew the assistance that they had afforded the lady, which reduced her to an extremity she had never before known.

Exclusive of this he instituted a suit before the lords of session, for the dissolution of the marriage; but when Mrs Cranstoun was heard, and the letters read, the artful

E*   *137*

contrivance was seen through, the marriage was confirmed, and Cranstoun was adjudged to pay the expences of the trial.

At the next sessions Captain Cranstoun preferred a petition, desiring to be heard by council, on new evidence which it was pretended had arisen respecting Miss Murray. This petition after some hesitation was heard; but the issue was, that the marriage was again confirmed, and Cranstoun was obliged to allow his wife a separate maintenance.

Still, however, he paid his addresses to Miss Blandy with the same fervency as before; which coming to the knowledge of Mrs Cranstoun, she sent her the decree of the court of session, establishing the validity of the marriage.

It is reasonable to suppose that this would have convinced Miss Blandy of the erroneous path in which she was treading. On this occasion she consulted her mother; and Cranstoun having set out for Scotland, the old lady advised her to write to him, to know the truth of the affair.

Absurd as this advice was, she wrote to him; but soon after the receipt of her letter, he returned to Henley, when he had impudence enough to assert that the cause was not finally determined, but would be referred to the house of Lords.

Mr Blandy gave very little credit to this assertion; but his wife assented at once to all he said, and treated him with as much tenderness as if he had been her own child; of which the following circumstance will afford ample proof.

Mrs Blandy and her daughter being on a visit to Mrs Pocock of Turville-court, the old lady was taken so ill as to be obliged to continue there for some days. In the height of her disorder, which was a violent fever, she cried, 'Let Cranstoun be sent for.' He was then with the regiment at Southampton; but, her request being complied with, she no sooner saw him, than she raised herself on the pillow, and hung round his neck, repeatedly exclaiming, 'My dear Cranstoun, I am glad you are come; I shall now grow well soon.' So extravagant was her fondness, that she insisted on having him as her nurse; and he actually administered her medicines.

On the following day she grew better; on which she said, 'This I owe to you, my dear Cranstoun; your coming has given me new health and fresh spirits. I was fearful I should die, and you not here to comfort that poor girl. How like death she looks!'

It would be ungenerous to the memory of Mrs Blandy to suppose that she saw Cranstoun's guilt in its true light of enormity; but certainly she was a most egregious dupe to his artifices.

Mrs Blandy and her daughter having come to London, the former wanted £40 to discharge a debt she had contracted unknown to her husband; and Cranstoun coming into the room while the mother and the daughter were weeping over their distresses, he demanded the reason of their grief; of which being informed, he left them, and soon returning with the requisite sum, he threw it into the old lady's lap. Charmed by this apparent generosity, she burst into tears, and squeezed his hand fervently: on which he embraced her, and said, 'Remember it is a son; therefore do not make yourself uneasy: you do not lay under any obligation to me.'

Of this debt of forty pounds, ten pounds had been contracted by the ladies while in London, for expences in consequence of their pleasures; and the other thirty by expensive treats given to Cranstoun at Henley, during Mr Blandy's absence.

Soon after this Mrs Blandy died; and Cranstoun now complaining of his fear of being arrested for the forty pounds, the young lady borrowed that sum, which she gave him; and made him a present of her watch; so that he was a gainer by his former apparent generosity.

Mr Blandy began now to shew evident dislike of captain Cranstoun's visits: but he found means to take leave of the daughter, to whom he complained of the father's ill treatment; but insinuated that he had a method of conciliating his esteem; and that when he arrived in Scotland he would send her some powders proper for the purpose; on which, to prevent suspicion, he would write 'Powders to clean the Scotch pebbles.'

It does not appear that the young lady had any idea that the powders he was to send her were of a poisonous nature. She seems rather to have been infatuated by her love: and this is the only excuse that can be made for her subsequent conduct, which appears otherwise totally inconsistent with that good sense for which she was celebrated.

Cranstoun sent her the powders, according to promise; and Mr Blandy being indisposed on the Sunday sevennight before his death, Susan Gunnel, a maid servant, made him some water-gruel, into which Miss Blandy conveyed some of the powder and gave it to her father; and repeating this draught on the following day, he was tormented with the most violent pains in his bowels.

When the old gentleman's disorder encreased, and he was attended by a physician, his daughter came into his room, and falling on her knees to her father, said, 'Banish me where you please; do with me what you please, so you do but forgive me; and as for Cranstoun, I will never see him, speak to him, or write to him, as long as I live, if you will but forgive me.'

In reply to this the father said, 'I forgive thee, my dear, and I hope God will forgive; but thou shouldst have considered before thou attemptedst any thing against thy father: thou shouldst have considered I was thy *own* father.'

Miss Blandy now acknowledged that she had put powder in his gruel, but that it was for an innocent purpose: on which the father turning in his bed, said, 'O such a villain! to come to my house, eat of the best, and drink of the best my house could afford, and in return take away my life, and ruin my daughter. O! my dear, thou must hate that man.'

The young lady replied, 'Sir every word you say is like a sword piercing to my heart; more severe than if you were angry; I must kneel and beg you will not curse me.' The father said, 'I curse thee, my dear! how couldst thou think I would curse thee? No, I bless thee, and hope God will bless thee, and amend thy life. Do, my dear, go out of the room; say no more, lest thou shouldst say any thing to thy own prejudice. Go to thy uncle Stephens; and take him for thy friend: poor man! I am sorry for him.'

Mr Blandy dying in consequence of his illness, it was suspected that his daughter had occasioned his death; whereupon she was taken into custody, and committed to the gaol at Oxford.

She was tried on the 3d of March, 1752, before Mr Baron Legge; and after many witnesses had been called to give evidence of her guilt, she was desired to make her defence, which she did in the following speech:

'My Lord,

'It is morally impossible for me to lay down the hardships I have received—I have been aspersed in my character. In the first place, it has been said, I spoke ill of my father; that I have cursed him, and wished him at hell, which is extremely false. Sometimes little family affairs have happened, and he did not speak to me so kind as I could wish. I own I am passionate, my lord, and in those passions some hasty expressions might have dropped: but great care has been taken to recollect every word I have spoken at different times, and to apply them to such particular purposes as my enemies knew would do me the greatest injury. These are hardships, my lord, such as yourselves must allow to be so. It was said too, my lord, that I endeavoured to make my escape. Your lordship will judge from the difficulties I laboured under:—I had lost my father;—I was accused of being his murderer;—I was not permitted to go near him;—I was forsaken by my friends—affronted by the mob,—and insulted by my servants.—Although I begged to have the liberty to listen at the door where he died, I was not allowed it. My keys were taken from me, my shoe-buckles and garters too,—to prevent me from making away with myself, as though I was the most abandoned creature. What could I do, my lord? I verily believe I must have been out of my senses. When I heard my father was dead, I ran out of the house, and over the bridge, and had nothing on but an half sack and petticoats, without a hoop,—my petticoats hanging about me;—the mob gathered about me. Was this a condition, my lords, to make my escape in? A good woman beyond the bridge seeing me in this distress, desired me to walk in, till the mob was dispersed: the town serjeant was there; I begged he would take me under his protection to have me home; the woman said it was not proper, the mob was very great, and that I had better stay a little. When I came home, they said I used the constable ill. I was locked up for fifteen hours, with only an old servant of the family to attend me. I was not allowed a maid for the common decencies of my sex. I was sent to gaol, and was in hopes there at least this usage would have ended; but was told it was reported I was frequently drunk; that I attempted to make my escape; that I did not attend at chapel. A more abstemious woman, my lord, I believe, does not live.

'Upon the report of my making my escape, the gentleman who was high sheriff last year (not the present) came and told me, by order of the higher powers, he must put an iron on me. I submitted as I always do to the higher powers. Some time after he came again, and said, he must put an heavier upon me, which I have worn, my lords, till I came hither. I asked the sheriff why I was so ironed? He said, he did it by the command of some noble peer, on his hearing that I intended making my escape. I told them I never had any such thought, and I would bear it with the other cruel usage I had received on my character. The Reverend Mr Swinton, the worthy clergyman who attended me in prison, can testify I was regular at the chapel whenever I was well; sometimes I really was not able to come out, and then he attended me in my room. They have likewise published papers and depositions, which ought not to have been published, in order to represent me as the most abandoned of my sex, and to prejudice the world against me. I submit myself to your lordships, and to the worthy jury—I do assure your lordship, as I am to answer it at the great tribunal, where I must appear, I am as innocent as the child unborn of the death of my father. I would not endeavour to save my life at the expence of truth. I really thought the powder an innocent, inoffensive thing, and I gave it to procure his love (meaning towards Cranstoun.)—It has been mentioned, I should say I was ruined. My lord, when a young woman loses her character, is not that her ruin? Why then should this expression be construed in so wide a sense? Is it not ruining my character to have such a thing laid to my charge? And, whatever may be the event of his trial, I am ruined most effectually.'

The trial lasted eleven hours, and then the judge summed up the evidence, mentioning the scandalous behaviour of some people respecting the prisoner, in printing and publishing what they called depositions taken before the coroner, relating to the affair before them: to which he added, 'I hope you have not seen them; but if you have, I must tell you, as you are men of sense and probity, that you must divest yourselves of every prejudice that can arise from thence, and attend merely to the evidence that has been now given.'

The judge then summed up the evidence with the utmost candour; and the jury, having considered the affair, found her guilty without going out of court.

After conviction, she behaved with the utmost decency and resignation. She was attended by the Reverend Mr Swinton, from whose hands she received the sacrament on the day before her execution, declaring that she did not know there was any thing hurtful in the powders she had given her father.

The night before her death she spent in devotion; and at nine in the morning she left her apartment, being dressed in a black bombazine, and having her arms bound with black ribbons.

The clergyman attended her to the place of execution, to which she walked with the utmost solemnity of deportment; and, when there, acknowledged her fault in administering the powders to her father, but declared that, as she must soon appear before the most awful tribunal, she had no idea of doing injury, nor any suspicions that the powders were of a poisonous nature.

Having ascended some steps of the ladder, she said, 'Gentlemen, don't hang me high, for the sake of decency.' Being desired to go something higher, she turned about, and expressed her apprehensions that she should fall. The rope being put round her neck, she pulled her handkerchief over her face, and was turned-off, on holding out a book of devotions which she had been reading.

The crowd of spectators assembled on this occasion was immense; and, when she had hung the usual time, she was cut down, and the body, being put into a hearse, was conveyed to Henley, and interred with her parents, at one o'clock on the following morning.

She was executed at Oxford, on the 6th of April, 1752.

It will be now proper to return to Cranstoun, who was the original contriver of this horrid murder. Having heard of Miss Blandy's commitment to Oxford gaol, he concealed himself some time in Scotland, and then escaped to Bologne in France. Meeting there with Mrs Ross, who was distantly related to his family, he acquainted her with his situation, and begged her protection: on which she advised him to change his name for her maiden name of Dunbar.

Some officers in the French service, who were related to his wife, hearing of his concealment, vowed revenge if they should meet with him, for his cruelty to the unhappy woman: on which he fled to Paris, whence he went to Furnes, a town in Flanders, where Mrs Ross had provided a lodging for his reception.

He had not been long at Furnes, when he was seized with a severe fit of illness, which brought him to a degree of reflection to which he had been long a stranger. At length, he sent for a father belonging to an adjacent convent, and received absolution from his hands, on declaring himself a convert to the Romish faith.

Cranstoun died on the 30th of November, 1752, and the fraternity of monks and friars looked on his conversion as an object of such importance, that solemn mass was sung on the occasion, and the body was followed to the grave, not only by the Ecclesiastics, but by the magistrates of the town.

His papers were then sent to Scotland, to his brother, lord Cranstoun; his cloaths were sold for the discharge of his debts; and his wife came into possession of the interest of the fifteen hundred pounds abovementioned.

This case is one of the most extraordinary that we shall have occasion to record in these volumes. The character and conduct of Cranstoun are infamous beyond all description. A married man seeking a young lady in marriage, deluding her by the vilest artifices, and the most atrocious falsehoods; and then murdering her father to obtain the object of his wishes, exhibits an accumulated picture of guilt to which no language can do justice. His sufferings afterwards appear to have been a providential punishment of his crimes. We are to hope that his penitence was sincere; but it is impossible to think highly of a religion that offers immediate pardon and absolution to a criminal, of whatever magnitude, on the single declaration of his becoming a convert to that religion.

With regard to Miss Blandy, the public have ever been divided in opinion on her case. Those who have presumed on her innocence have tacitly acknowledged that she was very weak, which contradicts the accounts we have of her genius and mental acquirements. On the contrary, those who have insisted on her guilt, have made no allowances for the weakness of the female mind; nor considered the influence of an artful man over the heart of a girl in love.

Her solemn declaration of her innocence would almost tempt one to think that she *was* innocent; for it is next to impossible to suppose that a woman of her sense and education would depart this life with a wilful lye in her mouth.

Be all this as it may, an obvious lesson is to be learnt from her fate.—Young ladies should be cautious of listening to the insidious address of artful love as they know not how soon, and how unsuspectedly, their hearts may be engaged to their own destruction, founded on the violation of all their nobler duties.

Those who are interested in this case should read *The Trial of Mary Blandy* in 'Notable British Trials,' edited by William Roughead, W.S., Edinburgh, and published by William Hodge and Co. Ltd. There is an Introduction reviewing all the circumstances and quoting the contemporary sources, which is of great value to any student of the life of the eighteenth century.

A Narrative of the Cases of MARY SQUIRES, who was convicted of robbery, and pardoned; and of ELIZABETH CANNING, who was convicted of, and transported for, Perjury, in swearing to that robbery.

THERE is so much of mystery in the following case, that it seems beyond the bounds of human sagacity to determine on which side the merit lies. The story, with all its particulars, must be within the memory of many of our readers, who have already formed their opinion of it; and it has been of such public notoriety, that few persons can be wholly unacquainted with it: we shall, therefore, only give an abridged account, fairly stated from the evidence as it arose, without favour or affection to either party.

If Elizabeth Canning's own story may be credited, she quitted the house of her mother, near Aldermanbury, on the first of January, 1753; and, having visited her uncle and aunt, who lived near Saltpetre-bank, was, on her return, assaulted in Moorfields by two men, who robbed her of half a guinea, which was in a small box in her pocket, and three shillings that were loose. They also took her gown, apron, and hat, which one of them put into the pocket of his great-coat; on which she screamed out; but he bound a handkerchief round her mouth, and tied her hands behind her, after which, she received a violent blow on the head, which, added to her former terror, occasioned her falling into a fit, a disorder to which she had been subject about four years.

On her recovery from the fit, and about half an hour before she reached Wells's house, she found herself by the road side, the two men dragging her forward. She observed water near the road, and arrived at the house where she said she was confined about three hours before day-light. When she came into the house, she did not see the mistress of it, Susannah Wells; but saw Mary Squires, a gipsey, and two girls.

Squires taking Canning by the hand, asked her if she chose to *go their way*, and, if she would, she should have fine cloaths. Canning, understanding that her meaning was to commence prostitute, replied in the negative; on which Squires took a knife from a drawer, cut the lace from her stays, and took them from her. Then Squires pushed her up a few stairs out of the kitchen, to a place called the Hayloft, and shut the door on her. On the approach of day-light, she found that the room had neither bed nor bedstead, and only hay to sleep on; that there was a black pitcher nearly full of water, and about twenty-four pieces of bread, in the whole about the quantity of a quartern-loaf; and that she had in her pocket a penny minced-pie, which she had bought to carry to her brother.

She said, that she covered herself with a bedgown and handkerchief, which she found in the grate; and that, for the space of twenty-eight days within a few hours, which she remained there, she had no food nor liquor except what is abovementioned, nor had the common evacuation of nature.

About four in the afternoon of Monday the 29th of January, she pulled down a board that was nailed on the inside of the window, and getting her head first out, she kept fast hold by the wall, and then dropped into a narrow place by a lane, behind which was a field.

Having got into the highway, she enquired her way to London, but did not stop. When she came into Moorfields the clock struck ten; and she thence proceeded to her mother's near Aldermanbury, where she told the above story to two gentlemen with whom she had lived as a servant: to which she added, that the place where she had been confined was near the Hertfordshire road, which was evident from her having seen a coachman drive by, who had frequently carried her mistress into Hertfordshire.

A number of circumstances giving reason to suspect that the house in which she had been confined was that of Susannah Wells, a warrant was issued to apprehend her and Squires, and such other people as might be found in the house.

Mr Lion, with whom she had lived servant, and several other persons, went with her to execute the warrant. When she came to the place, she fixed on Mary Squires as the person who had robbed her; and she said that Virtue Hall stood by while her stays were cut off.

On this, all the parties were carried before Justice Tyshmaker; when Hall so solemnly denied all knowledge of any such transaction having happened since she had been in the house, that she was discharged; but Squires was committed to New-prison for the robbery, and Wells for aiding and abetting her.

Soon afterwards, justice Fielding was applied to for a warrant for the apprehension of Hall, and she was examined before the magistrate for six hours, during which she continued in her former declaration. At length the justice said, that 'he would examine her no longer, but would commit her to prison, and leave her to stand or fall by the evidence that should be produced against her;' and he advised an attorney to prosecute her as a felon.

Hereupon she begged to be heard, and said she would tell the whole truth: and the substance of her declaration was, that Canning had been at Mrs Wells's, and was robbed in the manner that she herself had declared.

On this, Squires and Wells were brought to trial at the Old Bailey, and convicted, principally on the evidence of Virtue Hall, the first for assaulting and robbing Elizabeth Canning, and the latter for harbouring, concealing, and comforting her, well knowing her to have committed the robbery: and John Gibson, William Clark, and Thomas Grevil, having positively sworn that Squires was in Dorsetshire at the time when the robbery was said to have been perpetrated, they were committed to be tried for perjury.

Some gentlemen who had heard the trial, being dissatisfied with the evidence, made such application, that a free pardon was granted to Squires.

In the mean time, numbers of people were of opinion that the countrymen had sworn to the truth; and measures were accordingly taken to indict Canning for perjury: but, at the next sessions, her friends preferred bills of indictment against the men. Bills of indictment against the opposite parties being brought at the same time, the grand jury threw them all out; being resolved not to give any countenance to such a scene of perjury as must arise on one side or the other.

This happened at the sessions in April; but, at the next sessions, in June, bills of indictment were found against the countrymen: these, however, were intended to be removed into the court of King's Bench, by writ of certiorari; but the court refused to grant the writ, alledging, that the indictments ought to be tried at the Old Bailey, because the king's commission of gaol-delivery was directed to that court. Hereupon the countrymen were bailed; and, at the sessions held in the month of September following, they were arraigned, but were honourably acquitted, no person appearing to give evidence against them.

Squires being pardoned, and these men thus acquitted, the public opinion of this singular case became still more divided. Every one saw that there must have been perjury in the affair; but it was impossible to determine on which side it lay.

The lord mayor of London, at that time, was Sir Crisp Gascoyne, who exerted himself in the most vigilant manner to come at the truth of this mysterious affair; for which, as is but too common, he was abused with a degree of virulence that reflected the highest infamy on his calumniators; for, whatever might be their private opinion, or whatever his own, it was certainly the duty of a good magistrate to endeavour to investigate the truth.

In the month of May, 1754, Elizabeth Canning was indicted at the Old Bailey for wilful and corrupt perjury, in swearing, that she had been robbed by Mary Squires. A great number of witnesses swore that Squires was near Abbotsbury at the time that the robbery was said to have been committed: and, on the contrary, more than thirty persons of reputation declared on oath, that Canning's character stood so fair, that they could not conceive her capable of being guilty of such an atrocious crime as wilful perjury.

Ingenious arguments were used by the council on each side; and the jury, after mature deliberation, brought in a verdict, that she was guilty; in consequence of which, she received sentence to be transported for seven years.

No affair that was ever determined in a judicial way did, perhaps, so much excite the curiosity, or divide the opinion of the public, as that in question. The news-papers and magazines were for a long time filled with little else than accounts of Canning and Squires: prints of both parties were published, and bought up with great avidity. Canning was remarkable for what is called the plainness, and Squires for the ugliness, of person; and perhaps there never was a human face more disagreeable than that of the latter.

We should hardly be thought to exceed the truth, if we were to say that ten thousand quarrels arose from, and fifty thousand wagers were laid on, this business. All Great Britain and Ireland seemed to be interested in the event: and the person who did not espouse either one party or the other was thought to have no feeling. The first question in the morning was, 'What news of Canning?' and the last squabble at night was, whether she was honest or perjured; but this, however, could never be determined; and it will probably remain a mystery as long as the world endures.

Elizabeth Canning was transported to New England on the 31st of July, 1754, having first received some hundred pounds collected by the bounty of her friends and partizans.

She was afterwards reputably married in America; and the news-papers gave notice, that she died some years ago in that country.

From this story we may learn two useful lessons, on the fallibility of human testimony, and the horrid crime of perjury. If Canning was guilty, her crime was of the most enormous magnitude, that of endeavouring to swear away a life, in order to cover, perhaps, her own disgrace; for some persons thought that she had been debauched in her absence, and that the whole was a concerted scheme to conceal the truth. If she was innocent, what a variety of perjuries must have been committed by the opposite parties!

Upon the whole, we must end as we began: this story

is enveloped in mystery; and the truth of it must be left to
the discoveries of that important day, when all mists shall
be wiped from our eyes, and the most hidden things shall
be made plain. In the mean time, it is our duty to admire
and adore those inscrutable decrees of Providence, which
can bring good out of evil, and answer its own wise and
gracious purposes, by means least apparent to finite compre-
hension!

Usually described as 'The Mystery of Elizabeth Canning', this is
one of the most famous cases of the eighteenth century, and there exists
a very great literature dealing with the trial, and the circumstances of
Elizabeth Canning's life. In *Elizabeth is Missing*, by Lillian De La
Torre, published in 1947 by Michael Joseph Ltd., a full list of the
publications relating to the case is given, and the manuscript of the
book with complete notes and full annotated biography is deposited
in the Connecticut State Library at Hartford for the use of scholars.
Arthur Machen's *The Canning Wonder*, published in 1925, is one of
the best books on the subject. The case is also reported in Vol. 19 of
the State Trials. *Alibi Pilgrimage*, by F. J. Harvey Darton, is also a
most interesting book dealing with the central problem. Arthur
Machen says of the case:

> The case of Elizabeth Canning is one of the minor enigmas of
> the world. Like the song that the Sirens sang, and the name that
> Achilles bore when he dwelt among women, it may not be beyond
> all conjecture, but it is, assuredly, beyond all certitude. It is a
> puzzle. We may approximate, perhaps, to the answer; but we
> shall never possess it. In our investigation, however, there is one
> palmary clue which we must seize firmly at the beginning, and
> never allow to escape us, and this clue is the sure and undoubted
> fact that Elizabeth Canning was an infernal liar. That is, the
> whole tale she told on her return after a month's absence was a
> lie from beginning to end; a lie as a whole, a lie in all its parts.

In the State Trials, the report runs to 409 columns of small print,
but those who are interested will find it fascinating. The whole
country was divided into two parties, the Canaanites (the supporters
of Canning) amd the Egyptians (the supporters of Mary Squires the
gypsy). Henry Fielding took the greatest interest in the case and
wrote a pamphlet, *The clear state of the case of Elizabeth Canning*, and
many famous men, like Professor Kenny, the great authority on
Criminal Law, have followed in Fielding's footsteps.

In that very fascinating book by the late Lord Justice Mackinnon, *On Circuit*, after speaking of the present-day procedure at the criminal trials held at the Old Bailey, when the Lord Mayor or one of the Aldermen sits alongside the judge, he says: 'When Elizabeth Canning was convicted of perjury at the Old Bailey in 1754, Chief Justice Willes proposed seven years' transportation as her proper sentence. An Alderman, Sir John Barnard, moved an amended sentence of six months' imprisonment. The Chief Justice's proposal was only carried by six judges (including the Recorder), the Lord Mayor, and two Aldermen, against eight Aldermen. I cannot conceive what would happen if the Lord Mayor and an Alderman tried nowadays to over-rule the judge as to a sentence. I suspect that he would ignore them.'

The most extraordinary Case of EUGENE ARAM, who was hanged for Murder; together with the ingenious Defence which he made on his Trial.

THE murder for which Aram suffered, and his whole history, is so uncommon, that our readers will be equally pleased and astonished with a full and explicit relation of it.

One of the ancestors of this offender had been high sheriff of Yorkshire in the reign of king Edward the third; but, the family having been gradually reduced, Aram's father was but in a low station of life: the son, however, was sent to a school near Rippon, where he perfected himself in writing and arithmetic, and then went to London, to officiate as clerk to a merchant.

After a residence of two years in town, he was seized with the small-pox, which left him in so weak a condition, that he went back to Yorkshire for the recovery of his health.

On his recovery, he found it necessary to do something for immediate subsistence; and accordingly he engaged himself as usher to a boarding-school; but, not having been taught the learned languages in his youth, he was obliged to supply by industry what he had failed of through neglect; so that teaching the scholars only writing and arithmetic at first, he employed all his leisure hours in the most intense study, till he became an excellent Greek and Latin scholar; in the progress to which acquirements, he owed much to the help of a most extraordinary memory.

In the year 1734, he engaged to officiate as steward of an estate belonging to Mr Norton of Knaresborough; and while in this station he acquired a competent knowledge of the Hebrew. At this period he married; but was far from being happy in the matrimonial connexion.

We now proceed to relate the circumstances which led to the commission of the crime which cost Aram his life. Daniel Clarke, a shoemaker, at Knaresborough, after being married a few days, circulated a report, that his wife was entitled to a considerable fortune, which he should soon receive. Hereupon, Aram, and Richard Houseman, conceiving hopes of making advantage of this circumstance, persuaded Clarke to make an ostentatious shew of his own riches, to induce his wife's relations to give him that fortune of which he had boasted. There was sagacity, if not honesty, in this advice: for the world in general are more free to assist persons in affluence than those in distress.

Clarke was easily induced to comply with a hint so agreeable to his own desires; on which, he borrowed, and bought on credit, a large quantity of silver plate, with jewels, watches, rings, &c. He told the persons of whom he purchased, that a merchant in London had sent him an order to buy such plate for exportation; and no doubt was entertained of his credit till his sudden disappearance in February, 1745, when it was imagined that he had gone abroad, or at least to London, to dispose of his ill-acquired property.

When Clarke was possessed of these goods, Aram and Houseman determined to murder him, in order to share the booty; and, on the night of the 8th of February, 1745, they persuaded Clarke to walk with them in the fields, in order to consult with them on the proper method to dispose of the effects.

On this plan they walked into a field, at a small distance from the town, well known by the name of St Robert's Cave. When they came into this field, Aram and Clarke went over a hedge towards the cave, and when they had got within six or seven yards of it, Houseman (by the light of the moon) saw Aram strike Clarke several times, and at length beheld him fall, but never saw him afterwards. This was the state of the affair, if Houseman's testimony on the trial might be credited.

The murderers going home, shared Clarke's ill-gotten treasure, the half of which Houseman concealed in his garden for a twelvemonth, and then took it to Scotland, where he sold it. In the mean time, Aram carried his share to London, where he sold it to a Jew, and then engaged himself as an usher at an academy in Piccadilly; where, in the intervals of his duty in attending on the scholars, he made himself master of the French language, and acquired some knowledge of the Arabic, and other eastern languages.

After this, he was usher at other schools in different parts of the kingdom; but, as he did not correspond with his friends in Yorkshire, it was presumed that he was dead: but, in the year 1758, as a man was digging for lime-stones near St Robert's Cave, he found the bones of a human body; and a conjecture hereupon arose, that they were the remains of the body of Clarke, who, it was presumed, might have been murdered.

Houseman, having been seen in the company of Clarke a short time before his disappearance, was apprehended on suspicion; and, on his examination, giving but too evident signs of his guilt, he was committed to York-castle; and the bones of the deceased being shewn him, he denied that they were those of Clarke, but directed to the precise spot where they were deposited, and where they were accordingly found. The skull, being fractured, was preserved, to be produced in evidence on the trial.

Soon after Houseman was committed to the castle of York, it was discovered that Aram resided at Lynn in Norfolk; on which, a warrant was granted for taking him into custody; and, being apprehended while instructing some young gentlemen at a school, he was conveyed to York, and likewise committed to the castle.

At the Lent assizes following the prosecutors were not ready with their evidence, on which he was remanded till the Summer assizes, when he was brought to his trial.

When Houseman had given his evidence respecting this extraordinary affair, and all such collateral testimony had been given as could be adduced on such an occasion, Aram was called on for his defence: but, having foreseen that the perturbation of his spirits would incapacitate him to make such defence without previous preparation, he had written the following, which, by permission, he read in court:

'My Lord,

'I know not whether it is of right, or through some indulgence of your lordship, that I am allowed the liberty at this bar, and at this time, to attempt a defence, incapable and

uninstructed as I am to speak. Since, while I see so many
eyes upon me, so numerous and awful a concourse, fixed
with attention and filled with I know not what expectancy,
I labour not with guilt, my lord, but with perplexity. For
having never seen a court but this, being wholly unacquainted with law, the customs of the bar, and all judi-
ciary proceedings, I fear I shall be so little capable of speaking with propriety in this place, that it exceeds my hope, if
I shall be able to speak at all.

'I have heard, my lord, the indictment read, wherein I
find myself charged with the highest crime; with an enormity I am altogether incapable of; a fact, to the commission
of which there goes far more insensibility of heart, more
profligacy of morals, than ever fell to my lot. And nothing
possibly could have admitted a presumption of this nature,
but a depravity, not inferior to that imputed to me. However, as I stand indicted at your lordship's bar, and have
heard what is called evidence induced in support of such a
charge, I very humbly solicit your lordship's patience, and
beg the hearing of this respectable audience, while I,
single and unskilful, destitute of friends, and unassisted by
council, say something, perhaps like argument, in my
defence. I shall consume but little of your lordship's time;
what I have to say will be short, and this brevity, probably,
will be the best part of it; however, it is offered with all
possible regard, and the greatest submission to your lordship's consideration, and that of this honourable court.

'First, my lord, the whole tenor of my conduct in life
contradicts every particular of this indictment. Yet had I
never said this, did not my present circumstances extort
it from me, and seem to make it necessary. Permit me here,
my lord, to call upon malignity itself, so long and cruelly
busied in this prosecution, to charge upon me any im-
morality, of which prejudice was not the author. No, my
lord, I concerted no schemes of fraud, projected no violence, injured no man's person or property: my days were
honestly laborious, my nights intensely studious. And I
humbly conceive, my notice of this, especially at this time,
will not be thought impertinent, or unseasonable; but, at

least, deserving some attention, because, my lord, that any person, after a temperate use of life, a series of thinking and acting regularly, and without one single deviation from sobriety, should plunge into the very depth of profligacy, precipitately, and at once, is altogether improbable and unprecedented, and absolutely inconsistent with the course of things. Mankind is never corrupted at once; villainy is always progressive, and declines from right, step after step, till every regard of probity is lost, and every sense of all moral obligation totally perishes.

'Again, my lord, a suspicion of this kind, which nothing but malevolence could entertain, and ignorance propagate, is violently opposed by my very situation at that time, with respect to health; for but a little space before I had been confined to my bed, and suffered under a very long and severe disorder, and was not able, for half a year together, so much as to walk. The distemper left me indeed, yet slowly and in part; but so macerated, so enfeebled, that I was reduced to crutches; and so far from being well about the time I am charged with this fact, that I never, to this day, perfectly recovered. Could then a person in this condition take any thing into his head so unlikely, so extravagant? I, past the vigour of my age, feeble and valetudinary, with no inducement to engage, no ability to accomplish, no weapon wherewith to perpetrate such a fact; without interest, without power, without motive, without means.

'Besides, it must needs occur to every one, that an action of this atrocious nature is never heard of but, when its springs are laid open, it appears that it was to support some indolence, or supply some luxury, to satisfy some avarice, or oblige some malice, to prevent some real or some imaginary want: yet I lay not under the influence of any one of these. Surely, my lord, I may, consistent with both truth and modesty, affirm thus much; and none who have any veracity, and knew me, will ever question this.

'In the second place, the disappearance of Clarke is suggested as an argument of his being dead; but the uncertainty of such an inference from that, and the fallibility of all conclusions of such a sort, from such a circumstance, are too obvious, and too notorious, to require instances: yet, superseding many, permit me to procure a very recent one, and that afforded by this castle.

'In June, 1757, William Thompson, for all the vigilance of this place, in open day-light, and double-ironed, made his escape; and, notwithstanding an immediate enquiry set on foot, the strictest search, and all advertisement, was never seen or heard of since. If then Thompson got off unseen, through all these difficulties, how very easy was it for Clarke, when none of them opposed him? but what would be thought of a prosecution commenced against any one seen last with Thompson.

'Permit me, next, my lord, to observe a little upon the bones which have been discovered. It is said, which perhaps is saying very far, that these are the skeleton of a man. It is possible indeed it may: but is there any certain known criterion, which incontestably distinguishes the sex in human bones? Let it be considered, my lord, whether the ascertaining of this point ought not to precede any attempt to identify them.

'The place of their depositum too claims much more attention than is commonly bestowed upon it: for, of all places in the world, none could have mentioned any one, wherein there was greater certainty of finding human bones than a hermitage, except he should point out a churchyard; hermitages, in time past, being not only places of religious retirement, but of burial too. And it has scarce or never been heard of, but that every cell now known, contains, or contained these relicts of humanity; some mutilated, and some entire. I do not inform, but give me leave to remind your lordship, that here sat solitary sanctity, and here the hermit, or the anchoress, hoped that repose for their bones, when dead, they here enjoyed when living.

'All the while, my lord, I am sensible this is known to your lordship, and many in this court, better than to me. But it seems necessary to my case that others, who have not at all, perhaps, adverted to things of this nature, and may have concern in my trial, should be made acquainted with it. Suffer me then, my lord, to produce a few of many evidences, that these cells were used as repositories of the dead, and to enumerate a few, in which human bones have been found, as it happened in this in question; lest, to some, that accident might seem extraordinary, and, consequently, occasion prejudice.

'1. The bones, as was supposed, of the Saxon St Dubritius, were discovered buried in his cell at Guy's cliff near Warwick, as appears from the authority of Sir William Dugdale.

'2. The bones, thought to be those of the anchoress Rosia, were but lately discovered in a cell at Royston, entire, fair, and undecayed, though they must have lain interred for several centuries, as is proved by Dr Stukely.

'3. But my own country, nay, almost this neighbourhood, supplies another instance, for in January, 1747, were found, by Mr Stovin, accompanied by a reverend gentleman, the bones, in part, of some recluse, in the cell at Lindholm, near Hatfield. They were believed to be those of William of Lindholm, a hermit who had long made this cave his habitation.

'4. In February, 1744, part of Wooburn-abbey being pulled down, a large portion of a corpse appeared, even with the flesh on, and which bore cutting with a knife; though it is certain this had lain above 200 years, and how much longer is doubtful; for this abbey was founded in 1143, and dissolved in 1538 or 9.

'What would have been said, what believed, if this had been an accident to the bones in question?

'Farther, my lord, it is not yet out of living memory, that a little distance from Knaresborough, in a field, part of the 'manor of the worthy and patriot baronet, who does that borough the honour to represent it in parliament, were found, in digging for gravel, not one human skeleton only, but five or six deposited side by side, with each an urn placed at its head, as your lordship knows was usual in ancient interments.

'About the same time, and in another field, almost close to this borough, was discovered also, in searching for gravel, another human skeleton; but the piety of the same worthy gentleman ordered both pits to be filled up again, commendably unwilling to disturb the dead.

'Is the invention of these bones forgotten, then, or industriously concealed, that the discovery of those in question may appear the more singular and extraordinary? whereas, in fact, there is nothing extraordinary in it. My lord, almost every place conceals such remains. In fields, in hills, in highway sides, in commons, lie frequent and unsuspected bones. And our present allotments for rest for the departed is but of some centuries.

'Another particular seems not to claim a little of your lordship's notice, and that of the gentlemen of the jury; which is, that perhaps no example occurs of more than one skeleton being found in one cell: and in the cell in question was found but one; agreeable, in this, to the peculiarity of every other known cell in Britain. Not the invention of one skeleton, but of two, would have appeared suspicious and uncommon.

'But it seems another skeleton has been discovered by some labourer, which was full as confidently averred to be Clarke's as this. My lord, must some of the living, if it promotes some interest, be made answerable for all the bones that earth has concealed, and chance exposed? and might not a place where bones lay be mentioned by a person by chance, as well as found by a labourer by chance? or, is it more criminal accidentally to name where bones lie, than accidentally to find where they lie?

'Here too is a human skull produced, which is fractured; but was this the cause, or was it the consequence of death? was it owing to violence, or was it the effect of natural decay? if it was violence, was that violence before or after death? My lord, in May, 1732, the remains of William, lord archbishop of this province, were taken up, by permission, in this cathedral, and the bones of the skull were found broken; yet certainly he died by no violence offered to him alive, that could occasion that fracture there.

'Let it be considered, my lord, that, upon the dissolution of religious houses, and the commencement of the reformation, the ravages of those times both affected the living and the dead. In search after imaginary treasures, coffins were broken up, graves and vaults dug open, monuments ransacked, and shrines demolished; and it ceased about the beginning of the reign of queen Elizabeth. I entreat your lordship, suffer not the violences, the depredations, and the iniquities of those times, to be imputed to this.

'Moreover, what gentleman here is ignorant that Knaresborough had a castle; which, though now a ruin, was once considerable both for its strength and garrison? All know it was vigorously besieged by the arms of the parliament: at which siege, in sallies, conflicts, flights, pursuits, many fell in all the places round it, and where they fell were buried; for every place, my lord, is burial earth in war; and many, questionless, of these, rest yet unknown, whose bones futurity shall discover.

'I hope, with all imaginable submission, that what has been said will not be thought impertinent to this indictment; and that it will be far from the wisdom, the learning, and the integrity of this place, to impute to the living what zeal in its fury may have done; what nature may have taken off, and piety interred; or what war alone may have destroyed, alone deposited.

'As to the circumstances that have been raked together, I have nothing to observe; but that all circumstances whatsoever are precarious, and have been but too frequently found lamentably fallible; even the strongest have failed. They may rise to the utmost degree of probability, yet they are but probability still. Why need I name to your lordship the two Harrisons recorded by Dr Howel, who both suffered upon circumstances, because of the sudden disappearance of their lodger, who was in credit, had contracted debts, borrowed money, and went off unseen, and returned a great many years after their execution? Why name the intricate affair of Jacques du Moulin, under king Charles II related by a gentleman who was council for the crown? and why the unhappy Coleman, who suffered innocent, though convicted upon positive evidence, and whose children perished for want, because the world

F   *161*

uncharitably believed the father guilty? Why mention the
perjury of Smith, incautiously admitted king's evidence;
who, to screen himself, equally accused Faircloth and
Loveday of the murder of Dun; the first of whom, in 1749,
was executed at Winchester; and Loveday was about to
suffer at Reading, had not Smith been proved perjured, to
the satisfaction of the court, by the surgeon of the Gosport
hospital?

'Now, my lord, having endeavoured to shew that the
whole of this process is altogether repugnant to every part
of my life; that it is inconsistent with my condition of
health about that time; that no rational inference can be
drawn, that a person is dead who suddenly disappears;
that hermitages were the constant repositories of the bones
of the recluse; that the revolutions in religion, or the fortune of war, has mangled, or buried the dead; the conclusion remains perhaps no less reasonably than impatiently
wished for. I, at last, after a year's confinement, equal to
either fortune, put myself upon the candor, the justice, and
the humanity of your lordship, and upon yours, my countrymen, gentlemen of the jury.'

Aram was tried by Judge Noel, who, having remarked
that this defence was one of the most ingenious pieces of
reasoning that had ever fallen under his notice, summed up
the evidence to the Jury, who gave a verdict that Aram was
guilty; in consequence of which he received sentence of
death.

After conviction a clergyman was appointed to attend
him, to represent the atrociousness of his crime, to bring
him to a proper sense of his condition, and exhort him to
make an ample confession.

Aram appeared to pay proper attention to what was
said: but after the minister had retired, he formed the
dreadful resolution of destroying himself, having previously
written a letter, of which the following is a copy.

'My dear friend,

'Before this reaches you I shall be no more a living man
in this world, though at present in perfect bodily health;

but who can describe the horrors of mind which I suffer at this instant? Guilt! the guilt of blood shed without any provocation, without any cause, but that of filthy lucre, pierces my conscience with wounds that give the most poignant pains! 'Tis true, the consciousness of my horrid guilt has given me frequent interruptions in the midst of my business or pleasures; but still I have found means to stifle its clamors, and contrived a momentary remedy for the disturbance it gave me, by applying to the bottle or the bowl, or diversions, or company, or business; sometimes one, and sometimes the other, as opportunity offered: but now all these, and all other amusements, are at an end, and I am left forlorn, helpless, and destitute of every comfort; for I have nothing now in view but the certain destruction both of my soul and body. My conscience will now no longer suffer itself to be hoodwinked or browbeat; it has now got the mastery; it is my accuser, judge, and executioner; and the sentence it pronounceth against me, is more dreadful than that I heard from the bench, which only condemned my body to the pains of death, which are soon over; but conscience tells me plainly, that she will summon me before another tribunal, where I shall have neither power nor means to stifle the evidence she will there bring against me, and that the sentence which will then be denounced, will not only be irreversible, but will condemn my soul to torments that will know no end.

O! had I but hearkened to the advice which dear-bought experience has enabled me to give! I should not now have been plunged into that dreadful gulph of despair, which I find it impossible to extricate myself from; and therefore my soul is filled with horror inconceivable. I see both God and man my enemies, and in a few hours shall be exposed a public spectacle for the world to gaze at. Can you conceive any condition more horrible than mine? O, no! it cannot be! I am determined, therefore, to put a short end to trouble I am no longer able to bear, and prevent the executioner, by doing his business with my own hand, and shall, by this means at least, prevent the shame and disgrace of a public exposure; and leave the care of my soul in the hands of eternal mercy. Wishing you all health, happiness, and prosperity, I am, to the last moment of my life, yours, with the sincerest regard,   'EUGENE ARAM'

When the morning appointed for his execution arrived, the keeper went to take him out of his cell, when he was surprized to find him almost expiring through loss of blood, having cut his left arm above the elbow and near the wrist, with a razor; but he missed the artery. A surgeon being sent for, soon stopped the bleeding, and when he was taken to the place of execution he was perfectly sensible, though so very weak as to be unable to join in devotion with the clergyman who attended him.

He was executed near York on the 6th of August, 1759, and afterwards hung in chains on Knaresborough forest.

Such was the end of Eugene Aram: a man of consummate abilities, and wonderful erudition: the power of whose mind might have rendered him acceptable to the highest company, had not the foul crime of murder made him only an object of pity to the lowest!

How such a man, with abilities so superior, could think of embruing his hands in the blood of a fellow-creature, for the paltry consideration of gain, is altogether astonishing! It does not appear that he had any irregular appetites to gratify, or that he lived in any degree above his income. His crime, then, must be resolved into that of covetousness, which preys like a viper on the heart of him that indulgeth it.

From this vice, so repugnant to all the feelings of humanity, may the God of Benevolence protect us! But, while we pray against covetousness, let us recollect, that prudence, with regard to pecuniary concerns, is essential to our passing through this life with credit; and that the man who is not frugal of his own property, is seldom able to be generous, or even just, to others!

This case is included because it has exercised a curious fascination over the minds of men, a fascination which is due in some measure to the poem of Thomas Hood—'The Dream of Eugene Aram'—with its quite haunting verse :

164

Two stern-faced men set out from Lynn
Through the cold and heavy mist;
And Eugene Aram walked between
With gyves upon his wrist.

The murder took place in 1745, but Eugene Aram was not
arrested until 1758. For thirteen years he had carried his dreadful
secret about with him, and the imagination of Hood was touched by
the thought of this man acting as an usher in various schools with the
crime of murder on his hands. Eugene Aram was tried at the York
Assizes and made a most remarkable defence which may be read
here. The judge thought it to be one of the most ingenious pieces of
reasoning that he had ever heard. But the trial is important for
another reason. It was witnessed by William Paley who was then a
boy of 16 years of age, and it made the most powerful impression
upon him. Paley later produced his *Principles of Moral and Political
Philosophy* which had a very great influence on the criminal legislation
of his time. He believed that the end of all such legislation was the
prevention of crime, and supported capital punishment though he had
many suggestions for its amendment. Indeed, in some degree, he
supported the movement for the aggravation of the death penalty,
and was supposed to favour the idea of throwing offenders who had
been sentenced to death into a den of wild beasts. Many people in the
eighteenth century believed that death was not enough. There was an
anonymous pamphlet published with the title *Hanging Not Punishment Enough*, and there can be no doubt it represented a great body of
opinion. It did not go quite so far as to revive the punishment of the
sixteenth century when for seventeen years it was part of the law of
the land that poisoners should be boiled to death. This was actually
carried out at Smithfield and King's Lynn. But the pamphlet did
suggest that convicted men should be broken on the wheel, or flogged or
starved to death. It was all part and parcel of the idea that severity
of punishment could prevent crime, and is illustrated by the fact that
Eugene Aram's body was hung in chains in Knaresborough Forest.
This was in consequence of an Act of 1752 that allowed the bodies of
executed persons to be handed over to surgeons for dissection and to
be hung in chains. Strange as it may appear, these additional punishments seem to have struck a good deal of terror into people, though
one would have thought that what happened after death could not
have been of much concern to those who were to be executed. Dr
Radzinowicz's book, referred to above, is a perfect mine of information on these and kindred topics, and to those interested in the details
of the punishments of the eighteenth century it is quite indispensable.

A comprehensive Account of the Life, Trial, and Behavior of LAURENCE EARL FERRERS, who was hanged for the Murder of Mr JOHNSON, his Steward; with some Particulars of his Lordship's Family and Descent.

FROM the royal-blood of the Plantagenets was the house of Ferrers descended, and had been distinguished for ages. One of the family was slain while fighting on behalf of the crown, at the memorable battle of Shrewsbury, in the beginning of the reign of Henry the fourth; a circumstance that is mentioned by the immortal Shakespeare.

The second baronet of this family, Sir Henry Shirley, married one of the daughters of the famous earl of Essex who was beheaded in the reign of queen Elizabeth; and Sir Robert Shirley, son of the abovesaid Henry, died in the Tower, where he was confined by Oliver Cromwell, for his attachment to the cause of king Charles the first.

Sir Robert's second son succeeding to his title and estate, Charles the second summoned him to parliament by the title of lord Ferrers of Chartley, as the descendant of one of the coheiresses of Robert Earl of Essex, the title having been in abeyance from the death of the said earl, and the precedency of it as high as the 27th year of Edward the first.

In the year 1711, queen Anne created Robert Lord Ferrers Viscount Tamworth, and Earl Ferrers. This nobleman possessed a very large estate; but it was greatly diminished by making provision for his numerous family, which consisted of no less than fifteen sons and twelve daughters by two wives.

The titles were possessed by the second son of the first earl; but as he died without having any son, they fell to the next surviving brother, who was his father's ninth son: but as he did not marry, they fell, on his death, to the tenth son, who was father to the unfortunate earl whose crime gives rise to this narrative.

Laurence Earl Ferrers was a man of an unhappy disposition. Though of clear intellects, and acknowledged abilities when sober, yet an early attachment to drinking greatly impaired his faculties; and when drunk, his behaviour was that of a madman.[1]

Lord Ferrers married the youngest daughter of Sir William Meridith in the year 1752, but behaved to her with such unwarrantable cruelty, that she was obliged to apply to parliament for redress; the consequence of which was that an act passed for allowing her a separate maintenance, to be raised out of his estates.

At Derby races in the year 1756, Lord Ferrers ran his mare against Captain M——'s horse for £50, and was the winner. When the race was ended, he spent the evening with some gentlemen, and in the course of conversation the captain (who had heard that his lordship's mare was with foal) proposed, in a jocose manner, to run his horse against her at the expiration of seven months. Lord Ferrers was so affronted by this circumstance, which he conceived to have arisen from a preconcerted plan to insult him, that he quitted Derby at three o'clock in the morning, and went immediately to his seat at Stanton-Harold in Leicestershire.

He rang his bell as soon as he awaked; and a servant attending, he asked, if he knew how Capt. M—— came to be informed that his mare was with foal. The servant declared that he was ignorant of the matter, but the groom might have told it; and, the groom being called, he denied having given any information respecting the matter.

Previous to the affront presumed to have been given on the preceding evening, lord Ferrers had invited the captain and the rest of the company to dine with him as on that day; but they all refused their attendance, though he sent a servant to remind them that they had promised to come. Lord Ferrers was so enraged at this disappointment, that

[1] On this occasion it may not be improper to observe on that extravagance which is too frequently the consequence of inebriation. If a man did but consider how he reduces himself even below the level of a brute by drunkenness, surely he would never be guilty of such a low, such a pitiful vice !

he kicked and horse-whipped his servants, and threw at them such articles as lay within his reach.

The following will afford a specimen of the brutality of lord Ferrers's behaviour. Some oysters had been sent from London, which not proving good, his lordship directed one of the servants to swear that the carrier had changed them; but the servant declining to take such an oath, the earl flew on him in a rage, stabbed him in the breast with a knife, cut his head with a candlestick and kicked him on the groin with such severity, that he was incapable of a retention of urine for several years afterwards.

Lord Ferrers's brother and his wife paying a visit to him and his countess at Stanton-Harold, some dispute arose between the parties; and lady Ferrers being absent from the room, the earl ran up stairs with a large clasp-knife in his hand, and asked a servant whom he met, where his lady was. The man said, 'in her own room;' and being directed to follow him thither, lord Ferrers ordered him to load a brace of pistols with bullets. This order was complied with: but the servant, apprehensive of mischief, declined priming the pistols, which lord Ferrers discovering, swore at him, asked him for powder, and primed them himself. He then threatened that if he did not immediately go and shoot his brother the captain, he would blow his brains out. The servant hesitating, his lordship pulled the trigger of one of the pistols; but it missed fire. Hereupon the countess dropped on her knees, and begged him to appease his passions; but in return he swore at her, and threatened her destruction if she opposed him. The servant now escaped from the room, and reported what had passed to his lordship's brother, who immediately called his wife from her bed, and they left the house, though it was then two o'clock in the morning.

The unfortunate Mr Johnson, who fell a sacrifice to the ungovernable passions of lord Ferrers, had been bred up in the family from his youth and was distinguished for the regular manner in which he kept his accounts, and his fidelity as a steward.

When the law had decreed a separate maintenance for

the countess, Mr Johnson was proposed as receiver of the rents for her use; but he declined this office till urged to take it on him by the earl himself. It appears that Johnson now stood high in his lordship's opinion; but a different scene soon ensued; for the earl having conceived an opinion that Johnson had combined with the trustees to disappoint him of a contract for coal-mines, he came to a resolution to destroy the honest steward.

The earl's displeasure was first evinced by his sending notice to Johnson to quit a beneficial farm which he held under him; but Johnson producing a lease granted by the trustees, no farther steps were taken in the affair.

After this, lord Ferrers behaved in so affable a manner to Johnson, that the latter imagined all thoughts of revenge had subsided; but, on the 13th of January, 1760, his lordship called on Johnson, who lived about half a mile from his seat, and bid him come to Stanton between three and four in the afternoon of the Friday following.

His lordship's family now consisted of a gentlewoman named Clifford, with four of her natural children, three maid-servants, and five men-servants, exclusive of an old man and a boy.

After dinner on the Friday, lord Ferrers sent all the men-servants out of the house, and desired Mrs Clifford to go with the children to the house of her father, at the distance of about two miles.

Johnson coming to his appointment, one of the maids let him in, and, after waiting some time, he was admitted to his lordship's room, and, being ordered to kneel down, was shot with a pistol, the ball from which entered his body just beneath his ribs.

Lord Ferrers, alarmed at the crime he had committed, now called for the maid-servants, and directed them to put Mr Johnson to bed. He likewise sent to Mr Kirkland, a surgeon, who lived at Ashby de la Zouch, two miles from his seat. At the request of the wounded man, a person was also sent for his children.

Miss Johnson, the eldest daughter, soon came, and was followed by the surgeon, to whom lord Ferrers said, 'I

F* *169*

intended to have shot him dead; but, since he is still alive, you must do what you can for him.'

The surgeon soon found that Johnson had been mortally wounded; but knowing the earl's firy disposition, and dreading similar consequences to himself, he dissembled the matter, and told him, that there was no danger in the case.

Hereupon, the earl drank himself into a state of intoxication, and then went to bed; after which, Mr Johnson was sent to his own house in a chair, at two o'clock in the morning, and died at nine.

Mr Kirkland, being convinced that Johnson could not live, procured a number of persons to secure the murderer. When they arrived at Stanton-Harold, lord Ferrers was just arisen, and going toward the stables with his garters in his hand; but, observing the people, he retired to the house, and shifted from place to place, so that it was a considerable time before he was taken.

This happened on a Saturday, and he was conveyed to Ashby de la Zouch, and confined at a public-house till the Monday following, when the coroner's jury having set on the body, and delivered a verdict of 'Wilful Murder,' his lordship was committed to the gaol of Leicester.

After remaining in the above place about a fortnight, he was conveyed to London in his own landau. He behaved with the utmost composure during the journey, and, being taken before the house of peers, the verdict of the coroner's jury was read, on which he was committed to the Tower.

His lordship's place of confinement was the round tower, near the draw-bridge. Two wardens constantly attended in his room, and one waited at the door. At the bottom of the stairs two soldiers were placed, with their bayonets fixed; and a third was stationed on the draw-bridge: and the gates of the Tower were shut an hour before the usual time, on occasion of this imprisonment.

Mrs Clifford now brought her four children to London, and, taking lodgings in Tower-street, she sent messages to his lordship several times in the day, and answers being sent, the communication became troublesome; so that their messages were forbid to pass more than once in the day.

While in the Tower, lord Ferrers lived in a regular manner. His breakfast consisted of a muffin, and a bason of tea, with a spoonful of brandy in it. After dinner and supper, he drank a pint of wine mixed with water. His behaviour in general was very decent, but he sometimes exhibited evident proofs of discomposure of mind. His natural children were permitted to be with him some time; but Mrs Clifford was denied admittance, after repeated applications.

Preparations being made for lord Ferrers's trial, and lord Henley (the Chancellor) being created high steward on the occasion, the trial came on before the House of Peers, in Westminster-hall, on the 16th of April, 1760. The proof of the fact was sufficiently clear: but lord Ferrers cross-examined the witnesses in such a manner as gave sufficient proof of the sanity of his mind, of which some doubts had been entertained.

Being found guilty by the unanimous voice of the peers of Great-Britain, the lord high steward passed sentence that he should be executed on the 21st of April; but his sentence was respited to the 5th of May.

While in the Tower, lord Ferrers left sixty pounds a year to Mrs Clifford, a thousand pounds to each of his natural daughters, and thirteen hundred pounds to the children of Mr Johnson.[1]

This unhappy nobleman petitioned to be beheaded within the Tower: but, as the crime was so atrocious, the king refused to mitigate the sentence. A scaffold was erected under the gallows at Tyburn, and covered with black bays; and a part of this scaffold, on which he was to stand, was raised about eighteen inches above the rest.

On the morning of execution, he is said to have written the following lines, and to have been proceeding when the attendance of one of the wardens interrupted him;

> In doubt I live, in doubt I die;
> Yet, undismay'd, the vast abyss I'll try,
> And plunge into eternity.
> Through rugged paths——

[1] This legacy, we are assured, is still (1778) unpaid.

About nine o'clock the sheriffs attended at the Tower-gate; and lord Ferrers being told they were come, requested that he might go in his own landau, instead of a mourning-coach, which had been prepared for him. No objection being made to this request, he entered the landau, attended by the Reverend Mr Humphries, chaplain of the Tower. His lordship was dressed in a white suit, richly embroidered with silver, and when he put it on he said, 'This is the suit in which I was married, and in which I will die.'

Mr Sheriff Vaillant joined them at the Tower-gate, and, taking his seat in the landau, told his lordship how disagreeable it was to wait on him on so awful an occasion, but that he would endeavour to render his situation as little irksome as possible.

The procession now moved slowly, through an immense crowd of spectators. On their way, lord Ferrers asked Mr Vaillant, if he had ever seen such a croud: the sheriff answered in the negative; to which the unhappy peer replied, 'I suppose it is because they never saw a lord hanged before.'

The chaplain, observing that the public would be naturally inquisitive about his lordship's religious opinions; he replied, 'that he did not think himself accountable to the world for his sentiments on religion; but that he always believed in one God, the maker of all things; that whatever were his religious notions, he had never propagated them; that all countries had a form of religion, by which the people were governed, and whoever disturbed them in it, he considered as an enemy to society:—that he thought lord Bolingbroke to blame for permitting his sentiments on religion to be published to the world.'

And he made other observations of a like nature.

Respecting the death of Mr Johnson, he said, 'he was under particular circumstances, and had met with so many crosses and vexations, that he scarce knew what he did;' but he declared that he had no malice against the unfortunate man.

So immense was the croud, that it was near three hours before the procession reached the place of execution, on the way to which lord Ferrers desired to stop to have a glass of wine and water; but the sheriff, observing that it would only draw a greater crowd about him, he replied, 'that is true, I say no more; let us by no means stop.' He likewise observed, that the preliminary apparatus of death produced more terror than death itself.

At the place of execution he expressed a wish to take a final leave of Mrs Clifford; but the sheriff advised him to decline it, as it would disarm him of the fortitude he possessed; to which he answered, 'If you, Sir, think I am wrong, I submit;' after which he gave the sheriff a pocket-book, containing a bank-note, with a ring and a purse of guineas, which were afterwards delivered to the unhappy woman.

The procession was attended by a party of horse-grenadiers and foot-guards, and at the place of execution was met by another party of horse, which formed a circle round the gallows.

His lordship walked up the steps of the scaffold with great composure, and having joined with the chaplain in repeating the Lord's prayer, which he called a fine composition, he spoke the following words with great fervency: 'O God, forgive me all my errors!—pardon all my sins!'

He then presented his watch to Mr Vaillant, and gave five guineas to the assistant of the executioner, by mistake, instead of giving them to himself. The master demanding the money, a dispute arose between the parties, which might have discomposed the dying man, had not the sheriff exerted his authority to put an end to it.

The executioner now proceeded to do his duty. Lord Ferrers's neckcloth was taken off, a white cap which he had brought in his pocket put on his head, his arms secured with a black sash, and the halter put round his neck. He then ascended the raised part of the scaffold, and the cap being pulled over his face, the sheriff gave a signal, on which the raised scaffold was struck, and remained level with the rest.

After hanging an hour and five minutes, the body was received in a coffin lined with white sattin, and conveyed to surgeon's-hall, where an incision was made from the neck to the bottom of the breast, and the bowels were taken out, on inspection of which the surgeons declared that they had never beheld greater signs of long life in any subject which had come under their notice.

His lordship's hat and the halter lay near his feet in the coffin, on the lid of which were these words, 'LAURENCE EARL FERRERS, suffered May 5, 1760.' After the body had remained some time at surgeon's-hall, for public inspection, it was delivered to his friends for interment: but it would be unjust to his memory not to mention that, during his imprisonment, he had made pecuniary recompence to several persons whom he had injured during the extravagance of those passions to which he was unhappily subject.

This malefactor was executed at Tyburn on the 5th of May, 1760.

The case of lord Ferrers demands our serious attention. He was born to great hopes and high expectations, and was confessedly a man of superior abilities; but the unhappy indulgence of his passions led to his ruin. Hence, then, the due government of the passions ought to be learnt; for what is the man, who permits their unbounded gratification, but something lower than a brute?

Lord Ferrers appears to have been uninfluenced by the mild doctrines of Christianity. If these had held their proper weight on his mind, it would have been impossible that he could have acted as he did: but when Religion fails to produce its natural, its genuine effects, the man ceases to appear as such, and becomes an object of compassion, if not of contempt!

The report of this case makes very strange reading. There would appear to be little doubt that Earl Ferrers was not 'right in his head', but the quality of his cross-examination of the witnesses made a defence of insanity impossible. In *Letters of Horace Walpole* (The Folio Society, 1951), there is a reference to the case in a letter to George Montagu under date January the 28th, 1760, in which he says: 'You have heard, I suppose, a horrid story of another kind, of Lord Ferrers murdering his steward in the most barbarous and deliberate manner. He sent away all his servants but one, and like that heroic murderess Queen Christina, carried the poor man, through a gallery and several rooms, locking them after him, and then bid the man kneel down, for he was determined to kill him. The poor creature flung himself at his feet, but in vain, was shot and lived twelve hours. Mad as this action was, from the consequences, there was no frenzy in his behaviour. He got drunk, and at intervals talked of it coolly: but did not attempt to escape till the colliers beset his house and were determined to take him alive or dead. He is now in the gaol at Leicester, and will soon be removed to the Tower, then to Westminster Hall, and I suppose to Tower Hill; unless as Lord Talbot prophesied in the House of Lords, "Not being thought mad enough to be shut up till he had killed somebody, he will then be thought too mad to be executed." But that madman, Lord Talbot, was nó more honoured in his vocation, than other prophets are in their own country.'

Ferrers went to Tyburn in his own landau drawn by six horses, dressed in his embroidered silver suit. Many notorious criminals made a point of being especially well dressed for the journey to Tyburn, Dick Turpin even purchasing 'a new fustian frock and a pair of pumps' for the purpose.

A full and particular Narrative of the Cases of ANNE BEDDINGFIELD, and RICHARD RINGE, who were hanged for Petit Treason.

JOHN BEDDINGFIELD was the son of respectable parents at Sternfield in Suffolk, and having married a girl of seventeen years of age when he was about twenty-four, the young couple were placed in a good farm, which was carefully attended by Beddingfield, who bore the character of a man of industry and integrity. The young couple had two children, and lived in apparent happiness till near the time when the shocking event happened which gives rise to this melancholy tale.

Richard Ringe, a youth of nineteen, was engaged in the service of Mr Beddingfield; nor had he been long in the house before his mistress became so enamoured of him, that her husband was the object of her contempt. Her behaviour to Ringe was such that he could not long doubt of her favourable inclinations; nor had he virtue to resist the temptation; and they were so incautious in their proceedings, that four of the servants were occasional witnesses of their criminal intercourse.

At length Mrs Beddingfield, having formed the horrid design of destroying her husband, communicated her intention to Ringe, who hesitated on the dreadful proposal, nor consented till she promised that he should share her fortune as the reward of the deed.

Mrs Beddingfield, blinded by her passion, was now so much off her guard, as to say very indiscreet things to her servants, which might lead them to presume that she had determined on the most deliberate wickedness; of which the following is given as one instance. As she was dressing herself one morning, she said to her maid-servant, 'help me to put on my ear-rings; but I shall not wear them much longer, for I shall have new black ones. It will not be long before somebody in the house dies, and I believe it will be your master.'

Extravagant as this declaration was, the behaviour of

Ringe was not at all more prudent. He purchased some poison, and told one of the servant-maids, that he would be her constant friend if she would mix it with some rum and milk that her master drank in a morning; but the girl declined having any concern in so horrid a transaction; nor did she take any notice of the proposal that had been made till after the commission of the murder.

Mr Beddingfield happening to be indisposed, it was recommended to him to take a vomit; but the water which the servant-maid brought him to drink proving to be too hot, Ringe was directed to bring some cold water to mix with it; and he took this opportunity of putting arsenick into the water; but Beddingfield, observing a white sediment in the bason, would not drink, though no suspicion of the liquor being poisoned had occurred to him.

Henceforward the intentional murderers resolved not to think of having recourse to poison, but devised another scheme of dispatching the unfortunate object of their vengeance. Mr Beddingfield having been selling some cattle to another farmer, they had drank a sociable glass together, but not to such a degree as to occasion intoxication.

When Mr Beddingfield came home, he found that his wife was in bed with one of the maid-servants; on which he desired her to come to his chamber; but this she refused; and mutual recriminations passed between them.

It had been determined by Ringe to commit the murder on that night, while his master was asleep; whereupon, when he knew he was in bed, he quitted his own room, passed through that in which his mistress slept, and went to the bed-chamber of his master.

Ringe, observing that Mr Beddingfield was asleep, threw a cord round his neck to strangle him; but, being hurt by the weight of Ringe lying across him, he struggled so that they both fell off the bed together. However, the horrid deed of murder was soon perpetrated.

Mrs Beddingfield, being asleep in the next room, was awakened by the noise, and in her fright awakened the servant. At this instant Ringe entered the room, and said 'I have done for him;' to which the wife answered, 'Then I am easy.' The girl was greatly alarmed; but cried out, 'Master,' supposing Mr Beddingfield was present; for there was no light in the room: but Mrs Beddingfield commanded her to be silent.

Ringe asked the mistress if any one was acquainted with what had passed besides her and the maid; on which the girl asked, 'How came you here, Richard?' The villain, terrified by his guilt, replied, 'I was forced to it.' He now went to his own room, and laid down; and the mistress and maid getting up, the latter was charged not to utter a syllable of what had passed.

Mrs Beddingfield now directed the girl to call Ringe, who seemed offended at being disturbed; but, when he had struck a light, his mistress told him to go into his master's room, for she was afraid that he was indisposed. Ringe obeyed; but, on his return, said, with an air of surprize, that his master was dead.

By this time another maid-servant was got up, and the girls, going to their master's room, found the deceased lying on his face, and observed that part of his shirt-collar was torn off, and that his neck was black and swelled.

A messenger was instantly dispatched to Mr Beddingfield's parents, who proposed to send for a surgeon: but the wife insisted that it was unnecessary to send for a doctor, as her husband was already dead.

On the following day the coroner's jury took an inquisition into the cause of his death; but so superficial was the enquiry, that it lasted only a few minutes, and their determination was, that he died a natural death.

The guilty commerce between the murderers now became still more evident than before, but so fickle was Mrs Beddingfield's disposition, that in a few weeks she began to despise the man whom she had incited to the murder of her husband.

The servant-maid now resolved to discover the fact, but postponed the doing so till she had received the wages for her quarter's service. When her mistress had paid her, she went to her parents, and discovered all she knew of the matter; on which a warrant was issued for apprehending the murderers. They had an item of what was going forward, and therefore attempted to bribe the girl's mother to secrecy; but she rejected their offers; on which Mrs Beddingfield made her escape, but was apprehended at the end of two days. Ringe, however, seemed to disdain to consult his own safety, but remained in the house; and, after he was committed to prison, he confessed that he had deemed himself a dead man from the time of his perpetrating the murder.

At the Lent assizes, in 1763, the prisoners were brought to trial, when the surgeon and coroner were examined as to what fell within their knowledge. The former confessed that he saw evident marks of violence on the body; and being asked how he could depose before the coroner, that Mr Beddingfield had died a natural death, he replied, that he 'did not think much about it.' A strange, and almost unaccountable declaration!

The preceding part of this narrative will lead the reader to judge of the rest of the evidence that was given on the trial; and the prisoners, having nothing to alledge in extenuation of their crime, were capitally convicted, and sentenced to die.

After conviction, as well as before, Ringe freely confessed his guilt; but expressed the utmost anxiety at the thought of being dissected. Mrs Beddingfield refused to make any confession till the day before her death.

They were placed in one sledge on the morning of execution, and conveyed to a place near Ipswich, called Rushmore, where Ringe made a pathetic address to the surrounding multitude, advising young people to be warned, by his fate, to avoid the delusions of wicked women, and to consider chastity as a virtue.

After the fervent exercise of devotion he was turned off, while the body of Mrs Beddingfield, who had been first strangled at a stake, was burning to ashes, agreeable to the practice respecting women who are convicted of the murder of their husbands.

These malefactors suffered at Rushmore on the 8th of April, 1763.

From the fate of this woman girls should be taught never to think of giving their hands in marriage to a man, if they are not certain of his having full possession of their hearts: and if, after marriage, any disagreeable circumstances should arise, they should patiently recollect, that they have drawn an inevitable lot, and endeavour by a kind and obliging behaviour to conciliate the husband's affection; but by no means to think of violating the laws of chastity, without a proper observance of which, jealousy, and all its horrid train of consequences, must ensue; and marriage, otherwise the happiest state in life, be rendered the most miserable.

From the ignominious death of Ringe, young men should learn not to listen to the seducing tongue of female beauty; but, having lived a life of virtue till they can obtain each some worthy woman in marriage, do justice to the preference by which they may be distinguished!

A Narrative of the horrid Cruelties of ELIZABETH BROWNRIGG on her Apprentices; with an Account of her being apprehended, tried, convicted, and executed for Murder.

THIS wicked woman, after having been servant to a merchant in Goodman's-fields, married James Brownrigg, a painter, who went to settle at Greenwich, and after residing there six years came to London, and took a house in Fleur-de-lis Court, Fleet-street, where he carried on a considerable share of business, and had a little house at Islington for an occasional retreat.

Mrs Brownrigg had been the mother of sixteen children, three of whom were living when she forfeited her life to the justice of the laws.

As she practised midwifery, she was appointed by the overseers of the poor of St Dunstan's parish to take care of the poor women who were taken in labour in the workhouse; and it is but justice, to the memory of one who has but little else to be said in her favour, to declare that her character as a midwife remained unimpeached.

Mary Mitchell, a poor girl of the precinct of White-friars, was put apprentice to Mrs Brownrigg in the year 1765, and about the same time Mary Jones, one of the children of the Foundling-hospital, was likewise placed with her in the same capacity; and she had other apprentices.

As Mrs Brownrigg received pregnant women to lie-in privately, these girls were taken with a view of saving the expence of women servants. At first the poor orphans were treated with some degree of civility; but this was soon changed for the most savage barbarity. Having laid Mary Jones across two chairs in the kitchen, she whipped her with such wanton cruelty, that she was occasionally obliged to desist, from mere weariness. This treatment was frequently repeated; and Mrs Brownrigg used to throw water on her when she had done whipping her, and sometimes she would dip her head into a pail of water.

The room appointed for the girl to sleep in adjoined to the passage leading to the street-door, and as she had received many wounds on her head, shoulders, and various parts of her body, she determined not to bear such treatment any longer, if she could effect her escape. Observing that the key was left in the street-door when the family went to bed, she opened the door cautiously one morning, and escaped into the street.

Thus freed from her horrid confinement, she repeatedly enquired her way to the Foundling-hospital till she found it, and was admitted after describing in what manner she had been treated, and shewing the bruises she had received.

The child having been examined by a surgeon who found her wounds to be of a most alarming nature, the governors of the hospital ordered Mr Plumtree, their solicitor, to write to James Brownrigg, threatening a prosecution, if he did not give a proper reason for the severities exercised towards the child.

No notice of this letter being taken by Brownrigg, and the governors of the hospital thinking it imprudent to indict at common law, the girl was discharged in consequence of an application to the chamberlain of London.

Mary Mitchell, abovementioned, continued with her mistress for the space of a year, during which she was treated with such savage cruelty, that she also resolved to quit her service. Having got out of the house, she was met in the street by the younger son of Brownrigg, who forced her to return home, where her sufferings were greatly aggravated on account of her elopement.

In the interim, the overseers of the precinct of White-friars bound Mary Clifford to Brownrigg; nor was it long before she experienced similar cruelties to those inflicted on the other poor girls, and possibly still more severe. She was frequently tied up naked, and beaten with a hearth-broom, a horsewhip, or a cane, till she was absolutely speechless. This poor girl having a natural infirmity, the mistress would not permit her to lay in a bed, but placed her on a mat in a coal-hole that was remarkably cold; but after some time a sack and a quantity of straw formed her bed, instead of the mat.

During her confinement in that wretched situation she had nothing to subsist on but bread and water; and her covering during the night consisted only of her own cloaths, so that she sometimes lay almost perished with cold.

On a particular occasion, when she was almost starving through hunger, she broke open a cupboard in search of food, but found it empty; and on another occasion she broke down some boards, in order to procure a draught of water. Though she was thus pressed for the humblest necessaries of life, Mrs Brownrigg determined to punish her with rigour, for the means she had taken to supply herself with them.

On this she caused the girl to strip to the skin, and, during the course of a whole day while she remained naked, she repeatedly beat her with the but-end of a whip. In the course of this most inhuman treatment, a jack-chain was fixed round her neck, the end of which was fastened to the yard door, and then it was pulled as tight as possible, without strangling her. A day being passed in the practice of these savage barbarities, the girl was remanded to the coal-hole at night, her hands being tied behind her, and the chain still remaining about her neck.

The husband being obliged to find his wife's apprentices in wearing-apparel, they were frequently stripped naked, and kept so for whole days if their garments happened to be torn.

The elder son of Brownrigg had frequently the superintendence of the abovementioned wretched girl; but this was sometimes committed to the apprentice, who declared that she was totally naked one night when he went to tie her up.

The two poor girls were frequently so beaten, that their heads and shoulders appeared as one general sore; and when a plaister was applied to their wounds, the skin used to peel away: still, however, the savage mistress continued to treat them with her accustomed barbarity.

Sometimes Mrs Brownrigg, when resolved on uncommon

183

severity, used to tie their hands with a cord, and draw them up to a water-pipe which ran across the ceiling in the kitchen; but that giving way, she desired her husband to fix a hook in the beam, through which a cord was drawn, and their arms being extended, she used to horsewhip them till she was weary, and till the blood followed every stroke.

The elder son of Brownrigg having one day directed Mary Clifford to put up a half-tester bedstead, the poor girl was unable to do it, on which he beat her till she could no longer support his severity; and at another time, when the mother had been whipping her in the kitchen till she was absolutely tired, the son renewed the savage treatment.

Mrs Brownrigg would sometimes seize the poor girl by the cheeks, and, forcing the skin down violently with her fingers, would cause the blood to gush from her eyes.

Mary Clifford, unable to bear these repeated severities, complained of her hard treatment to a French lady who lodged in the house; and she having represented the impropriety of such behaviour to Mrs Brownrigg, the inhuman monster flew at the girl, and cut her tongue in two places with a pair of scissars.

On the morning of the 13th of July, Mrs Brownrigg went into the kitchen, and, after obliging Mary Clifford to strip to the skin, drew her up to the staple, and, though her body was almost one general sore, from former bruises, yet this barbarian mistress renewed her cruelties with the accustomed severity.

After whipping her till the blood streamed down her body, she let her down, and made her wash herself in a tub of cold water; Mary Mitchell, the other poor girl, being present during this transaction. While Clifford was washing herself, Mrs Brownrigg struck her on the shoulders, already sore with former bruises, with the but-end of a whip; and she treated the poor child in the manner abovementioned five times in the same day; as if she was determined to set no bounds to her inhumanity.

The poor girl's wounds now began to shew evident signs of mortification; and it is probable that she might have been privately buried, and the murderess escaped detection, but for the following circumstance. Mary Clifford's mother-in-law, who had resided some time in the country, came to town, and enquired after the child; and being informed that she was placed at Brownrigg's, she went thither, but was refused admittance by Mr Brownrigg, who even threatened to carry her before the lord-mayor if she came there to make farther disturbances.

Hereupon the mother-in-law was going away, when Mrs Deacon, wife of Mr Deacon, baker at the adjoining house, called her in, and informed her that she and her family had often heard moanings and groans issue from Brownrigg's house, and that she suspected the apprentices were treated with unwarrantable severity.

Mrs Deacon likewise promised to exert herself to come at the truth of the affair.

At this juncture Mr Brownrigg, going to Hampstead on business, bought a hog, which he sent home. This hog was put into a covered yard, to which there was a sky-light, which it was thought necessary to remove, in order to give air to the animal.

As soon as it was known that the sky-light was removed, Mr Deacon ordered his servants to watch, in order, if possible, to discover the girls. Deacon's servant-maid, looking from a window, saw one of the girls stooping down; on which she called her mistress, and she desired the attendance of some of the neighbours, who, having been witnesses of the shocking scene, some men got upon the leads, and dropped bits of dirt, to induce the girl to speak to them; but she seemed wholly incapable.[1]

Hereupon Mrs Deacon sent to the girl's mother-in-law, who going to the overseers who had placed out the child, they called on Mr Grundy, one of the overseers of St

---

[1] It will seem strange, that when suspicions of a murderous intention arose, the neighbours could hesitate a moment in procuring proper authority to search the house ; but the fact is, that people in general are afraid to interest themselves in any matter that may become an object of legal discussion.

Dunstan's, and all of them going together, they demanded a sight of Mary Clifford: but Brownrigg, who had nicknamed her Nan, told them that he knew no such person, but if they wanted to see Mary (meaning Mary Mitchell), they might; and accordingly produced her.

Mr Deacon's servant now declared that Mary Mitchell was not the girl who had been seen in the shocking situation abovementioned; on which Mr Grundy sent for a constable, to search the house, which was done; but no discovery was then made.

Mr Brownrigg threatened highly; but Mr Grundy, with the spirit that became the officer of a parish, took Mary Mitchell with him to the workhouse, where, on the taking off her leathern-boddice, it stuck so fast to her wounds, that she shrieked with the pain: but, on being treated with great humanity, and told that she should not be sent back to Brownrigg's, she gave an account of the horrid treatment that she and Mary Clifford had sustained; and confessed that she had met the latter on the stairs just before they came to the house.

On this Mr Grundy and some others returned to the house, to make a stricter search; on which Brownrigg sent for a lawyer, in order to intimidate them, and even threatened a prosecution, unless they immediately quitted the house.

Unterrified by these threats, Mr Grundy sent for a coach to carry Brownrigg to the compter; on which the latter promised to produce the girl in half an hour, if the coach was discharged. This being consented to, the girl was produced from a cupboard, under a beauset in the dining-room, after a pair of shoes, which young Brownrigg had in his hand during the proposal, had been put upon her.

It is not in language to describe the miserable appearance this poor girl made: almost her whole body was ulcerated. Being taken to the workhouse, an apothecary was sent for, who pronounced her to be in danger.

Brownrigg was conveyed to Wood-street compter; but his wife and son made their escape, taking with them a gold watch and some money.

Mr Brownrigg was now carried before Mr alderman Crosby, who fully committed him, and ordered the girls to be taken to St Bartholomew's hospital, where Mary Clifford died within a few days; and the coroner's inquest being summoned, found a verdict of wilful murder against James and Elizabeth Brownrigg, and John their son.

In the mean time, Mrs Brownrigg and her son shifted from place to place in London, bought cloaths in Rag-fair, to disguise themselves, and then went to Wandsworth, where they took lodgings in the house of Mr Dunbar, who kept a chandler's-shop, where they remained till they were apprehended, carefully screening themselves from public view.

Mr Dunbar, happening to read a newspaper[1] on the 15th of August, saw an advertisement which so clearly described his lodgers, that he had no doubt but they were the murderers. On this he went to London the next day, which was Sunday, and, going to church, sent for Mr Owen, the churchwarden, to attend him in the vestry, and gave him such a description of the parties, that Mr Owen desired Mr Deacon and Mr Wingrave a constable, to go to Wandsworth, and make the necessary enquiry.

On their arrival at Dunbar's house, they found the wretched mother and son in a room by themselves. They gave evident signs of confusion at the first interview; but a coach being procured, they were conveyed to London, without any person in Wandsworth having knowledge of the affair, except Mr and Mrs Dunbar.

At the ensuing sessions at the Old Bailey the father, mother, and son, were indicted; when Elizabeth Brownrigg, after a trial of eleven hours, was found guilty of murder, and ordered for execution: but the man and his son, being acquitted of the higher charge, were detained to take their

---

[1] This is one, of ten thousand instances, that proves the importance of the liberty of the press; and it is evident that those who seek to abridge it, can be no true friends to the liberties of their country. It may be sometimes abused, but will be always of the highest importance.

trials for a misdemeanour, of which they were convicted, and imprisoned for six months.

After sentence of death was passed on Mrs Brownrigg, she was attended by a clergyman, to whom she confessed the enormity of her crime, and acknowledged the justice of the sentence by which she had been condemned.

The parting between her and her husband and son, on the morning of her execution, was affecting beyond description. The son falling on his knees, she bent herself to him, and embraced him. The husband was kneeling on the other side; she also kneeled down, and, having besought the Almighty to have mercy on her soul, said 'Dear James, I beg that God, for Christ's sake, will be reconciled, and that he will not leave me, nor forsake me, in the hour of death, and in the day of judgment.'

On her way to the place of execution the people expressed their abhorrence of her crime in terms which, though not proper for the occasion, testified their astonishment that such a wretch could have existed: they even prayed for her damnation instead of her salvation: they doubted not but that 'the devil would fetch her,' and hoped that 'she would go to hell.' Such were the sentiments of the mob.

At the place of execution this miserable woman joined in prayers with the ordinary of Newgate, whom she desired to declare to the multitude, that she confessed her guilt, and acknowledged the justice of her sentence.

After execution her body was put into a hackney-coach, conveyed to surgeons-hall, dissected and anatomized; and her skeleton may be yet seen in a nitch in the hall.

Elizabeth Brownrigg was hanged at Tyburn on the 14th of September, 1767.

What is it possible to say on this subject that will not have occurred to every reader of feeling and humanity? This more than common murder—this murder by inches, has something so shocking in its nature, something so infernal in its progress, that there is no language in which to express our abhorrence of it.

That Mrs Brownrigg, a midwife by profession, and herself the mother of many children, should wantonly murder the children of other women, is truly astonishing, and can only be accounted for by that depravity of human nature, which philosophers have always disputed, but which true christians will be ready to allow.

Let her crimes be buried, though her skeleton be exposed; and may no one hereafter be found hardy enough to copy those crimes!

Women who have the care of children from parish workhouses, or hospitals, should consider themselves at once as mistresses and as mothers; nor ever permit the strictness of the former character to preponderate over the humanity of the latter.

A particular Account of the Trial of Mr BA-RETTI, an Italian, who was indicted for the wilful Murder of EVAN MORGAN, and acquitted; together with the Defence which he made in Court.

AT the sessions held at the Old Bailey in November, 1769, Mr Baretti was brought to his trial, for the murder of Evan Morgan, on the 6th of October preceding; when the substance of the evidence against him was to the following effect.

Elizabeth Ward deposed, that, between nine and ten at night on the 6th of October, she heard a woman, whom she had never seen before, ask the prisoner to give her a glass of wine, and at the same time take hold of him in a manner inconsistent with decency:—that the prisoner proceeded forward, but, soon turning back, doubled his fist and struck this deponent a violent blow on the face:—that, on her screaming out, three men came up, and demanded 'how he could strike a woman,' and, shoving him once or twice, pushed him off the pavement. At this time, she said, Baretti drew a knife, while the men followed him, calling out 'Murder! he has a knife out!' and this deponent believed that the deceased was stabbed at this juncture.

The deposition of Thomas Patman was to the following effect. That he had been in company with a Mr Clark and the deceased on the night abovementioned; that he saw Mr Baretti strike a woman, whom he did not know, on the head; and, on her screaming out, Morgan and Clark pushed Patman, though not with much violence, against Baretti, who gave him a blow on the left side, in consequence of which the blood ran down into his shoe:—that he then called out he was stabbed; that Baretti retreated; that Morgan followed him about half-way up Panton-street, where Morgan received a wound from the prisoner in Patman's presence, in consequence of which he fell to the ground.

The testimony of John Clark confirmed, in several particulars, that of the preceding evidence; but, on his being cross-examined, he acknowledged that Patman did not know he was stabbed till Mr Baretti ran into Panton-street. He likewise owned, that himself had sworn before the coroner, 'that Morgan collared Baretti before he knew Patman was wounded; and that one of the women said the prisoner ought to have a knock over the head with her patten.'

The evidence of Mr Lambert, a tallow-chandler in Panton-street, was to the following effect. He said, that Mr Baretti ran into a grocer's shop, opposite his house; that Patman was standing at the door, with the blood running down his shirt, and said that a gentleman in the shop had stabbed him. Mr Baretti had at that time a knife in one hand, and a silver case over the blade, which was bloody. Mr Lambert, who at that time was in the office of constable, called to Baretti to surrender, and, immediately running towards him, seized him, and took him into custody, in order to convey him before a magistrate.

Morgan having been carried to the Middlesex-hospital, one of the patients, who had been there at the time, declared, that he had heard the deceased say, that he saw a gentleman assault two women; on which, without intending to give offence, he went to assist them; when Baretti stabbed him in two places, and that he then turned round, and stabbed him a third time; and that the third wound hurt him more than the two former.

The testimony of Mr Wyatt, the surgeon who attended Morgan, imported, that the deceased had received three wounds, one of which, being in the belly, was the immediate occasion of his death. He farther said, that, while he was dressing Patman, Clark being present, and enquiring into what gave rise to the misfortune, Clark said, that they saw a gentleman abusing a lady who was acquainted with Morgan; that Morgan pushed Clark against Patman, and that Clark pushed him against the prisoner; that he was not struck by either of them, but he believed the woman damned him for a French bougre, and said he ought to have his head cloven with a patten.

A short time after this, Mr Wyatt demanded of Clark whether the woman was of his acquaintance; and he replied in the negative, and then denied that she was even acquainted with Morgan; though, not more than two minutes before, he had confessed that she was.

This being the substance of the evidence on the trial, Mr Baretti read the following defence, which will probably be deemed to give more insight into the real state of the case, than all that has preceded it.

'On Friday the 6th I spent the whole day at home, correcting my Italian and English dictionary, which is actually reprinting and working off; and upon another book in four volumes, which is to be published in February next, and has been advertised in the news-papers. I went a little after four to the club of royal academicians in Soho, where I stopped about half an hour, waiting for my friends, and warming myself in the club-room.

'Upon nobody's coming, I went to the Orange coffee-house, to see if a letter was come for me (for my letters come there) but there was none. I went back to go to the club, and going hastily up the Haymarket, there was a woman at a door: they say there were two, but I took notice of but one, as I hope God will save me; there might have been two, though I only saw one; that is a fact. There was a woman eight or ten yards from the corner of Panton-street, and she clapped her hands with such violence about my private parts, that it gave me great pain. This I instantly resented, by giving her a blow on the hand, with a few angry words. The woman got up directly, raised her voice, and finding by my pronunciation I was a foreigner, she called me several bad names, in a most contumelious strain; among which, French bougre, d—ned Frenchman, and a woman-hater, were the most audible.

'I had not quite turned the corner, before a man made me turn back, by giving me a blow with his fist, and asking me how I dare strike a woman; another pushed him against me, and pushed me off the pavement; then three or four more joined them. I wonder I did not fall from the high step which is there. The path-way is much raised from the

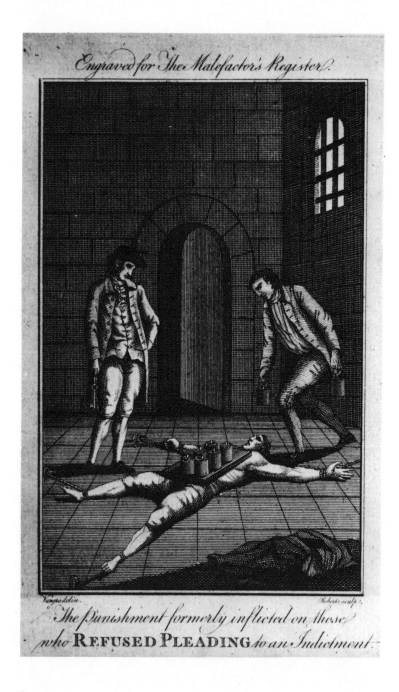

Engraved for The Malefactor's Register.

The Punishment formerly inflicted on those who REFUSED PLEADING to an Indictment.

coach-way. A great number of people surrounded me presently, many beating me, and all d—ning me on every side, in a
most frightful manner. I was a Frenchman in their opinion,
which made me apprehensive I must expect no favour nor
protection, but all outrage and blows.

'There is generally a great puddle in the corner of Panton-
street, even when the weather is fine; but that day it had
rained incessantly, which made it very slippery. I could
plainly perceive my assailants wanted to throw me into the
puddle, where I might be trampled on; so I cried out,
murder! There was a space in the circle, from whence I
ran into Panton-Street, and endeavoured to get into the
footway. I was in the greatest horror, lest I should run
against some stones, as I have such bad eyes. I could not
run so fast as my pursuers, so that they were upon me,
continually beating and pushing me, some of them attempting to catch me by the hair-tail: if this had happened, I
had been certainly a lost man. I cannot absolutely fix the
time and place where I first struck. I remember, somewhere
in Panton-street I gave a quick blow to one who beat off
my hat with his fist.

'When I was in Oxendon-street, fifteen or sixteen yards
from the Haymarket, I stopped, and faced about. My
confusion was great, and seeing a shop open, I ran into it
for protection, quite spent with fatigue. I am certainly
sorry for the man; but he owed his death to his own daring
impetuosity. Three men came into the shop, one of them
cried to me to surrender myself to him, who was a constable. I asked them if they were honest men, and friends;
they said yes. I put up my knife, desired them to arrest me,
begged they would send for a coach, and take me to Sir
John Fielding.

'I appeal to them how I behaved when I surrendered,
and how thankful I was for their kind protection. Sir John
heard what I and the men had to say. They sent me into a
room below, from whence I dispatched a man to the club
in Gerrard-street, when Sir Joshua Reynolds and other
gentlemen came to me.

'A messenger was dispatched to the Middlesex hospital,

where they said Morgan was carried. A surgeon came, and took his oath that Morgan was in danger. Sir John committed me to Tothill-fields-bridewell. Two gentlemen, as well as the constable, can witness to my behaviour when the coachman lost his way, which forced us to alight in the mire and darkness, in order to find the way to Tothill-fields-bridewell. I humbly conceive this will shew I had no intention of escaping. That woeful night I passed without rest.

'My face had been observed to be hurt, while I was at Sir John Fielding's; and the constable was the first who took notice of a blow I had received on my chin. But when the heat and fear had subsided, I found a great pain in divers parts of my body. Mr Molini and Mr Low, being with me, desired me to let them see what was the matter with my back, which I complained of. I stripped, and they saw several bruises.

'This, my lord and gentlemen of the jury, is the best account I can give of my unfortunate accident: for what is done in two or three minutes, in fear and terror, is not to be minutely described; and the court and the jury are to judge. I hope your lordship, and every person present, will think that a man of my age, character, and way of life, would not spontaneously quit my pen, to engage in an outrageous tumult. I hope it will easily be conceived that a man almost blind could not but be seized with terror on such a sudden attack as this. I hope it will be seen that my knife was neither a weapon of offence or defence; I wear it to carve fruit and sweatmeats, and not to kill my fellow-creatures.

'It is a general custom in France not to put knives upon the table, so that even ladies wear them in their pockets for general use. I have continued to wear it after my return, because I have found it occasionally convenient. Little did I think such an event would ever have happened. Let this trial turn out as favourable as my innocence may deserve, still my regret will endure as long as life shall last.

'A man who has lived full fifty years, and spent most of that time in a studious manner, I hope, will not be supposed to have voluntarily engaged in so desperate an affair. I beg leave, my lord and gentlemen, to add one thing more. Equally confident of my own innocence, and English discernment to trace out truth, I did resolve to waive the privilege granted to foreigners by the laws of this kingdom: nor was my motive a compliment to this nation: my motive was my life and honour; that it should not be thought I received undeserved favour from a jury, part my own country. I chose to be tried by a jury of this country; for, if my honour is not saved, I cannot much wish for the preservation of my life. I will wait for the determination of this awful court with that confidence, I hope, which innocence has a right to obtain. So God bless you all.'

Several gentlemen now appeared in behalf of Mr Baretti; among whom, Mr Lambert proved that he had received a blow, that his hat was lost, and that his face was swelled.

Mr Molini swore that, on the day after the affray, he had observed a swelling on Mr Baretti's cheek, and several bruises on his back and shoulder; and Mr Low deposed, that, when he visited Mr Baretti in prison, he had seen six or seven bruises on different parts of his body.

Justice Kelynge, major Alderton, and Mr Petrin, deposed, that some abandoned women, attended by bullies, had severally attacked them in an indelicate way in the Haymarket.

To the character of Mr Baretti appeared Sir Joshua Reynolds, doctor Johnson, Mr Fitzherbert, and Edmund Burke, esquire, all of whom represented him as a man of benevolence, sobriety, modesty, and learning. The honourable Mr Beauclerk, Mr Garrick, and Mr Molini, all confirmed this testimony, adding, that persons who travel in foreign countries are accustomed to carry such knives as that which had been unhappily made use of by the prisoner.

After considering the whole matter, the jury acquitted Mr Baretti of murder and manslaughter, and gave a verdict of 'Self-defence.'

This case of Mr Baretti may be deemed one of the extraordinary kind. It seems evident, from the depositions made on his trial, and from the substance of his defence, that he had been assaulted by people of abandoned character; but the question is, whether he had a right to defend himself with such a weapon as he made use of; however, we shall not presume to decide on this question, as the jury solemnly determined that he *had*, by the verdict they gave.

Mr Baretti's character was of the utmost service to him on this solemn occasion. His learning, his connexions, his disposition, were all of the highest importance to him; and though the alledged crime was no less than murder, we well remember that he was bailed by four gentlemen of distinguished character; so that he did not lay in Newgate even a single hour.

His generous refusal to accept of the usual favour of being tried by a jury composed of an equal number of Foreigners with Englishmen, furnishes an admirable proof of his disdain of taking any advantage; nor is it a small presumptive proof of his innocence: and his declaration that his regret would endure as long as life should last, though the trial should turn out as favourably as innocence might deserve, is greatly in favour of his humanity: and indeed no man of liberal feelings can have been even the accidental occasion of the death of a fellow creature, without sincerely lamenting the misfortune.

The people of this country may wonder that Mr Baretti, an Italian by birth, should make his defence in such correct English: but it is to be remembered, that he had lived long among us, had studied our language with critical attention, and wrote it with a degree of purity scarce ever equalled by a Foreigner; to whom the English language, of all others, is said to be the most difficult of acquisition.

Upon the whole, this inference should be drawn from the present case:—those who would consult their own safety should avoid giving offence to others in the streets. The casual passenger has, at least, a right to pass unmolested; and he or she that may insult him cannot deserve pity, whatever consequences may follow.

Foreign gentlemen, however, should consider, that the best method of escaping the fury of a mob is to take shelter in the first house they may see open: there are few people who could be so hard of heart as not to afford them protection; and we must think, for the honour of our country, that the generality would protect them against their assailants.

The number of abandoned women, who infest the streets of the metropolis every evening, are in some measure to be pitied; but, when they add insult to indecent application, they ought to be punished with the utmost severity. But what must those men think of themselves, whose seductive arts have reduced women to a state so deplorable? If they have any sensibility left, horror and remorse must seize their minds: yet, however great their sufferings, they are not deserving of pity.—Violators of all the laws of honour, they have no claim to our compassion!

In Vol. 2 of Birkbeck Hill's *Boswell's Life of Johnson* at page 97 is to be found the evidence as to character given at this trial by Sir Joshua Reynolds, Dr Johnson, Edmund Burke, David Garrick and Oliver Goldsmith. Boswell records the trial in these words: 'Never did such a constellation of genius enlighten the aweful Sessions House, emphatically called JUSTICE HALL; Mr Burke, Mr Garrick, Mr Beauclerk and Dr Johnson: and undoubtedly their favourable testimony had due weight with the Court and Jury. Johnson gave his evidence in a slow, deliberate and distinct manner, which was uncommonly impressive. It is well known that Mr Baretti was acquitted.'

An Account of the Cases of SAMUEL ROBERTS and THOMAS BACCHUS, who were hanged for High Treason, in counterfeiting the current Coin of this Realm.

THE first mentioned of these malefactors was a native of Shrewsbury. He was descended of parents of very fair character, but in circumstances rather contracted; however, they gave him what education was in their power, and then apprenticed him to a baker.

After the expiration of the term of his apprenticeship, he repaired to the metropolis, and laboured as a journeyman with different masters for a considerable time, still supporting the character of an industrious and honest man. Some friends, observing the goodness of his disposition, advanced him money, with which he took a shop in Grays-inn-lane, and met with such success in business as rewarded his assiduity.

At length, very unhappily for himself, he became acquainted with the father of Bacchus, from the casual meeting him at a public house. Soon after their acquaintance the old man advised him to remove into Southwark, where he said an excellent house and shop offered for his accommodation. Roberts being married, and having four children, listened to this advice, in the hope of making a better provision for his family.

A very short time after his residence in Southwark, the elder Bacchus and his son, with some other people who were coiners, told Roberts that they would be ready to assist him with money on any emergency. It happened that, some little time afterwards, Roberts wanted some money to make up a bill due for flour, on which he mentioned the affair to the elder Bacchus, and he was immediately furnished with the requisite sum.

This circumstance had not long taken place, when the younger Bacchus informed Roberts that his father was out of town, and begged his assistance in coining, on the condition of which he should be amply supplied with such money as he might want.

Roberts hesitated for a while to comply with a scheme big with such evident destruction; but the prospect of gain becoming at length too strong for his more virtuous resolutions, he fatally consented, and ruin was the consequence. The nature of the partnership, for such it may be deemed, was this: Bacchus was generally the immediate coiner of the counterfeit money, which Roberts put off to unsuspecting people. They had imitated a variety of gold and silver coin, which was so well executed that it could hardly be distinguished from the real money made at the Tower; yet the adulteration was so great, that, in many pieces, the intrinsic value was not a fourth of the nominal.

Great part of this counterfeit money was put off at country-fairs, where the agents employed to dispose of it (for there were others besides Roberts) appeared as horse-dealers, and found several country tradesmen ready enough to traffic with them for this false coin.

The coiners used to sell this money by weight to the countrymen, who circulated it in the course of their connexions; so that the evil spread wide, to the injury of many an unfortunate individual.

In the interim Bacchus and Roberts lived in a very handsome manner on the profits of their iniquitous trade. Their neighbours could not conceive how they procured a subsistence; and it is possible that they might have continued their practices a considerable time longer, but that one of their accomplices gave such hints as led to the ready means of detecting them.

Some constables being employed to search the house, they found Bacchus, with all the implements proper for coining, in the act of making counterfeit money, while Roberts was assisting him in this unlawful transaction; on which both the parties were taken into custody, and being carried before Sir John Fielding, that magistrate committed them to Newgate.

It may be now proper to mention that Bacchus was a native of the town of Stafford, and was, at a very early age, initiated into the art of coining by his father, who seems purposely to have trained him to the gallows. The younger Bacchus never followed any business but coining, except occasionally dealing in smuggled goods when he happened to have a considerable sum of money in his possession.

The prisoners remained in Newgate several months before they were brought to trial; but at length they were convicted on the clearest evidence, and sentenced to die.

The behaviour of Roberts after conviction was exceedingly well adapted to his unhappy situation. He was regular and devout in his attendance on religious duties, employed much time in reading books of devotion, and was regardful of the instructions given him by the ordinary of Newgate. On learning that the warrant for his execution was arrived, his seriousness and penitence appeared to be augmented, and he looked forward to eternity in the humble hope of the divine pardon.

Nor was the behaviour of Bacchus less regular, penitent, and devout. He made a decent preparation for his approaching death. The father of Bacchus had retired into the country, whence he sent his son a letter after condemnation, of which the following is a copy:

'My dear Child,
'I send you these few lines to comfort you; I should have sent you some money before, but I hope, my dear child, you will forgive me, as you hope to be forgiven in heaven. There you will find a better father than you have found in me. Be as happy as you can;—you are going to happiness, and leave me behind to be miserable. I hope you will die happy, because you know you are innocent. Thou art now going, I shall soon follow thee. I hope you will meet your dear mother in heaven. As we shall soon part in this world, may my prayers be heard for you in heaven!
'From your loving father till death,
WILLIAM BACCHUS'

'P.S. My dear love to Roberts; and tell him, if it should be in my power to serve his family, I will, I shall think it a pleasure. May heaven receive you both!'

The unhappy convicts received the holy sacrament on the morning of execution, and behaved in a manner suitable to their calamitous circumstances. They were drawn to the gallows on a sledge, as is usual in the case of coiners. They warned the multitude not to follow their evil example, and acknowledged the justice of that sentence by which they had been condemned to an ignominious death.

After the customary exercises of devotion, the prisoners underwent the final sentence of the law; and when the bodies had hung the usual time, they were delivered to their relations, in order that the bodies might be deposited with the parent earth.

Samuel Roberts and Thomas Bacchus were hanged at Tyburn on the 21st of May, 1772.

There is something singular in the affair before us. We see that the counterfeit money was sold by weight to people in the country, who could be mean enough to make such purchases from avaricious motives, though they must know that their neighbours would be ultimately defrauded.

The young Bacchus, though a professed coiner, appears to have been in some measure an object of pity. His father had trained him to the business from his early youth: but surely that father ought to be the general object of execration. It is difficult to form an idea of the aggravated guilt of that man who can wilfully train his own child to destruction. The paternal and the filial duty ought to be mutual: a failure on either side is usually fatal to the happiness of one of the parties.

In this case, Bacchus made the false money, and Roberts uttered it. They were both charged with High Treason and hanged. The first statute making the offence of counterfeiting the King's money High Treason was in 1350, and many statutes followed making various coinage offences Treason, although some were merely felonies without benefit of clergy. In 1832 the law relating to coinage offences was overhauled and amended, and the death penalty for all coinage offences was abolished.

Account of the Trials and Convictions of Robert Perreau, and Daniel Perreau, for Forgery, attended with very extraordinary Circumstances.

In order to preserve, as near as possible, the chronological disposition of this work, we insert the following in this place, though the brothers Perreau were not executed till a considerable time after conviction, nor till after the acquittal of Mrs Rudd; but it is necessary that their trials should precede that of Mrs Rudd, as the former were in some measure productive of the latter.

On the 10th of March, 1775, discovery was made of a series of forgeries, said to have been carried on for a length of time by Robert and Daniel Perreau, twin brothers; the one an apothecary of great practice, and the other living in the stile of a gentleman.

The above parties, together with Mrs Margaret Caroline Rudd, who lived with Daniel Perreau as his wife, and who was deemed to have been a principal agent in the forgeries, were taken into custody, and carried before the bench of magistrates in Bow-street, where the crowd attending to hear their examination was so great, that it became necessary to adjourn to the Guildhall, Westminster.

The evidence there adduced tended to prove that the parties had raised considerable sums by bonds forged in the name of the well-known agent, William Adair, Esquire, which they imposed on several gentlemen of fortune, as collateral securities with their own notes, for the payment of the said sums.

This transaction was discovered by the following means. Robert Perreau, whose character had been hitherto unimpeachable, applied to Mr Drummond, the banker, to lend him £5,000 and offered a bond for £7,500 which he said Mr Adair had given to his brother, as a security for the payment.

It will now be proper to remark, that, in order to give

colour to the validity of these bonds, it had been artfully suggested that Mrs Rudd had near connexions with Mr Adair; and it was even insinuated, that she was his natural daughter: but Mr Drummond, to whom Mr Adair's writing was familiar, had no sooner looked at the signature, than he doubted its authenticity and very politely asked Robert Perreau, if he had seen Mr Adair sign it? The latter said he had not, but had no doubt but it was authentic, from the nature of the connexion that subsisted.

To this Mr Drummond said, that he could not advance such a sum without consulting his brother, and desired Perreau to leave the bond, promising to return it the next morning, or advance on it the sum required.

Mr Perreau made no scruple to leave the bond, and call in the morning. In the interim Mr Drummond examined the bond with greater attention; and Mr Stephens, secretary of the Admiralty, happening to call, his opinion was demanded; when comparing the signature of the bond with letters he had lately received from Mr Adair, he was firmly convinced that it was forged.

When Perreau came, Mr Drummond spoke more freely than he had done before, and told him that he imagined he had been imposed on; but begged that, to remove all doubt, he would go with him to Mr Adair, and get that gentleman to acknowledge the validity of the bond; on which the money should be advanced.

Perreau made not the least objection. They went together; and Mr Adair was asked if the bond was his. He declared it was not; but Perreau smiled, and said he jested.

Mr Adair told him that it was no jesting matter, and that it was his duty to clear up the affair. Perreau said, 'if that was the case, he had been sent on a fine errand!' He desired to have the bond, and said he would make the necessary enquiries: but this was refused, and it was thought a point of prudence to watch the motions of Robert Perreau, till Daniel and his pretended wife were produced.

Soon after he returned home, the three parties went into a coach; and, if Mrs Rudd's testimony may be credited, she took with her what money and valuables she could conveniently carry; and said, that the brothers had taken her money, gold watch, and jewels, into their possession; but no reason was assigned for their doing so.

Their escape, however, if such was intended, was prevented; for an information being laid against them, they were apprehended, carried before Sir John Fielding, and examined at the Guildhall, Westminster, as above-mentioned. The facts already mentioned were attested by Mr Adair, Mr Drummond, and other persons; and Sir Thomas Frankland charged them with obtaining from him £4,000 on the first application, which they honestly repaid before the money became due; afterwards £5,000 and then £4,000 on similar bonds, all signed with the name of Mr Adair.

Mr Watson, a money-scrivener, said that he had drawn eight bonds, all of them ordered by one or other of the brothers; but he hesitated to fix on either, on account of their great personal resemblance; but being pressed to make a positive declaration, he fixed on Daniel as his employer.

Dr Brooke charged the brothers with obtaining from him fifteen bonds of the bank of Air, each of the value of £100 upon the security of a forged bond for £3,100.

On the strength of this evidence the brothers were committed, the one to New Prison, and the other to Clerkenwell Bridewell; and Mrs Rudd was admitted an evidence for the crown.

On her future examination she declared that she was the daughter of a nobleman in Scotland; that, when young, she married an officer in the army, named Rudd, against the consent of her friends; that her fortune was considerable; that, on a disagreement with her husband, they resolved to part; that she made a reserve of money, jewels, and effects, to the amount of £13,000 all of which she gave to Daniel Perreau, whom she said she loved with the tenderness of a wife; 'that she had three children by him; that he had returned her kindness in every respect till lately, when having been unfortunate in gaming in the alley, he had become uneasy, peevish, and much altered to her; that he cruelly constrained her to sign the bond now in question, by holding a knife to her throat, and swearing that he would murder her if she did not comply; that, being struck with remorse, she had acquainted Mr Adair with what she had done, and that she was now willing to declare every transaction with which she was acquainted, whenever she should be called upon by law so to do.'

At the sessions held at the Old Bailey in June, 1775, Robert Perreau, Esquire, was indicted for forging a bond for the payment of £7,500 in the name of William Adair, Esquire, and also for feloniously uttering and publishing the said bond, knowing it to be forged, with intention to defraud Robert and Henry Drummond, Esquires.

After what we have mentioned above respecting this transaction, we shall be as concise as possible in the recital of the evidence. Henry Drummond, Esquire, deposed, that Robert Perreau requested the loan of £1,400 having made a purchase in Suffolk or Norfolk to the amount of £12,000. He said he had a house in Harley-street, Cavendish-square, which cost £4,000 the deeds of which house he would leave as a security. These he did leave, and promising to return in ten days, the money was paid him. He came some time afterwards, and apologized for not having kept his appointment; and said he then came to borrow £5,000 on the bond, out of which he would pay the £1,400 abovementioned.

Mr Drummond and his brother doubting the validity of the bond, Perreau said there were family-connexions between him and Mr Adair, who had money of his in his hands, for which he paid interest.

A great part of what Mr Drummond delivered in evidence has been already given in the former part of this narrative. Mr Drummond going with the prisoner to Mr Adair's, Mrs Daniel Perreau (Mrs Rudd) was sent for, when Robert asked her, if she had not given the bond to him. She owned that she had, took the whole on herself, and acknowledged that she had forged the bond.

The counsel for the prisoner asking Mr Drummond if he was certain that the prisoner said it was *his* money that Mr Adair paid interest for, he answered in the affirmative. He declared likewise, that Mr Perreau did not make the

205

least objection to leaving the bond with him, nor shewed any reluctance in going with him to Mr Adair's house.

He likewise said that Mrs Rudd took the whole on herself, begged them, 'for God's sake to have mercy on an innocent man;' and that she said no injury was intended to any person, and that all would be paid; and that she acknowledged delivering the bond to the prisoner.

The counsel demanding if Mr Drummond and Mr Adair, after hearing what Mrs Rudd said, had not expressed themselves as considering the prisoner as her dupe; the answer was, 'We both expressed ourselves to that effect. A constable had been sent for, and we discharged him.'

The identity of the bond was proved by Mr Wheatley, Clerk to Messieurs Drummond.—The evidence of Mr Robert Drummond was not, in any very essential point, different from that of his brother. He deposed, that when Mrs Rudd had acknowledged that she forged the bond, he expressed his doubt, the hand-writing being so different from that of a woman, and said nothing would convince him of it but her shewing, on a piece of paper, that she could write that sort of hand. He said he did not mean to ensnare her, and would immediately throw the writing into the fire. Mrs Rudd instantly wrote William Adair, or part of the name, so very like the signature of the bond, that it satisfied him, and he burnt the paper. Robert Perreau then said, that 'he hoped that the information she had given sufficiently acquitted him;' but he was told that he had better not inquire into that; and on this occasion he shewed the first sign of anxiety.

Sir Thomas Frankland deposed, that the prisoner brought him two bonds at different times, one to Daniel Perreau for £6,000 and the other to himself (Robert) for £5,300; that for £5,300 on which he lent him £4,000 was to be repaid on the 26th of March, with the three days grace; the other was due on the 8th of March.[1]

[1] The intent of this evidence seems to have been, to show that the money to be borrowed of Mr Drummond was designed to repay the money actually borrowed of Sir Thomas; and that there was no intention of defrauding either of them.

Mr Wilson declared that he filled up the bond at the desire of the prisoner; and produced his instructions for so doing. He likewise acknowledged that he had filled up other bonds for the prisoner.

That the hand-writing at the bottom of the bond was not the hand writing of William Adair was proved by Scroope Ogilvie and James Adair, esquires. Mr James Adair was now questioned by counsel respecting a private interview he had with Mrs Rudd, but the court doubted if this might be allowed as evidence. After some observations made by the counsel for the prisoner, a letter was read, which he presumed had been sent him by William Adair, esquire, but which appeared to have been written by Mrs Rudd, but it was scarcely intelligible.

The prisoner now proceeded to make his defence in the following terms:—'My Lords, and gentlemen of the jury; If I had been wanting in that fortitude which is the result of innocence, or had found any hesitation in submitting my proceedings to the strictest scrutiny, I need not at this day have stood before my country, or set my life upon the issue of a legal trial. Supported by the consciousness of my integrity, I have forced that transaction to light, which might else have been suppressed, and I have voluntarily sought that imprisonment which guilt never invites, and even innocence has been known to fly from; ardently looking forward to this hour; as the sure, though painful, means of vindicating a character, not distinguished, indeed, for its importance, but hitherto maintained without a blemish. There are many respectable witnesses at hand (and many more, I persuade myself, would be found, if it had been necessary to summon them upon a point of such notoriety), who will inform your Lordships and the court, how I have appeared to them to act; what trust has been reposed in me, and what credit I had in their opinions, for my diligence, honesty, and punctuality. In truth, my Lords, I am bold to say that few men, in my line of life, have carried on their business with a fairer character, not many with better success. I have followed no pleasures, nor launched into any expences: there is not a man living who can charge me

with neglect or dissipation. The honest profits of my trade
have afforded me a comfortable support, and furnished me
with the means of maintaining, in a decent sort, a worthy
wife, and three promising children, upon whom I was
labouring to bestow the properest education in my power:
in short, we were as happy as affluence and innocence could
make us, till this affliction came upon us by surprize, and
I was made the dupe of a transaction from whose[1] criminality,
I call God, the searcher of all human hearts, to witness, I
am now as free as I was at the day of my birth.—My Lords,
and gentlemen of the jury, men who are unpractised in
deceit will be apt to credit others for a sincerity which they
themselves possess. The most undesigning characters have
at all times been the dupe of craft and subtilty. A plain
story, with the indulgence of the court, I will relate, which
will furnish strong instances of credulity on one part, and
at the same time will exhibit a train of such consummate
artifices on the other, as are not to be equalled in the annals
of iniquity, and which might have extorted an equal confidence from a much more enlightened understanding than I
can claim.'

Having said thus much, the unhappy man proceeded to
relate a variety of circumstances relative to the imposition
practised on him by Mrs Rudd, of which the following are
the most remarkable.

He said that she was constantly conversing about the
Interest she had with Mr W. Adair; and that Mr Adair
had, by his interest with the king, obtained the promise of
a baronetage for Daniel Perreau, and was about procuring
him a seat in parliament. That Mr Adair had promised to
open a bank, and take the brothers Perreau into partnership
with him: that the prisoner received many letters signed
William Adair, which he had no doubt came from that
gentleman; in which were promises of giving them a

[1] If Mr Perreau had spoken English, he would have said 'from
the criminality of which'; but we presume this must have been a
mistake of the short-hand writer; as the other parts of his defence do
not appear deficient in point of grammar.

considerable part of his fortune during his life, and that he was to allow Daniel Perreau £2,400 a year for his houshold expences, and £600 a year for Mrs Rudd's pin-money. That Mr Daniel Perreau purchased a house in Harley-street for £4,000, which money Mr William Adair was to give them. That, when Daniel Perreau was pressed by the person he bought the house of for the money, the prisoner understood that they applied to Mr William Adair, and that his answer was that he had lent the king £70,000, and had purchased a house in Pall Mall at £7,000, in which to carry on the banking business, and therefore could not spare the £4,000 at that time.

The prisoner now related a variety of circumstances, which would tempt an ingenuous mind to suppose him innocent, and that the guilt of the transaction rested with Mrs Rudd. The unfortunate man then proceeded in his defence in the following terms:

'My lords, and gentlemen of the jury, I have now faith-fully laid before you such circumstances as have occurred to my memory, as necessary for your information, in order as they happened during my acquaintance with Mrs Rudd, under the character of my brother's wife. Many have been the sufferers by artifices and impostors, but never man appeared, I believe, in this, or any other tribunal, upon whom so many engines were set at work to interest his credulity. It will not escape the notice of this splendid[1] court, that my compassion was first engaged by the story of Mrs Rudd's sufferings, before my belief was invited to her representations. Let me have credit with you for yielding up by pity in the first instance, and you cannot wonder I did not withhold my credulity afterwards. It is in this natural, this necessary consequence, I rest my defence. I was led from error to error by such insensible degrees, that every step I took strengthened my infatuation. When Mr Drummond first hesitated at the hand-writing at the foot of the bond, if it did not so alarm me as to shake my belief in

---

[1] *Splendid* is an awkward word on this occasion: perhaps *awful* would have been more proper.

this artful woman, let it be considered that I had been prevailed upon to negociate other bonds of hers, depositing them in the hands of bankers who had never spied any defect, or raised the least objection. These bonds have been regularly and punctually paid in due time. The letters sent to me, as if from William Adair, critically agreed with the hand-writing of the bond. Mr Adair did not keep money at Mr Drummond's; opportunities of comparing his hand-writing for many years had not occurred, and the hesitation upon his part appeared to me no more than the exceptions and minute precautions of a banker, which could not so suddenly overturn the explicit belief that I had annexed to all that was told me in Harley-street. Can any greater proof be given than my own proposal to Mr Drummond of leaving the bond in his hands till he had satisfied his credulity? Can your lordships, or gentlemen of the jury, for a moment suspect, that any man would be guilty of such a crime, whose proceedings were so fair and open? that single circumstance, I am satisfied, will afford my total exculpation. The resort to Mr Adair was as easy to Mr Drummond, as to the books in his compting-house; it does not come within the bounds of common sense, much less does it fall within the possibility of guilt, that any man living should voluntarily, with his eyes open, take a step so directly and absolutely centering in his certain destruction. But this circumstance, strong as it is, is not all my case. I bless God, the protector of innocence, that, in my defence, proofs arise upon proofs: the least of them, I trust, will be thought incompatible with guilt. It should seem impossible that a guilty person would propose to Mr Drummond to retain the bond for the satisfaction of his scruples; but that the same person should, after so long a time for consideration had passed after my leaving the bond, which was full twenty-four hours, openly, and in the face of day, enter the shop of Mr Drummond, and demand if he had satisfied all his scruples, unless a man from mere desperation had been weary of his life, and sought a dissolution; this, I humbly apprehend, would be an absolute impossibility: but, my lords, and gentlemen of the jury, I had neither in my breast

the principle of guilt, nor had I that desperate loathing of
existence as should bring a shameful condemnation on my
head. It is true I have invited this trial; but it is equally
true I have done it in the consciousness of my integrity,
because I could not otherwise go through the remainder of
my days with comfort and satisfaction, unless I had the
verdict of my countrymen for my acquittal, and rested my
innocence upon the purest testimony I could have on this
side the grave. It is plain I had an opportunity of with-
drawing myself. How many men are there, with the clearest
intentions, yet from the apprehension of being made the
talk of the public, and, above all, the dread of imprisonment, and the terror of a trial, would have thought themselves happy to have caught at any opportunity of saving
themselves from such a series of distress? greater confidence
can no man be in, of the integrity of his case, and the justice
of his country. When it was found necessary to the designs
of Mrs Rudd, that I and my family should be made the
dupes of her connexions with the house of Adair, it may
well be believed that nothing but the *strongest interdictions*
could prevent my endeavours to obtain an interview. In
fact, this point was laboured with consummate artifice,
and nothing less than ruin to my brother and his affairs
was denounced upon my breaking this injunction. It was
part of the same error to believe her in this also. A respectable witness has told you, and I do not controvert his
evidence, that my confidence in her assertion, and *in the
testimonials that she exhibited under the hand,* as I believed,
of Mr Adair, were such, in my mistaken judgement, as to
be equal to the evidence of my own senses, pressed by the
forms of business to say to Mr Drummond that I had seen
Mr Adair myself; but I neither went to Mr Adair, nor
disclosed those pressing motives which prevented me. No
less free to confess my faults, than I am confident to assert
my innocence, I seek no palliation for this circumstance,
except my temptation and my failings; and I trust it will
rather be a matter of surprize, that, in the course of a
negotiation, through the whole of which I was acted upon
by the most artful of impostors, that this only deviation was

to be found: and yet this very circumstance carries with it a clearer conviction of my being the dupe of Mrs Rudd's intrigues, than any I have to offer in my defence; and if my subsequent proceedings, and the alacrity I shewed in going with Mr Drummond to Mr Adair, together with my conduct before this gentleman, is, as I apprehend it is, absolutely irreconcileable with a consciousness of guilt, the circumstances abovementioned will serve to shew with what a degree of credulity the artifices of Mrs Rudd had furnished me.—Upon the whole, if, in the above detail, no circumstances are discovered in which an innocent man, under the like delusion with myself, might not have acted as I have acted, and, at the same time, if there be very many particulars in which no guilty man would have conducted himself as I have conducted myself, I should be wanting in respect to your Lordships and the jury, if I doubted the justice of their verdict, and which is inseparable from it, my honourable accquittal.'

The prisoner now proceeded to call his witnesses, the substance of whose evidence we shall give in the most concise manner. George Kinder deposed, that Mrs Perreau[1] told him 'that she was a near relation of Mr James Adair; that he looked upon her as his child, had promised to make her fortune, and with that view had recommended her to Mr William Adair, a near relation, and intimate friend of his, who had promised to set her husband and the prisoner up in the banking business.' He likewise deposed, that the said Mr Daniel Perreau was to be made a baronet, and described how she would act when she became a lady. This witness deposed, that Mrs Rudd often pretended that Mr William Adair had called to see her, but that he never had seen that gentleman on any visit.

John Moody, a livery-servant of Daniel Perreau, deposed, that his mistress wrote two very different hands, in one of which she wrote letters to his master, as from Mr William Adair, and in the other the ordinary business of the family; that the letters written in the name of William Adair were

_____

[1] The only name by which he knew Mrs Rudd.

pretended to have been left in his master's absence; that his mistress ordered him to give them to his master, and pretend that Mr Adair had been with his mistress for a longer or shorter time, as circumstances required. This witness likewise proved that the hand at the foot of the bond and that of his mistress's fictitious writing were precisely the same:[1] that she used different pens, ink, and paper, in writing her common and fictitious letters; and that she sometimes gave the witness half a crown, when he had delivered a letter to her satisfaction. He said he had seen her go two or three times to Mr J. Adair's, but never to William's; and that Mr J. Adair once visited his mistress on her lying in.

Susanna Perreau (the prisoner's sister) deposed to the having seen a note delivered to Daniel Perreau, by Mrs Rudd, for £19,000 drawn as by William Adair, on Mr Croft, the banker, in favour of Daniel Perreau.

Elizabeth Perkins swore that, a week before the forgery was discovered, her mistress gave her a letter to bring back to her in a quarter of an hour, and say it was brought by Mr Coverley, who had been servant to Daniel Perreau: that she gave her mistress this letter, and her master instantly broke the seal.

Daniel Perreau declared that the purport of this letter was ' that Mr Adair desired her to apply to his brother, the prisoner, to procure him £5,000 upon his (Adair's) bond, in the same manner as he had done before; that Mr Adair was unwilling to have it appear that the money was raised for him, and therefore desired to have the bond lodged with some confidential friend, that would not require an assignment of it; that his brother, on being made acquainted with his request, shewed a vast deal of reluctancy, and said it was a very unpleasant work; but undertook it with a view of obliging Mr William Adair.'

The counsel for the prosecution demanding, 'if he did not disclaim all knowledge of the affair before Mr Adair,'

---

[1] If this evidence was credited, was it not conclusive against Mrs Rudd, and in favour of the Perreaus?

he said, he denied ever having seen the bond before, nor had he a perfect knowledge of it till he saw it in the hands of Mr Adair.

David Caffady, who assisted Mr R. Perreau as an apothecary, deposed, that he lived much within the profits of his profession, and that it was reported he was going into the banking business.

John Leigh, clerk to Sir John Fielding, swore to the prisoner's coming voluntarily to the office, and giving information that a forgery had been committed,[1] on which Mrs Rudd was apprehended. Mr Leigh was asked, if she 'ever charged the prisoner with any knowledge of the transaction till the justices were hearing evidence to prove her confession of the fact.' Mr Leigh answered, that he did not recollect that circumstance, but that on her first examination she did not accuse the prisoner.

Mr Perreau now called several persons of rank to his character. Lady Lyttleton being asked, if she thought him capable of such a crime, *supposed she could have done it as soon herself.* Sir John Moore, Sir John Chapman, General Rebow, Capt. Ellis, Capt. Burgoyne, and other gentlemen, spoke most highly to the character of the prisoner; yet the jury found him guilty.

After this copious account of the trial of Robert, a very short abstract of that of the other brother may suffice, especially as that of Mrs Rudd is to follow.

Daniel Perreau was indicted for forging and counterfeiting a bond, in the name of William Adair, for £3,300, to defraud the said William Adair; and for uttering the same, knowing it to be forged, with intent to defraud Thomas Brooke, doctor of physic. Mr Scroope Ogilvie, who had been clerk to Mr William Adair nine or ten years, proved the forgery; and Dr Brooke proved the uttering of the forged bond.

By way of defence, the prisoner declared that Mrs Rudd had given him the bond as a true one; that he believed it genuine, authentic and valid; and protested, by all his

---

[1] Surely this evidence ought to have had great weight with the jury.

hopes of happiness in this life and in a future, that he had
never conceived an idea of any thing so base as the defrauding any man of his property. He added, 'I adjure
the Almighty so to assist me in my present dangerous situation, as I speak here before you.'[1]

Mr Daniel Perreau called several persons to prove the
artifices which Mrs Rudd had practised to deceive him.
Many persons of fortune and credit appeared to his character; and spoke of his conduct previous to the fatal event
in terms of the highest approbation; but the jury brought in
a verdict of guilty; and the unfortunate brothers received
sentence of death, but were not executed till January, 1776,
because though Mrs Rudd had been admitted an evidence,
yet the judges committed her as a principal, as will be seen
more at large in the account of the subsequent trial.

After conviction, the behaviour of the brothers was, in
every respect, proper for their unhappy situation. Great
interest was made to obtain a pardon for them, particularly
for Robert, in whose favour 78 bankers and merchants of
London signed a petition to the king; the newspapers were
filled with paragraphs, evidently written by disinterested
persons, in favour of men whom they thought dupes to the
designs of an artful woman: but all this availed nothing.

On the day of execution the brothers were favoured with
a mourning coach, and it was thought that 30,000 people
attended. They were both dressed in mourning, and behaved with the most christian resolution. When they
quitted the coach and got into the cart, they bowed res-
pectfully to the sheriffs, who waved their hands as a final
adieu.

After the customary devotions, they crossed their hands,
joining the four together, and in this manner were launched
into eternity. They had not hung more than half a minute
when their hands dropped asunder, and they appeared to
die without pain.

[1] This is an odd phrase; but so it is recorded by the short-hand
writer. Perhaps the word *truth* should have been inserted instead of
here.

Each of them delivered a paper to the ordinary of Newgate, which declared their innocence, and ascribed the blame of the whole transaction to the artifices of Mrs Rudd; and, indeed, thousands of people gave credit to their assertions, and a great majority of the public thought Robert wholly innocent.

Daniel Perreau and Robert Perreau were executed at Tyburn on the 17th of January, 1776.

On the Sunday following the bodies were carried from the house of Robert in Golden-square, and, after the usual solemnities, deposited in the vault of Saint Martin's Church. The coffins were covered with black cloth and nails, and a black plate on each, inscribing their names, the day of their death, and their ages (42), being twin brothers. They were carried in separate hearses, their friends attending in mourning coaches. The croud was so great, that the company could with difficulty get into the church; but at length the ceremony was decently performed, and the mob dispersed.

A few reflections naturally arise on this occasion. There was great guilt somewhere, but where it lay the public will determine. One would imagine that, if Robert Perreau had been guilty, he would not have returned to Drummond's, nor went to Adair's, after being suspected. Charity will suppose that he fell a victim to his friendship for his brother, and lost his life through the telling of a lye; a strong argument for a strict adherence to truth in all we say.

A very ingenious writer on this subject says, 'Upon a dispassionate review of the above trial, is it not possible that the plausible promises of an artful impostor, aided by the vain hope of being made rich and great by her pretended connexions, may have operated on a credulous, though otherwise sensible, mind; like as a gypsey's tale is frequently found to do on weak and unsuspecting women? If so, it will naturally account for the absurdity of the prisoner's pretending an acquaintance with Mr William Adair, whom he had never seen, and was strictly enjoined not to see, and for all the fallacious pretences that followed.'

After this quotation, we shall say no more on this business, but proceed to the trial of Mrs Rudd.

An Account of the Trial and Acquittal of MARGARET CAROLINE RUDD, on a Charge of Forgery.

ON the 16th of September, 1775, Mrs Rudd was put to the bar at the Old Bailey, to be tried for forgery; but the counsel for the prisoner pleading that, as she had been already admitted an evidence for the crown, it was unprecedented to detain her for trial, and the judges differing in opinion on the point of law, she was remanded to prison, till the opinion of the judges could be taken on a subject of so much importance.

On the 8th of December, 1775, Margaret Caroline Rudd was indicted for feloniously forging a bond, purporting to be signed by William Adair, and for feloniously uttering and publishing the same.

Having been brought to the bar in September sessions, to plead to the said indictment, and her counsel contending that she ought not to be tried, as she had acknowledged herself an accomplice, and had been admitted an evidence by the magistrates; and the judges 'differing in opinion on the point of law: reference was had to the opinion of all the judges, that the matter might be finally settled, how far, under what circumstances, and in what manner, an accomplice, received as a witness, ought to be entitled to favour and mercy.'

Mr justice Aston now addressed the prisoner, informing her that eleven of the judges had met (the chief justice of the Common Pleas being indisposed), 'and were unanimous in opinion, that, in cases not within any statute, an accomplice, who fully discloses the joint guilt of himself and his companions, and is admitted by justices of the peace as a witness, and who appears to have acted a fair and ingenuous part in the disclosure of all the circumstances of the cases in which he has been concerned, ought not to be prosecuted for the offences so by him confessed, but cannot by law plead this in bar of any indictment, but merely as an equitable claim to mercy from the crown: and nine of the judges were of opinion, that all the circumstances relative to this claim *ought* to be laid before the court, to enable the judges to exercise their discretion, whether the trial should proceed or not. With respect to the case before them, the same nine judges were of opinion, that if the matter stood singly upon the two informations of the prisoner, compared with the indictments against her, she ought to have been tried upon all, or any of them, for from her informations she is no accomplice: she exhibits a charge against Robert and Daniel Perreau, the first soliciting her to imitate the hand-writing of William Adair, the other forcing her to execute the forgery under the threat of death. Her two informations are contradictory: if she has suppressed the truth, she has no equitable claim to favour; and if she has told the truth, and the whole truth, she cannot be convicted. As to the indictments preferred against her by Sir Thomas Frankland, as her informations before the justices have no relation to his charges, she can claim no sort of advantage from these informations.'

The trial was now proceeded on. The principal evidences were, the wife of Robert Perreau, and John Moody a servant to Daniel. The first endeavoured to prove that the bond was published, the latter that it was forged. Sir Thomas Frankland proved that he had lent money on the bond. It was objected by the counsel for the prisoner, that Mrs Perreau was an incompetent witness, as she would be interested in the event; but the court over-ruled this objection.

Mrs Perreau deposed, that, on the 24th of December, she saw Mrs Rudd deliver a bond to her husband, which he laid on the table while he brushed his coat; that it was for £5,300 payable to Robert Perreau, and signed William Adair; and that it was witnessed in the names of Arthur Jones and Thomas Start, or Hart. Mrs Perreau being asked when she again saw the bond, said it was brought to her on the 8th of March (the day after her husband was convicted), when she selected it from other bonds delivered to him on the 24th of December. She made her mark on it and deposed that, when it was delivered to Mr Perreau, Mrs

Rudd said, 'Mr Adair would be very much obliged to Mr Perreau to try to raise upon that bond the sum of £4,000 of Sir Thomas Frankland.'

Serjeant Davy cross-examined Mrs Perreau. She acknowledged that till the 24th of December she had never seen a bond in her life, and that, on her first sight of that in question, she had no suspicion 'that any thing was wrong.' Being asked how she could recollect, at the distance of three months, the names, the sum, and the several circumstances respecting the bond, she said, 'I have the happiness to have a good memory.' Being asked if she had not examined the other bonds at the same time, she said, she had. It was demanded if her memory had retained the date or sum in any other paper produced to her. She replied, 'I do not remember.'

John Moody, who had been servant with Mrs Rudd, deposed that his mistress wrote two different hands, a common and a feigned one; that in her common hand she noted the usual business of the house; but that, when she wrote letters as coming from William Adair, she wrote her feigned hand. A bond signed William Adair was now shewn him; and he said, 'the name appears to be the same hand the letters were wrote in, which I gave to Daniel Perreau, as coming from Mr William Adair, and which I saw Mrs Rudd write the directions of.' He was asked if he thought Mr Adair's name was of the prisoner's writing. He replied, 'I believe it is her hand-writing.'

On his cross-examination he owned that he had never seen Mrs Rudd write Mr Adair's name.[1]

Thus stood the evidence. Sir Thomas Frankland proved the lending Robert Perreau £4,000 on the bond in question, and that he had given him a draught for £3,890, deducting the discount of £5,000 formerly lent, with the discount of the money then borrowed, and £15 10s. for a lottery ticket: that he had since received, among other things, jewels to the value of £2,800, with women's wearing-apparel, &c.

[1] No doubt this was true.—If she wrote it at all, she had too much art to let a servant be witness of such a transaction.

which might, for what he knew, be the prisoner's, but were sold to him by the two Perreaus by a bill of sale.

Christian Hart deposed, that she had received a paper from the prisoner, tending to prove that there was a combination against her life to have been concerted at the house of this witness, by Sir Thomas Frankland and the friends of the Perreaus. Our readers will give what credit they please to this evidence.

It was now demanded of Mrs Rudd, what she would say in her defence. She addressed the jury in a short, but sensible speech, and concluded in these words, 'Gentlemen, ye are honest men, and I am safe in your hands.'

The jury, after a short consultation, gave their verdict in the following singular, and perhaps unprecedented words: '*According to the evidence before us*, NOT GUILTY.'

The verdict was no sooner given, than Mrs Rudd quitted the court, and retired to the house of a friend at the west end of the town.

There is a mystery in the story of the brothers Perreau, and Mrs Rudd, that no person but the latter can clear up. We are told that she is yet living;[1] but we hope that, before she quits this world, she will discover the secrets of a transaction concerning which the public opinion has been so much divided. The Perreaus were guilty, or they were not; and it is only from Mrs Rudd the truth can be known. A declaration of the fact, if she *was* guilty, could not now affect her, as she was acquitted by the laws of her country.

[1] In March, 1779.

An authentic Account of the Proceedings in the House of Peers on the Trial of ELIZABETH DUTCHESS of KINGSTON, for Bigamy.

ABOUT nine o'clock in the morning of Monday the 15th of April, 1776, the peeresses, foreign ambassadors, &c. concluded the ceremony of assuming their respective places in Westminster hall: and at half past ten her majesty, accompanied by the prince of Wales, the bishop of Osnaburgh, two other young princes, and the princess royal, and attended by lord and lady Holdernesse, lord Hinchinbroke, and others of the nobility, entered the hall from the duke of Newcastle's house in New Palace Yard, and took her seat in the centre of his grace's gallery.

The procession came into the hall in the following order at a quarter past eleven: the eldest sons of peers, preceded by the domestics of the lord high steward, masters in chancery, king's serjeants and judges, barons, bishops, viscounts, earls, marquisses and dukes; the serjeant at arms, the lord high steward with black rod on his right, and garter on his left; the lord president, and the lord privy-seal. The barons proceeded to their seats next the bar, the junior barons taking the left hand seat next the bar, and the other barons following in that order till the seats were filled in the front of the court. The archbishops and bishops occupied the side benches on the right, and the dukes the benches extending from the throne to the table.

The persons who composed the court having taken their seats with the usual formalities, the lord high steward directed the clerk of the crown to read the *certiorari*, the return thereof, the caption of the indictment, the indictment itself, and other official papers; which being done, the serjeant at arms made proclamation for the usher of the black rod to place the prisoner at the bar.

The dutchess then came forward, attended by Mrs Egerton, Mrs Barrington, and Miss Chudleigh, three of the ladies of her bedchamber, and her chaplain, physician, and apothecary; and as she approached the bar she made three reverences, and then dropped on her knees, when the lord high steward said, 'Madam, you may rise.' Having risen, she curtsied to the lord high steward and the house of peers; and her compliments were returned.

Proclamation being made for silence, the lord high steward mentioned to the prisoner the fatal consequences attending the crime of which she stood indicted, signifying that, however alarming and awful her present circumstances, she might derive great consolation from considering that she was to be tried by the most liberal, candid, and august assembly in the universe.

The dutchess then read a paper, setting forth that she was guiltless of the offence alledged against her, and that the agitation of her mind arose, not from the consciousness of guilt, but from the painful circumstance of being called before so awful a tribunal on a criminal accusation; begging, therefore, that if she was deficient in the observance of any ceremonial points, her failure might not be understood as proceeding from wilful disrespect, but be attributed to the unfortunate peculiarity of her situation. It was added in the paper that she had travelled from Rome in so dangerous a state of health, that it was necessary for her to be conveyed in a litter; and that she was perfectly satisfied that she should have a fair trial, since the determination respecting her cause, on which materially depended her honor and fortune, would proceed from the most unprejudiced and august assembly in the world.

The lord high steward desired the lady to give attention while she was arraigned on an indictment for bigamy. Proclamation for silence being made, the dutchess (who had been permitted to sit) arose, and read a paper, representing to the court that she was advised by her counsel to plead the sentence of the ecclesiastical court in the year 1769, as a bar to her being tried on the present indictment. The lord high steward informed her that she must plead to the indictment; in consequence of which she was arraigned; and, being asked by the clerk of the crown whether she was guilty of the felony with which she stood charged, she answered with great firmness, 'Not guilty, my lords.' The clerk of the crown then asking her how she would be tried, she said, 'by God and her peers;' on which the clerk said, 'God send your ladyship a good deliverance.'

The serjeant at arms made proclamation for all persons who had evidence to produce against the prisoner to appear. The lord high steward requested, that, as his seat was so distant from the bar, he might be allowed, for the convenience of hearing, to go to the table; to which the court readily acquiesced.

Mr Dunning, in a concise speech, opened the pleadings in support of the prosecution. He was followed by Mr Thurloe, the attorney general, who learnedly animadverted on the plea advanced by the prisoner, and said that, being counsel for the prosecution, it became his duty to declare his opinion on the case in question, which was, that he could not discover any reasonable foundation for the plea urged by the prisoner; and he desired that, if there were reasons sufficient to support it, they might be produced by the counsel on the opposite side.

Lord Mansfield moved, that a proper officer from Doctors Commons might read the sentence of the ecclesiastical court. Hereupon the attorney general said that it would be necessary for all the allegations, replications, &c. on which the sentence was founded, to be read; and the clerk of the crown read the allegations, and was proceeding with the replications, when Lord Mansfield observed, that it would not be necessary to read the latter papers, since the counsel, in the course of their pleadings, would introduce the material arguments therein contained.

Mr Wallace rose to reply to the attorney general, and in an eloquent strain of forcible argument endeavoured to prove the determination of the ecclesiastical court to be conclusive. Mr Wallace was followed by Mr Mansfield, who displayed great ingenuity and learning in support of the same doctrine.

Doctor Calvert, a civilian, spoke nearly for the space of two hours, and produced many precedents to prove the sentence of the consistory court to be definitive and irrevocable. The same ground of argument was pursued by

Doctor Wynne, another civilian, who also quoted several cases in point in behalf of the Dutchess; and on the conclusion of this gentleman's speech the court was adjourned on the motion of Lord Gower.

The business of the second day was opened by the lord high steward, who desired the counsel for her Grace to reply to the arguments advanced on the preceding day against evidence being admitted in support of the prosecution.

The attorney general entered upon a minute examination of the pleadings on the other side, and endeavoured to confute the arguments of the counsel and civilians, and to prove that the cases they had quoted were ill-applied, and undeserving authority. This gentleman spoke about an hour and twenty minutes.

The solicitor general then arose, and delivered a learned and elaborate speech, wherein he was extremely severe on the consistory court, saying he could not allow authority to that doctrine which puts the decisions of that court above the cognizance of the temporal ones. He said, that if the sentences of the ecclesiastical court were to be deemed conclusive, persons addicted to indulge a disposition to variety might each, by the exercise of industry and ingenious collusion, gratify his passions with seventy-five wives before attaining his thirtieth year. His witty and humorous allusions frequently provoked a general laugh at the expence of Doctors Commons; and he concluded with giving it as his opinion that the supreme court of legislature was invested with an indisputable power of reversing the decisions of the consistory courts. Mr Dunning spoke next, strongly supporting the arguments of the solicitor general, and producing several authorities from the law-books in justification of his opinion, that the plea could not be admitted as a bar against calling evidence to prove the criminality of the prisoner.

Doctor Harris, a civilian, rose in behalf of the prosecution; and, taking an extensive view of the pleadings of the Doctors Calvert and Wynne, exerted his utmost power to prove them nugatory.

Lord Talbot then addressed the court, observing, that as

Dodd delin.

White sculp.

Mode of punishment by BRANDING, or burning on
the HAND, at the New Sessions House.

the matter in agitation was of the utmost importance both
to the noble prisoner, and the right honourable court in
general, the pleadings on both sides could not be weighed
with too minute an attention; and lest the memory should
be encumbered (candidly acknowledging that he had already
heard more than he believed his mind would retain) he
moved for the court to adjourn to the chamber of parliament.
Hereupon the lord high steward came from the table to the
throne, and requested to be informed whether it was the
pleasure of the house to adjourn; and the question being put,
it passed in the affirmative.

On Friday, the 19th of April Mr Wallace was called
upon by the lord high steward to reply in behalf of the
prisoner. Lord Ravensworth then begged he might propose
a question to the counsel at the bar. His lordship's question
was, 'Is the sentence of the ecclesiastical court in this case
final and conclusive, or is it not?' Upon this Lord Mansfield
said, 'If the noble lord means—Is there any precedent for
reversing the sentence of the ecclesiastical court? the answer
must certainly be in the negative. As to any other meaning,
the question is in debate among the counsel at the bar, and
has been so these three days.'

Mr Wallace then largely expatiated in support of his
former cases, and pleaded powerfully in refutation of the
arguments advanced by the counsel on the opposite side,
producing many other cases in point, and urging that they
were incontrovertible. The next speaker was Doctor
Calvert, who pleaded very ably in support of the power of the
ecclesiastical court: he concluded with insisting that the
sentence of the consistory court was indisputably a legal
plea in bar of evidence being produced against the prisoner.

It being intimated that the counsel for the Dutchess had
concluded their replies, a motion was made by Lord Gower
for adjourning to the parliament chamber, and for allowing
her Grace permission to retire to her apartment till the
peers should return into court; upon which the lord high
steward adjourned the court about half past three o'clock.

The peers having taken their seats in the parliament
chamber, Lord Camden proposed the following questions

H

to the judges:—'Whether it was their opinion that the court had power to call evidence in support of the prosecution? or whether they deemed the sentence of the ecclesiastical court conclusive and irrevocable? and whether the prosecutor could or could not proceed in this court against the prisoner for obtaining the decision of the consistory court by collusion and fraud?' The opinion of the judges was, 'That in either case the prosecutor was authorised to enter into evidence in support of the indictment on which the prisoner stood arraigned.'

In consequence of the above determination, the house, after having withdrawn for about half an hour, returned into court; and the lord high steward informed the attorney general, that he was directed by their lordships to order him to proceed with the trial.

Mr Attorney then explained the nature of the evidence he meant to produce, and recapitulated a great number of facts and circumstances from the year 1742, previous to the supposed marriage of her Grace with Mr Hervey, to the time of her marriage with the late Duke of Kingston.

The solicitor general rose to examine the witnesses, and Anne Craddock being called to the bar, the Duke of Richmond observed that it would be proper for her to stand at a greater distance from the prisoner, and, after some debate on this head, Mr Quarme, deputy usher of the black rod, was placed between them. One of the clerks of the house put the questions from the counsel, and delivered the answers of the witness with an audible voice.

The evidence of Anne Craddock was to the following purpose:—I have known her Grace the Dutchess of Kingston ever since the year 1742; at which time she came on a visit to Mr Merrill's, at Launceston in Hampshire, during the Winchester races. At that time I lived in the family of Mrs Hanmer, Miss Chudleigh's aunt, who was then on a visit at Mr Merrill's, where Mr Hervey and Miss Chudleigh first met, and soon conceived a mutual attachment towards each other. They were privately married one evening about eleven o'clock in Launceston church, in the presence of Mr Mountney, Mrs Hanmer, the Reverend

Mr Ames, the rector, who performed the ceremony, and myself. I was ordered out of the church, to entice Mr Merrill's servants out of the way. I saw the bride and bridegroom put to bed together; and Mrs Hanmer obliged them to rise again: they went to bed together the night following. In a few days Mr Hervey was under the necessity of going to Portsmouth, in order to embark on board Sir John Danvers's fleet, in which he was a lieutenant; and being ordered to call him at five o'clock in the morning, I went into the bed chamber at the appointed hour, and found him and his lady sleeping in bed together, and was unwilling to disturb them, thinking the delay of an hour or two would not be of any consequence. My husband, to whom I was not married till after the time I have mentioned, accompanied Mr Hervey in the capacity of his servant. When Mr Hervey returned from the Mediterranean, his lady and he lived together. I then thought her in a state of pregnancy. Some months after, Mr Hervey went again to sea, and during his absence, I was informed that the lady was brought to bed. She herself told me she had a little boy at nurse, and that his features greatly resembled those of Mr Hervey.

The Duke of Grafton asked the witness, whether she had seen the child? and she answered in the negative. His Grace also asked, whether, as the ceremony was performed at night, there were any lights in the church? In reply to which she said, Mr Mountney had a wax light fixed to the crown of his hat. In reply to questions proposed by Lord Hillsborough, the witness acknowledged that she had received a letter from Mr Fossard, of Piccadilly, containing a promise of a sinecure place, on condition of her appearing to give evidence against the lady at the bar, and expressing that if she thought proper she might shew the letter to Mr Hervey.

On Saturday the 20th of April Anne Craddock was further examined. The Lords Derby, Hillsborough, Buckinghamshire, and others, questioning her whether she had not been promised a reward by the prosecutor on condition of her giving evidence to convict the prisoner; her answers were evasive, but she was at length brought to acknowledge

H*   227

that pecuniary offers had been made to induce her to give evidence in support of the prosecution.

Mrs Sophia Pettiplace, sister to Lord Howe, was next examined; but her evidence was of no consequence. She lived with her Grace at the time when her supposed marriage took place with Mr Hervey, but was not present at the ceremony; and she only believed that the Dutchess had mentioned the circumstance to her.

Cæsar Hawkins, Esquire, deposed, that he had been acquainted with the Dutchess several years, he believed not less than thirty. He had heard of a marriage between Mr Hervey and the lady at the bar, which circumstance was afterwards mentioned to him by both parties, previous to Mr Hervey's last going to sea. By the desire of her Grace he was in the room when the issue of the marriage was born, and once saw the child. He was sent for by Mr Hervey soon after his return from sea, and desired by him to wait upon the lady, with proposals for procuring a divorce, which he accordingly did; when her Grace declared herself absolutely determined against listening to such terms; and he knew that many messages passed on the subject. Her Grace some time after informed him, at his own house, that she had instituted a jactitation suit against Mr Hervey in Doctors Commons. On another visit she appeared very grave, and desiring him to retire into another apartment, said she was exceedingly unhappy in consequence of an oath, which she had long dreaded, having been tendered to her at Doctors Commons to disavow her marriage, which she would not do for ten thousand worlds. Upon another visit, a short time after, she informed him, that a sentence had passed in her favour at Doctors Commons, which would be irrevocable, unless Mr Hervey pursued certain measures within a limited time, which she did not apprehend he would do. Hereupon he enquired how she got over the oath; and her reply was, that the circumstance of her marriage was so blended with falsities that she could easily reconcile the matter to her conscience; since the ceremony was a business of so scrambling and shabby a nature, that she could as safely swear she was *not*, as that she *was* married.

Judith Philips being called, swore, that she was the widow of the Reverend Mr Ames; that she remembered when her late husband performed the marriage ceremony between Mr Hervey and the prisoner; that she was not present, but derived her information from her husband; that some time after the marriage the lady desired her to prevail upon her husband to grant a certificate, which she said she believed her husband would not refuse; that Mr Merrill, who accompanied the lady, advised her to consult his attorney from Worcester; that in compliance with the attorney's advice a register-book was purchased, and the marriage inserted therein, with some late burials in the parish. The book was here produced, and the witness swore to the writing of her late husband.

The writing of the reverend Mr Ames was proved by the reverend Mr Inchin, and the reverend Mr Dennis; and the entry of a caveat to the duke's will was proved by a clerk from Doctor's Commons. The book in which the marriage of the duke of Kingston with the lady at the bar was registered on the 8th of March, 1769, was produced by the reverend Mr Trebeck of St Margaret's, Westminster; and the reverend Mr Samuel Harpur, of the Museum, swore, that he performed the marriage ceremony between the parties on the day mentioned in the book produced by Mr Trebeck.

Monday the 22d of April, after the attorney-general had declared the evidence in behalf of the prosecution to be concluded, the lord high steward called upon the prisoner for her defence, which she read; and the following are the most material arguments it contained to invalidate the evidence adduced by the prosecutor:—she appealed to the Searcher of all hearts, that she never considered herself as legally married to Mr Hervey; she said that she considered herself as a single woman, and as such was addressed by the late duke of Kingston; that, influenced by a legitimate attachment to his grace, she instituted a suit in the ecclesiastical court, where her supposed marriage with Mr Hervey was declared null and void; but, anxious for every conscientious as well as legal sanction, she submitted an authentic state of her case to the archbishop of Canterbury, who, in the most decisive and unreserved manner, declared that she was at liberty to marry, and afterwards granted, and delivered to doctor Collier, a special licence for her marriage with the late duke of Kingston. She said that, on her marriage, she experienced every mark of gracious esteem from their majesties, and her late royal mistress, the princess dowager of Wales, and was publicly recognized as dutchess of Kingston. Under such respectable sanctions and virtuous motives for the conduct she pursued, strengthened by a decision that had been esteemed conclusive and irrevocable for the space of seven centuries, if their lordships should deem her guilty, on any rigid principle of law, she hoped, nay, she was conscious, they would attribute her failure as proceeding from a mistaken judgment and erroneous advice, and not censure her for intentional guilt.

She bestowed the highest encomiums on the deceased duke, and solemnly assured the court, that she had in no one instance abused her ascendency over him; and that, so far from endeavouring to engross his possessions, she had declared herself amply provided for by that fortune for life which he was extremely anxious to bequeath in perpetuity. As to the neglect of the duke's eldest nephew, she said it was entirely the consequence of his disrespectful behaviour to her; and she was not dissatisfied at a preference to another nephew, whose respect and attention to her had been such as the duke judged to be her due, in consequence of her advancement to the honour of being the wife of his uncle.

The lord high steward desired Mr Wallace to proceed with the evidence. The advocate stated the nature of the evidence he meant to produce to prove that Anne Craddock had asserted to different people that she had no recollection of the marriage between Mr Hervey and the lady at the bar; and that she placed a reliance on a promise of having a provision made for her in consequence of the evidence she was to give on the present trial; and, to invalidate the depositions of Judith Phillips, he ordered the clerk to read a letter, wherein she supplicated her grace to exert her influence to prevent her husband's discharge from the duke's service, and observed, that Mrs Phillips had, on the preceding day, swore, that her husband was not dismissed, but voluntarily quitted his station in the household of his grace.

Mr Wallace called Mr Berkley, Lord Bristol's attorney, who said his lordship told him he was desirous of obtaining a divorce, and directed him to Anne Craddock, saying she was the only person then living who was present at his marriage; and that, a short time previous to the commencement of the jactitation suit, he waited upon Anne Craddock, who informed him that her memory was bad and that she could remember nothing perfectly in relation to the marriage, which must have been a long time before.

Anne Pritchard deposed that about three months had elapsed since being informed by Mrs Craddock that she expected to be provided for soon after the trial, and of being enabled to procure a place in the custom-house for one of her relations.

The lord high steward addressed himself to the court; saying, that their lordships had heard the evidence on both sides, and that the importance and solemnity of the occasion required that they should severally pronounce their opinions in the absence of the prisoner, observing that the junior baron was to speak first.—Their lordships declared the prisoner to be guilty.

Proclamation being made for the usher of the Black-rod to bring the prisoner to the bar, she no sooner appeared than the lord high steward informed her that the lords had maturely considered the evidence adduced against her, and likewise all that had been advanced in her favour, and had pronounced her guilty of the felony for which she was indicted. He then requested whether she had any thing to urge against judgment being pronounced. Hereupon the lady delivered a paper containing the following words, to be read by the clerk:

'I plead the privilege of the Peerage.'

After this the lord high steward informed her grace, that the lords had considered the plea, and agreed to allow it;

adding words to this effect, 'Madam, you will be discharged on paying the usual fees.'

The lady appeared to be perfectly composed and recollected during the greatest part of her long and important trial; but when sentence was pronounced she fainted, and was carried out of Court.

Sentence was pronounced upon Elizabeth Dutchess of Kingston on Monday the 22d of April, 1776.

Some years subsequent to the transaction on which the above trial was founded, the legislature made ample provision against every species of clandestine and collusive marriages; and therefore we shall, contrary to our usual practice, wave the introduction of concluding remarks, since there can be no necessity for dissuasives against crimes that can be no longer committed.

This case is perhaps notable for this reason, that the Editors of *The Malefactor's Register* conclude ' . . . we shall, contrary to our usual practice, wa[i]ve the introduction of concluding remarks . . .' But the case is noteworthy in many respects. Elizabeth Chudleigh was a great wit and beauty and had been a Maid-of-Honour to the Princess of Wales. She married the Duke of Kingston, but it was alleged in the charge of bigamy that she had been secretly married at an early age, that she was the mother of a child, and was already married when she married the Duke.

The trial here recorded took place in the House of Lords. The privilege of peerage belonged to the wives of peers, and if the wife of a peer was charged with felony she was bound to be tried by the House of Lords and there was no power to waive the privilege. If Parliament was sitting, she would be tried by the House of Lords as the Court of the King in Parliament; and if Parliament was not sitting she would be tried in the Court of the Lord High Steward constituted by special commission. In this case, the commission was issued to Earl Bathurst as Lord High Steward, and the description in the early part of the case is of the procession from the House of Lords to Westminster Hall. The present report says—'Proclamation being made for silence, the Lord High Steward mentioned to the prisoner the fatal consequences attending the crime of which she stood indicted . . .' but the full report in the State Trials makes it plain that the Lord High Steward informed her that the death penalty had been abolished and added: 'This consideration must necessarily tend to lessen the perturbation of your spirits on this awful occasion.' Indeed the whole trial in some respects was a solemn farce, for everybody knew how it was to end in case the Duchess should be convicted.

Before the evidence was called, there was an extremely lengthy argument which ran into several days, some of which is here reported. The short point of the argument was this: it was necessary for the prosecution to prove the secret marriage of 1744, and there was a decree of the Consistory Court in 1769 that no such marriage existed. Thirteen speeches were made by counsel in support of the view that it was not competent to the prosecution to call evidence to contradict the decree of the Consistory Court. The Common Law judges who were in attendance were asked to advise their Lordships and did so, and their advice was followed by the House of Lords. They said in effect that the decree was no bar and so the trial proceeded.

At the end of the evidence each peer announced his vote in the time-honoured words 'Guilty upon my honour' except the Duke of Newcastle who said 'Guilty erroneously, but not intentionally, upon my honour'. Then came the farce. The Duchess claimed the privilege of the peerage. Peers enjoyed complete immunity from punishment if the offence was one to which benefit of clergy applied. They were not asked to read the 'necking verse', they were not branded in the hand, and they could not be imprisoned. They enjoyed all these privileges by statute. A further great argument arose whether the wife of a peer was entitled to the same privileges, and the judges advised the House that she was so entitled. So after five days of great pomp and solemnity she was discharged without any punishment at all. But there can be little doubt that she had been advised that this would be the end of it all, for she would not leave Calais to come for the trial until she had got the necessary assurances.

Those who are interested in this trial should certainly read the account of it in Vol. 20 of the State Trials. There all the arguments are set out fully with the opinions of the judges. These opinions had been carefully prepared beforehand, for as they said: ' . . . from the first appointment of this trial it was easy to see that a question of this sort would probably arise . . .' It is scarcely necessary to add that the privilege of the peerage has now been abolished, as has the trial of peers in the House of Lords.

It is not possible within the limits of a short note such as this to give the full details of this most interesting case. The secret first marriage to a younger son of the Earl of Bristol at a lonely church as midnight was approaching, is quite a romance in itself. The steps taken to obtain the decree of the Consistory Court, and the purpose of it, are equally full of interest. The reason for the prosecution for bigamy after the death of the Duke of Kingston was that the husband of the only daughter of the Duke was incensed at the terms of the Duke's will and alleged in the Chancery Division that the Duchess, his step-mother, had exerted undue influence over the Duke when he made his will. In those proceedings the facts of the secret marriage came to light, and out of revenge, the Bill for bigamy was presented. The account in the State Trials, in addition to the legal arguments, sets out the history of the life of Elizabeth Chudleigh at length.

In *Letters of Horace Walpole* referred to above there are several references to Elizabeth Chudleigh and the Duchess of Kingston which are of the greatest interest. Writing to Horace Mann on May the 3rd 1749 (that is five years after the secret marriage), Walpole describes a subscription masquerade and the people who attended it and the costumes they adopted. He says: 'Miss Chudleigh was IPHIGENIA, but so naked that you would have taken her for ANDRO-MEDA.' It somehow brings the sprightly Elizabeth to life and reveals her daring character in a few words.

The extraordinary Case, Trial, Conviction, and Execution, of Dr WILLIAM DODD, for Forgery.

O N the 8th of February, 1777, the reverend Dr Dodd, and Mr Robertson, a broker, were charged before the lord mayor, by Henry Fletcher, and Samuel Peach, Esquires, with forging and uttering as true a counterfeit bond, purporting to be the bond of the earl of Chesterfield, for the payment of £4,200, with an intent to defraud, &c.

The history of this affair is as follows. Dr Dodd being in want of cash to pay his Tradesmen's bills, and having been preceptor to the earl of Chesterfield, he pretended that his lordship had an urgent occasion to borrow £4,000, but did not chuse to be his own agent, and begged that the matter might be secretly and expeditiously conducted. The doctor employed Mr Robertson, a broker, to whom he presented a bond, not filled up or signed, that he might find a person who would advance the requisite sum to a young nobleman who had lately come of age. After applying to several persons who refused the business, because they were not to be present when the bond was executed, Mr Robertson, absolutely confiding in the doctor's honour, applied to Messrs. Fletcher and Peach, who agreed to lend the money. Mr Robertson returned the bond to the doctor, in order to its being executed; and on the following day the doctor produced it as executed, and witnessed by himself.

When Mr Robertson was examined before the lord mayor, he said, 'I, knowing Mr Fletcher to be a particular man, and one of those who would object to one subscribing witness only, put my name under the doctor's. I then went and received the money, which I paid into the hands of Dr Dodd, £3,000 in notes of Sir Charles Raymond and Company, the remaining £1,200 in bank-notes.'

The money being thus in the doctor's possession, he gave Mr Robertson a *hundred pounds*[1] for his trouble, and paid some of his own debts with a part of the remainder: but it does not appear but that he intended to replace the money,

[1] Was not this a handsome consideration for transacting such a business?

and pay off the bond in a short time, without the knowledge of any Person but the broker, and the gentlemen of whom the money had been borrowed. It happened, however, that the bond being left with Mr Manly (attorney for Messrs Fletcher and Peach), he observed, in the condition of the bond, 'a very remarkable blot in the first letter E, in the word SEVEN, which did not seem to be the effect of chance, but done with design. He thought it remarkable, but did not suspect a forgery; yet he shewed Mr Fletcher the bond and blot, and advised him to have a clean bond filled up, and carried to lord Chesterfield for execution.'

Mr Fletcher consented; and Mr Manly went on the following day to his lordship, who, having previous notice of the intended business, asked him if he had called about the bond. Mr Manly said he had; and his lordship answered, 'I have burnt the bond.'

This appeared very extraordinary; but was soon explained, by lord Chesterfield's saying he thought the gentleman called about a bond for £500 which he had given some years before, and had taken up and burnt.

When Mr Manly produced the bond in question, lord Chesterfield was surprized, and immediately disowned it. Upon this Mr Manly went directly to Mr Fletcher, to consult what steps to take. Mr Fletcher, a Mr Innis, and Mr Manly, went to Guildhall, to prefer an information respecting the forgery against the broker and Dr Dodd. Mr Robertson was taken into custody, and with Fletcher, Innis, Manly, and two of the lord mayor's officers, went to the house of Dr Dodd in Argyle-street. They opened the business; Dr Dodd was very much struck and affected. Manly told him, if he would return the money, it would be the only means of saving him. He instantly returned six notes of £500 each, making £3,000. He drew on his banker for £500. The broker returned £100. The doctor gave a second draught on his banker for £200 and a judgement on his goods for the remaining £400 which judgement was carried immediately into execution.[1]

[1] After this full restitution, does there not appear a kind of cruelty in trying Dr. Dodd at all? But justice *must* be done.

All this was done by the doctor in full reliance on the honour of the parties that the bond should be returned to him cancelled: but notwithstanding this restitution, he was taken before the lord mayor, and charged as abovementioned, when his defence was expressed in the following terms: 'I had no intention to defraud my lord Chesterfield, or the gentleman who advanced the money. I hope that the satisfaction I have made in returning the money will atone for the offence. I was pressed exceedingly for £300 to pay some bills due to tradesmen. I took this step as a temporary resource: I should have repaid it in half a year. My lord Chesterfield cannot but have some tenderness for me, as my pupil: I love him, and he knows it. There is nobody wishes to prosecute. I am sure my lord Chesterfield don't want my life: I hope he will shew clemency to me. Mercy should triumph over justice.'

This defence was not allowed to have any weight; and the Doctor was committed to the Compter, in preparation for his trial.

On the 19th of February, 1777, Doctor Dodd, being put to the bar at the Old Bailey, addressed the court in the following terms:—'My lords, I am informed that the bill of indictment against me has been found on the evidence of Mr Robertson, who was taken out of Newgate, without any authority or leave from your lordships, for the purpose of procuring the bill to be found. Mr Robertson is a subscribing witness to the bond, and, as I conceive, would be swearing to exculpate himself, if he should be admitted as a witness against me; and as the bill has been found upon his evidence, which was surreptitiously obtained, I submit to your lordships that I ought not to be compelled to plead on this indictment, and upon this question I beg to be heard by my counsel. My lords, I beg leave also further to observe to your lordships, that the gentlemen on the other side of the question are bound over to prosecute Mr Robertson.'

It is now proper to remark, that, 'previous to the arguments of the counsel, an order which had been surreptitiously obtained from an officer of the court, dated Wednesday, February the 19th, and directed to the keeper of

Newgate, commanding him to carry Lewis Robertson to Hicks's-hall, in order to his giving evidence before the grand inquest on the present bill of indictment; likewise a resolution of the court, reprobating the said order; and also the recognizance entered into by Mr Manly, Mr Peach, Mr Innis, and the right hon. the earl of Chesterfield, to prosecute and give evidence against Dr Dodd and Lewis Robertson for the said forgery; should be read; and the clerk of the arraigns was directed to inform the court whether the name Lewis Robertson was indorsed as a witness on the back of the indictment, which was answered in the affirmative.'

The counsel now proceeded in their arguments for and against the prisoner. Mr Howarth, one of Dr Dodd's advocates, contended that not any person ought 'to plead or answer to an indictment, if it appears upon the face of that indictment that the evidence upon which the bill was found was not legal or competent to have been adduced before the grand jury.'

Mr Cowper, of counsel on the same side, followed this idea, and hoped that Dr Dodd might not be called on to plead to the bill of indictment, and that the bill might be quashed.

Mr Buller, who was likewise retained for Dr Dodd, spoke as follows; and his arguments are so ingenious, that we think it our duty to transcribe them literally:—'My lords, I am of counsel on the same side with Mr Howarth and Mr Cowper. It is the established law of this land, that no man shall be put upon his trial for any offence, unless there be a bill first properly found by a grand jury: I say *properly* found; for if there be any objection whatsoever to the finding the indictment, and the most familiar that are to be found in our books are those that go to the objection of the grand jury; for instance, where only one person of the grand jury has been incompetent, where only eleven of the jury have found the bill, that therefore it shall not be tried. I take it the objections go universally. I am aware that the objections I have been alluding to, and which are particularly stated in Lord Hale, go to the grand jury only; but

I will beg leave to consider whether the reason that governs the one does not govern the other. Another case put by my Lord Hale is this: if one of the grand jury is outlawed, these objections go to the persons of the grand jury: I am aware that that is not the present objection; but I will beg leave, with your lordships' permission, to consider whether this does not fall within the same reason; for I cannot conceive that the law, which is so peculiarly watchful over the personal qualifications of the grand jury, should not be equally attentive to the evidence which is laid before them, and upon which they are to decide the fate of the bill which is offered to their consideration. I take it to be as essential to the finding of the bill, that the evidence offered to the grand jury should be such as the law allows, as it is when the indictment afterwards comes to be tried before your lordships; and if that rule holds, I trust I shall have very little difficulty in convincing your lordships that this bill has been improperly found. My lords, the prosecutor has thought it so material to admit Mr Robertson a witness in this cause, that though, in my humble apprehension, he stands in a much more criminal light than the prisoner at the bar, yet they have thought fit to bargain with him, to let him off from a capital felony of the most dangerous sort to society, the most peculiarly so from his situation in life, of any man that can be charged with such an offence. Mr Robertson stands in this business as a sworn broker of the city of London: as such it was his peculiar duty to preserve good faith between man and man; he is bargained with by the prosecutor to be let off in a case where he stands upon the appearance against him, now as the most criminal, for the purpose of procuring evidence against the prisoner at the bar. My lords, if that evidence be improper, there remains but one thing more to be enquired into; that is, whether your lordships can say that that evidence has not had an improper effect when it was admitted before the grand jury: it is not improbable that the bill might be found wholly upon his evidence: if I have a right to assume that as a fact, because the prosecutor has thought it material and absolutely necessary to produce him before the grand jury, why then your lordships sitting here cannot say but this indictment may have been found upon his evidence only: if it be so, is Robertson a person whose evidence ought to have been received? If I am right in saying that the same evidence, and the same evidence only, is legal before a grand jury, which is legal upon a trial, I apprehend the case which was mentioned yesterday in Lord Hale, folio 303, is decisive upon this point. My lords, there are more passages in that folio book; the first was the case mentioned yesterday of "Henry Trew, was indicted for a burglary, and (by the advice of Keeling, chief justice; Brown, justice; and Wilde, recorder) Perrin was sworn a witness against Trew as to the burglary, which he confessed, but was not indicted for the other felony." Here he was admitted because he confessed himself guilty. The passage before that in Lord Hale seems to me still stronger:—"If two defendants be charged with a crime, one shall not be examined against the other to convict him of an offence, unless the party examined confess himself guilty."—Now, has Robertson confessed himself guilty? No, he has not; then there is an express authority by Lord Hale, that not having done it he is no witness, he does not stand in that predicament which Lord Hale states the man to be there. He says that they were both charged with the crime; that is the case here; the prisoner and Robertson were both committed for the same crime; he stands now charged with that crime, and he has not pleaded guilty; therefore upon this authority I take it to be clear, that he cannot be admitted a witness upon the trial; and if not, I must leave it to the ingenuity of the learned counsel to shew why a man, who the law says shall not be a witness upon the trial, shall be admitted a witness to find the bill upon, against a man whom there is no other evidence to affect.'

Mr Mansfield, and the other counsel employed for the prosecution, replied to these arguments in a manner that did honour to their ingenuity and professional knowledge. It would greatly exceed our limits to give their arguments at length; and it will therefore be sufficient to say, that it was agreed on all hands that the trial should be proceeded

on; the question respecting the competency of Robertson's
evidence being reserved for the opinion of the twelve judges.

Hereupon Dr Dodd was indicted for forging a bond, for
the payment of £4,200 with intent to defraud, &c. as
mentioned at the head of this article.

As we have already recited the leading particulars of this
business, it will be unnecessary to be more minute; but only
to say, that when the evidence was gone through, the court
told the doctor that was the time for him to make his defence; on which he spoke as follows:

'My lords, and gentlemen of the jury;—Upon the
evidence which has been this day produced against me, I
find it very difficult to address your lordships: there is no
man in the world who has a deeper sense of the heinous
nature of the crime, for which I stand indicted, than myself.
I view it, my lords, in all its extent of malignancy towards
a commercial state, like ours; but, my lords, I humbly apprehend, though no lawyer, that the moral turpitude and
malignancy of the crime always, both in the eye of the law,
of reason, and of religion,[1] consists in the intention. I am
informed, my lords, that the act of parliament on this head
runs perpetually in this stile, *with an intention to defraud.*
Such an intention, my lords, and gentlemen of the jury, I
believe, has not been attempted to be proved upon me, and
the consequences that have happened, which have appeared
before you, sufficiently prove that a perfect and ample
restitution has been made. I leave it, my lords, to you, and
the gentlemen of the jury, to consider, that if an unhappy
man ever deviates from the law of right, yet, if in the single
first moment of recollection, he does all that he can to make
a full and perfect amends, what, my lords, and gentlemen of
the jury, can God and man desire further? My lords, there
are a variety of little circumstances, too tedious to trouble
you with, with respect to this matter. Were I to give a
loose to my feelings, I have many things to say which I am

[1] This is a strange phrase; it is what an Irishman would call
'*both* all *three*'; but it is thus printed; and if Dr Dodd made use of it,
his situation must be allowed for.

sure you would feel with respect to me: but, my lords, as it appears on all hands, as it appears, gentlemen of the jury, in every view, that no injury, intentional or real, has been done to any man upon the face of the earth, I hope that therefore you will consider the case in its true state of clemency. I must observe to your lordships, that though I have met with all candour in this court, yet I have been pursued with excessive cruelty; I have been prosecuted after the most express engagements, after the most solemn assurances, after the most delusive, soothing arguments of Mr Manly; I have been prosecuted with a cruelty scarcely to be paralleled : a person, avowedly criminal in the same indictment with myself, has been brought forth as a capital witness against me; a fact, I believe, totally unexampled. My lords, oppressed as I am with infamy, loaded as I am with distress, sunk under this cruel prosecution, your lordships, and the gentlemen of the jury, cannot think life a matter of any value to me : no, my lords, I solemnly protest, that death of all blessings would be the most pleasant to me after this pain. I have yet, my lords, ties which call upon me; ties which render me desirous even to continue this miserable existence :—I have a wife, my lords, who for twenty-seven years has lived an unparalleled example of conjugal attachment and fidelity, and whose behaviour during this trying scene would draw tears of approbation, I am sure, even from the most inhuman. My lords, I have creditors, honest men, who will lose much by my death: I hope, for the sake of justice towards them, some mercy will be shewn to me. If, upon the whole, these considerations at all avail with you, my lords, and you gentlemen of the jury; if, upon the most partial survey of matters, not the slightest intention of injury can appear to any one; and I solemnly declare it was in my power to replace it in three months; of this I assured Mr Robertson frequently; and had his solemn assurances that no man should be privy to it but Mr Fletcher and himself, and, if no injury was done to any man upon earth; I then hope, I trust, I fully confide myself in the tenderness, humanity, and protection of my country.'

The discerning reader will easily see, by the defence, that

Dr Dodd was not a man of superior abilities; and the defence itself appears to be little else than a confession of guilt.

The jury retired for about ten minutes, and then returned with a verdict, that 'The prisoner was GUILTY;' but at the same time presented a petition, humbly recommending the convict to the royal mercy.[1]

On the first day of the sessions held at the Old Bailey in May, 1777, Dr Dodd, being put to the bar, was addressed by Mr Justice Aston in the following terms:

'Doctor William Dodd,

'When you was brought up in last February sessions, to plead to an indictment found by the grand jury of Middlesex for forgery, before you pleaded, or the trial was proceeded upon, a question was submitted to the court by you, with the advice of your counsel, which was reserved for the opinion of the judges; that is, whether you was bound to plead to, and ought to be tried upon that indictment, as the name of Lewis Robertson, committed for the same forgery, appeared to be indorsed as a witness upon the bill of indictment, and that he had been taken before the grand jury to be examined as a witness by means of an order directed to the keeper of Newgate, which had been improperly obtained, on the 19th of February, and which was afterwards vacated by the court.

'The judges have met, and have fully considered the whole matter of this objection; and they are unanimously of opinion, that the necessity of some proper authority to carry a witness who happened to be in custody before the grand jury to give evidence, regards the justification of the gaoler only; but that no objection lies upon that account in the mouth of the party indicted, for in respect of him the finding of the bill is right, and according to law.

'Whether a private prosecutor, by using an accomplice in or out of custody as a witness, gives such a witness a

[1] It seems highly probable that this petition was previously prepared by the friends of Dr Dodd; for an absence of ten minutes was insufficient to agree on a verdict, and prepare the petition.

plea not to be prosecuted, or can entitle himself, the prosecutor, to have his recognizance discharged, is a matter very fit for consideration under all the circumstances of the particular case, when that question shall arise; but it is a matter in which the party indicted has no concern, nor can he make any legal objection to the producing such a person as a witness, for the accomplice is, against him, a legal and competent witness, and so was Lewis Robertson upon the bill of indictment preferred against you.

'The judges, therefore, are of opinion, that the proceedings upon that indictment against you were legally had, and that you was thereupon duly convicted according to law. Of this opinion I thought it most proper thus early to apprize you, that you may be prepared for the consequence of it at the close of the sessions.'

To this address Dr Dodd replied in the following terms: My lord, I humbly thank your lordship, and the rest of the learned judges, for the consideration you have been pleased to give to the objections made by my counsel on that awful day of my trial; and I rest fully satisfied, my lord, in the justice of your lordship's opinion.'

On the last day of the sessions Dr Dodd was again put to the bar, when the clerk of the arraigns said, 'Dr William Dodd, you stand convicted of forgery; what have you to say why this court should not give you judgement to die according to law?'

Hereupon Dr Dodd addressed the court in the following terms. 'My lord, I now stand before you a dreadful example of human infirmity. I entered upon public life with the expectations common to young men whose education has been liberal, and whose abilities have been flattered; and when I became a clergyman, I considered myself as not impairing the dignity of the order. I was not an idle, nor, I hope, an useless minister: I taught the truths of christianity with the zeal of conviction, and the authority of innocence. My labours were approved; my pulpit became popular; and, I have reason to believe, that of those who heard me some have been preserved from sin, and some have been reclaimed. Condescend, my lord, to think, if these considerations aggravate my crime, how much they must embitter my punishment!

'Being distinguished and elevated by the confidence of mankind, I had too much confidence in myself, and thinking my integrity, what others thought it, established in sincerity, and fortified by religion, I did not consider the danger of vanity, nor suspect the deceitfulness of my own heart. The day of conflict came, in which temptation seized and overwhelmed me! I committed the crime, which I entreat your lordship to believe that my conscience hourly represents to me in its full bulk of mischief and malignity. Many have been overpowered by temptation, who are now among the penitent in heaven!

'To an act now waiting the decision of vindictive justice, I will not presume to oppose the counterbalance of almost thirty years, (a great part of the life of man) passed in exciting and exercising charity; in relieving such distresses as I now feel; in administering those consolations which I now want. I will not otherwise extenuate my offence, than by declaring, what I hope will appear to many, and what many circumstances make probable, that I did not intend finally to defraud: nor will it become me to apportion my own punishment, by alledging, that my sufferings have been not much less than my guilt. I have fallen from reputation which ought to have made me cautious, and from a fortune which ought to have given me content. I am sunk at once into poverty and scorn: my name and my crime fill the ballads in the streets; the sport of the thoughtless, and the triumph of the wicked!

'It may seem strange, my lord, that, remembering what I have lately been, I should still wish to continue what I am:— but contempt of death, how speciously soever it may mingle with heathen virtues, has nothing in it suitable to christian penitence.

'Many motives impel me to beg earnestly for life. I feel the natural horror of a violent death, the universal dread of untimely dissolution. I am desirous to recompence the injury I have done to the clergy, to the world, and to religion; and to efface the scandal of my crime, by the example of my repentance:—but, above all, I wish to die with thoughts more composed, and calmer preparation.

'The gloom and confusion of a prison, the anxiety of a trial, the horrors of suspence, and the inevitable vicissitudes of passion, leave not the mind in a due disposition for the holy exercises of prayer, and self-examination. Let not a little life be denied me, in which I may, by meditation and contrition, prepare myself to stand at the tribunal of Omnipotence, and support the presence of that judge, who shall distribute to all according to their works; who will receive and pardon the repenting sinner; and from whom the merciful shall obtain mercy.

'For these reasons, my lords, amidst shame and misery, I yet wish to live; and most humbly implore, that I may be recommended by your lordship to the clemency of his Majesty.'

The RECORDER now proceeded to pass sentence in the following terms:—'Dr William Dodd; you have been convicted of the offence of publishing a forged and counterfeit bond, knowing it to be forged and counterfeited; and you have had the advantage which the laws of this country afford to every man in that situation, a fair, an impartial, and an attentive trial.

'The jury, to whose justice you appealed, have found you guilty; their verdict has undergone the consideration of the learned judges, and they found no ground to impeach the justice of that verdict; you yourself have admitted the justice of it; and now the very painful duty that the necessity of the law imposes upon the court, to pronounce the sentence of that law against you, remains only to be performed.

'You appear to entertain a very proper sense of the enormity of the offence which you have committed; you appear too in a state of contrition of mind, and I doubt not have duly reflected how far the dangerous tendency of the offence you have been guilty of is encreased by the influence of example, in being committed by a person of your character, and of the sacred function of which you are a member. These sentiments seem to be yours; I would wish to cultivate such sentiments; but I would not wish to add to the anguish of a person in your situation by dwelling upon it.

'Your application for mercy must be made elsewhere; it would be cruel in the court to flatter you; there is a power of dispensing mercy where you may apply. Your own good sense, and the contrition you express, will induce you to lessen the influence of the example by publishing your hearty and sincere detestation of the offence of which you are convicted; and that you will not attempt to palliate or extenuate, which would indeed add to the degree of the influence of a crime of this kind being committed by a person of your character and known abilities; I would therefore warn you against any thing of that kind. Now, having said this, I am obliged to pronounce the sentence of the law, which is—That you Dr William Dodd be carried from hence to the place from whence you came; that from thence you are to be carried to the place of execution, where you are to be hanged by the neck until you are dead.'— To this Dr Dodd replied, 'Lord Jesus, receive my soul!'

We will now proceed to an account of the execution of Dr Dodd, then relate some farther particulars respecting him, and conclude with remarks proper to the occasion.

This unhappy clergyman was attended to the place of execution, in a mourning coach, by the Rev Mr Villette, ordinary of Newgate, and the Rev Mr Dobey. Another criminal, named Joseph Harris, was executed at the same time. It is impossible to give an idea of the immense crouds of people that thronged the streets from Newgate to Tyburn. When the prisoners arrived at the fatal tree, and were placed in the cart, Dr Dodd exhorted his fellow-sufferer in so generous a manner as testified that he had not forgot the duty of a clergyman, and was very fervent in the exercise of his own devotions. Just before the parties were turned off, Dr Dodd whispered to the executioner. What he said cannot be known; but it was observed that the man had no sooner driven away the cart, than he ran immediately under the gibbet, and took hold of the doctor's legs, as if to steady the body; and the unhappy man appeared to die without pain; but the groans, prayers, and tears, of thousands attended his exit.

Dr Dodd was executed on the 27th of June, 1777.

Thus perished all that was mortal of William Dodd, doctor of divinity, late prebendary of Brecon, and chaplain in ordinary to his Majesty. This man, with all his faults, was not without his virtues; he was the promoter of many charities, and the institutor of some of them. The Magdalen hospital, the society for the relief of poor debtors, and that for the recovery of persons apparently drowned, will, we trust, be perpetual monuments to his credit: but it is our duty not to conceal or disguise his faults, the principal of which appear to have been vanity, and a turn for extravagance, which ruined his circumstances, and urged him to commit the crime which cost him his life.

After conviction, the exertions made to save Dr Dodd were perhaps beyond all example in any country. The news-papers were filled with letters, and paragraphs in his favour. Individuals of all ranks and degrees exerted themselves in his behalf: parish officers went, in mourning, from house to house, to procure subscriptions to a petition to the king; and this petition, which, with the names, filled 23 sheets of parchment, was actually presented. Even more than this:—the lord mayor and common council went in a body to St James's, to solicit mercy for the convict. But all this availed nothing: it was necessary to make an example of a man who had set but too bad an one to others; and who, from the fairest prospect of rising to the highest honours of the church, sunk to the lowest degree of abasement.

Surely this tale will be a lesson against extravagance, and will teach us to be content in the station of life in which Providence hath placed us. The fate of this unhappy man furnishes, likewise, the strongest argument against the crime of forgery; for if all the interest that was exerted to save Dr Dodd could have no weight, no one hereafter guilty of it ought to expect a pardon. If, then, any one should be tempted to the commission of it, let him reflect on this case; let him, moral and religious considerations apart, stay the hasty hand, and let him retract the rash resolution.

We shall conclude this narrative with an extract from

an address which Dr Dodd wrote, after conviction, to his fellow prisoners; because we deem it well worthy the public attention.—'There is always,' says the doctor, 'a danger lest men, fresh from a trial in which life has been lost, should remember with resentment and malignity the prosecutor, the witnesses, or the judges. It is indeed scarcely possible, with all the prejudices of an interest so weighty, and so affecting, that the convict should think otherwise than that he has been treated, in some part of the process, with unnecessary severity. In this opinion he is perhaps singular, and therefore probably mistaken: but there is no time for disquisition; we must try to find the shortest way to peace. It is easier to forgive than to reason right. He that has been injuriously or unnecessarily harrassed, has one opportunity more of proving his sincerity, by forgiving the wrong, and praying for his enemy.

'It is the duty of a penitent to repair, as far as he has the power, the injury he has done. What we can do is commonly nothing more than to leave the world an example of contrition. On the dreadful day, when the sentence of the law has its full force, some will be found to have affected a shameless bravery, or negligent intrepidity. Such is not the proper behaviour of a convicted criminal. To rejoice in tortures is the privilege of a martyr; to meet death with intrepidity is the right only of innocence, if in any human being innocence could be found. Of him whose life is shortened by his crimes, the last duties are humility and self-abasement. We owe to God sincere repentance; we owe to man the appearance of repentance. Men have died with a steadfast denial of crimes, of which it is very difficult to suppose them innocent. By what equivocation or reserve they may have reconciled their consciences to falsehood it is impossible to know: but if they thought that, when they were to die, they paid their legal forfeit, and that the world had no farther demand upon them; that therefore they might, by keeping their own secrets, try to leave behind them a disputable reputation; and that the falshood was harmless because none were injured; they had very little considered the nature of society. One of the principal parts of national felicity arises from a wise and impartial administration of justice. Every man reposes upon the tribunals of his country the stability of possession, and the serenity of life. He therefore who unjustly exposes the courts of judicature to suspicion, either of partiality or error, not only does an injury to those who dispense the laws, but diminishes the public confidence in the laws themselves, and shakes the foundation of public tranquillity.

'For my own part, I confess, with deepest compunction, the crime which has brought me to this place; and admit the justice of my sentence, while I am sinking under its severity.'

The case of Dr Dodd is extremely interesting for a variety of reasons. Public opinion was very deeply roused. Dodd was the son of the Vicar of Bourne in Lincolnshire, and at the time of his execution he was a distinguished figure in the life of London, and was Chaplain to the King. He was a preacher of great renown and moved in the highest social circles. He had made full confession of his guilt, and had also made full restitution. He was no criminal in the ordinary use of that term, and the most extraordinary efforts were made to save him from the gallows. No doubt it was the personality of Dodd which aroused this nation-wide outburst on his behalf, but men everywhere were awakened to the fact that there was no alternative punishment provided to the penalty of death. Dr Johnson exerted himself to try and save Dodd, although he had no great admiration for him, as may be seen in the somewhat acid comments recorded by Boswell. The address which Dodd made to the Court, and the address to his fellow convicts in prison (both of which are printed here), were written by Johnson. The Corporation of London presented a petition on Dodd's behalf and this also was drafted by Johnson. On the eve of Dodd's execution, Johnson sent to the newspapers a finely-worded letter headed: 'Observations on the Propriety of pardoning Dr Dodd.' Johnson's activities were due to his dissatisfaction with the state of the existing criminal law and in particular to the system which provided no alternative in a case like this. The real difficulty was that Dr Dodd could only be saved by the exercise of the royal clemency. George the Third and those advising him were quite unmoved by all the public clamour, and indeed the more the clamour grew the more were they determined to see the sentence confirmed and carried out. Lord Mansfield in particular was strongly opposed to any commutation of the sentence of death, believing that if clemency were shown to Dodd it would have to be shown to others. The King was also powerfully influenced by the fact that Daniel and Robert Perreau had been executed at Tyburn about eighteen months before (see pp. 214-215), and is reported to have said that if he pardoned Dodd he should regard himself as the moral murderer of the Perreaus. This was the reason why the unprecedented agitation came to nothing, and on 27th June, 1777, Dodd was driven to Tyburn in his own carriage preceded by a hearse with his own coffin inside it. The privilege of riding in a private carriage was granted to people of some standing in the world, though the usual practice was for convicts to go to Tyburn in a cart, manacled, and sitting on their own coffins.

The case of Dr Dodd is noteworthy, therefore, because it marked the beginning of the prolonged agitation against the rigours of capital punishment which resulted in the reforms of the nineteenth century. It also brought into great prominence the necessity for a well-devised system of secondary punishments, and it showed plainly that the exercise of the royal prerogative of mercy was an unsatisfactory means of correcting any shortcomings of the law itself.

Particulars of the Trial of JOSEPH RELPH, who was indicted for Murder, and found guilty of Manslaughter.

AT the sessions held at the Old Bailey, in December, 1778, Joseph Relph, mariner, was indicted for the wilful murder of Andrew Schultz on the 26th of November preceding; and he likewise stood charged on the coroner's inquisition, for feloniously killing and slaying the said Andrew.

The prisoner was employed in the impress service, and the following is the state of the evidence adduced on the trial.—John Clear swore, that he was a beadle of Wapping; that Mr James Stewart, a tallow-chandler, called him from the Mason's lodge, and told him a man was murdered: that he went to the sign of the Gibraltar, where he found the prisoner leaning down in a box, having the fingers of his left hand, which were bloody, tied in a handkerchief: that on this deponent's asking what was the matter, Relph said he had been used ill, and cut to pieces; that he went with him quietly to the Round-house, and the next day before a magistrate, who committed him to New prison.

John Hageman deposed, that he was a servant to Mr Compton, sugar-baker, in Brewer's-lane; there were five of his companions, all of whom were going home to Mr Compton's; that they were all on the foot-pavement, and the deceased was running before him: that he saw a woman with a lantern in her hand crossing the way, and a girl about eight years old with her; and that Hardwicke (one of the company) lifted up the woman's peticoats behind.

The counsel now interposed, and said he should prove that the woman and child were the wife and daughter of the prisoner.

Hageman proceeded, and said that the woman having walked a hundred yards, the prisoner overtook them; on which his wife pointed to Hardwicke, and said 'This is the young man that laid hold of my gown.' The prisoner crossed to Hardwicke, and asked him what business he had to meddle with the woman's gown. Hardwicke made no reply; and one Kello coming up at the juncture, said to the lieutenant, (Relph) 'Sir, I am your prisoner, and will go with you where you like.' This evidence farther deposed, that the lieutenant took Hardwicke by the neck, and pulled his hat off.

John Kello was now sworn; but not being perfect in the English language, an interpreter was sworn to deliver his evidence, which was to the following effect: that Andrew Schultz was one of the party, returning with his fellow-servants to Mr Compton's; that he himself was sober, but doubted if Hardwicke was not somewhat in liquor: that he did not see the prisoner till he came and put a hanger to his breast; on which this deponent acknowledged himself his prisoner, and consented to go where he ·pleased; but that he thrust the hanger through his cloaths, and slightly wounded him in the breast.

When this deponent felt the sword hurt him, he jumped aside; and then Schultz said 'You had better put your sword by.' After some struggling Kello took the hanger from the lieutenant, but did not observe whether Schultz was wounded or not; that the prisoner went to a public-house, and afterwards heard that Schultz was wounded; and that the lieutenant was cut in the hand.

Frederick Hardwicke, being sworn, acknowledged that he had touched the bottom of the woman's gown as he was passing her; owned he was a little disguised in liquor, and that, after he had touched the woman's gown, he received a blow from behind on his neck, and his hat fell off; but he could not tell by whom the blow was given. When he recovered himself, and got to his companions, he observed that Schultz was wounded, and that the lieutenant was going to the public house with a drawn hanger in his hand; he followed him, and staid there two minutes: he observed that the lieutenant's hand was bloody, and immediately went home to his own lodgings.

Sarah Hoskins, an oyster woman, wife of William Hoskins of Bell-dock, saw four young men in the highway, and observed the lieutenant collar Hardwicke, and likewise saw a woman on the other side of the way, whom she heard say 'you dirty fellow, how dare you meddle with my gown?' or petticoat, the deponent could not be sure which. Her husband, the lieutenant, then came up, and said 'My dear, what is the matter?' to which she replied, 'the dirty fellow has been pulling my gown,' or words to that purpose.

Mrs Hoskins then saw the lieutenant collar Frederick Hardwicke, and say 'If you don't go along with me, I will draw my sword and stab you.' They then struggled from the Bell ale-house door, till they got between a brazier's and tin-shop, at the distance of nine or ten yards. In the mean time one of the men, who had a stick, hit the lieutenant on the back while Hardwicke and he were struggling. During this commotion the lieutenant's wife was hanging round his neck in the highway; but this deponent did not see the sword drawn, only heard the threat that it should be done: nor did she know whether the sword was drawn before or after the lieutenant was struck.

About five or six minutes after the lieutenant was struck with the stick, she heard somebody cry out, 'Stop him, stop him, the young man is dead in the tin-shop.' The lieutenant then went into the ale-house.

This was the substance of the evidence; and the judge then said to the counsel for the prisoner, 'Do you mean to make this less than manslaughter?' To which the counsel replied in the following words: 'No, my lord, we cannot make it less than manslaughter. The lieutenant was used very ill while his wife was hanging round his neck to prevent any further fighting. She was cut a-cross her neck, and the lieutenant had his hand and his coat cut in two places, and was beat all over his arm and shoulders.'

The court now observing that, if the jury were satisfied, nothing farther need be heard, but if not they would proceed; the jury said, 'My lord, we are all satisfied; and soon afterwards they gave a verdict that the prisoner was 'Not guilty of the murder, but guilty of manslaughter only;' on which he was branded and discharged.

We see that, in the instance before us, a life had been lost, yet the party accused could not be convicted of murder; and we have the rather inserted this trial, to caution people to avoid occasional quarrels in the streets, which can never be attended with any good consequences, and are frequently productive of the most fatal.

In the present case we find that the accused party was what is called a lieutenant of a press-gang; that is, the principal savage among savages. The custom of impressing, let counsellors plead, and senators debate till they are hoarse, is incompatible with every idea we can frame of the natural right to that freedom which God has bestowed equally on us all; and which, from the very nature of the donation, it appears to be every man's duty to support.

There is nothing very particular in the case before us which tends to prove any insolence on the part of the lieutenant; but these volumes are growing to a conclusion, and we could not think of putting a period to them, without entering our protest against a practice which opposes every sentiment of humanity, and militates against all the finer feelings of the soul.

What! because a man has served his country faithfully for a series of years by sea, and has at length retired in the fond hope of enjoying the sweets of domestic felicity, shall he be dragged from the fond wife, and the helpless innocents, when he wishes not again to tempt the danger of the seas? Honour, common honesty, plain sense, humanity, and even law, reprobate the idea!

We have had of late two or three instances of freemen of London being impressed; but they have been discharged: the hardiest, the most callous of our lawyers dare not bring the matter to a legal issue: they know that sound sense and the laws of the realm are against the practice; they therefore fly from the subject, and, like the Parthians, conquer in retreat.

Setting aside all moral considerations, and permitting even humanity to sleep on this subject, sound policy forbids this infernal practice. The British tars are full free to serve their country. Let proper bounties be offered, let proper encouragements be held forth, and the navy will never want a man. It will be said that the giving high bounties to sailors will occasion an increase of those taxes which are already nearly insupportable. No doubt but our taxes are very burthensome; but let our pensioners be reduced in number and in pay, and we shall not want a sum to reward our daring sailors. Besides, the bounties given to these men, politically considered, cost nothing. Every man knows that a seaman carries nothing abroad with him but his jacket, his trowsers, and his valour. He spends his bounty-money where he receives it; and the cash circulates among those who gave it.

Let BRITISH GENEROSITY vie with BRITISH VALOUR, and we may bid DEFIANCE to the WORLD!

The Editors gave their reasons for inserting this case in the following words: ' . . . to caution people to avoid occasional quarrels in the streets, which can never be attended with any good consequences, and are frequently productive of the most fatal.' The reason it is included here is because of the plate showing the punishment of branding in the hand being inflicted. Branding as a punishment dates back to the year 1487, and the Act of Henry the Seventh said: 'Every Person, not being within Orders, which once hath been admitted to the Benefit of Clergy, eftsoons [i.e., afterwards] arraigned of an offence be not admitted to have the benefit or Privilege of his Clergy. And that every person convicted of Murder be marked with an M upon the braun of his left thumb; and if he be for any other felony, the same person to be marked with a T in the same place of the left thumb, and these marks to be made by the gaoler openly in the Court before the Judge.' In the Criminal Court at Lancaster there are still kept the instruments formerly used for branding. There can be seen in the dock the brazier, the branding irons and the iron contraption into which the prisoner's hand was forced.

In 1669, an Act of Parliament provided that instead of branding on the thumb, the convict was to be branded on the most visible part of the left cheek nearest the nose. This method only lasted for seven years. Quite obviously, people who had been branded on the face would find it difficult to get employment when their bad character was so openly displayed, and were likely to continue a life of crime because no other way of life was open to them. Branding on the hand was resumed, but in the reign of Anne it was provided that convicts could be burnt in the hand and be sent to a House of Correction. In 1717 a further alteration was made, and in place of burning

in the hand, a convict could be transported to the colonies in America
for seven years. In 1779, the Court was empowered to impose a fine
or a whipping in place of the branding. The preamble to the Act of
Parliament which made this change spoke of the branding as being
'disregarded or ineffectual'. With the approval of the judges, the
branding was being carried out with a cold iron, but the plate here
reproduced shows the burning being done with a hot iron. The case
of Relph is interesting, too, because of the observations of the Editors
about the forcible impressing of men for the British fleet. The press
gang was the name given to these naval parties who carried out the
forcible impressment until the beginning of the nineteenth century.

Concluding Note, by the Editors.

THUS have we endeavoured, and we hope not unsuccessfully, to compleat this work, in conformity to the proposals originally offered to the public. We trust we have not omitted any trials of great importance, nor inserted many of a trifling nature.

Those who wish well to Society will be pleased to see vice exposed in every shape, and reprobated under all the variety of forms it may assume. Too much cannot be said to discountenance its propagation, or to enhance the charms of true religion and virtue.

To advance these important purposes should be the aim and end of every publication. The book that does not tend to make people wiser and better is a nuisance to society, and a disgrace to the press.

As the reformation of prisoners, rather than the punishment of them, should be the great aim of our legislators, we beg leave to submit to our readers some extracts from letters written by a gentleman to a Member of Parliament, both of them of the most amiable private characters, and both of them zealous promoters of every public good.

Jonas Hanway, Esq; in a letter to Sir Charles Bunbury, says, 'In the general view of our prisons, I beg leave to make a few remarks, which to those who have not considered the subject may carry some degree of information. Of all the abuses which ever crept into civil society, professing Christianity, considering the evil propensities of the common run of our malefactors, the *tap-house* seems to stand in a distinguished rank. What reformation can be expected, where it is the interest of the keeper of a prison to promote inebriety and dissipation of thought? If he is suffered to sell strong liquors for his own emolument, he will be tempted to shut his gates against every one who would relieve the real crying wants of those who are in need, and open them wide to all such as will supply the means of drunkenness. There can be no good reason for an indulgence, which, scattering the thoughts, will create a desperate repugnance to the calls of heaven. When the

258

foul ought to tremble, as being on the verge of eternity, such a conduct is abominable beyond all expression.

'Doth not the magistrate prostitute his authority, in granting licences, on the puerile presumption that he shall increase the revenue? Or is it that knowing how scanty the allowance is to the keepers of prisons, he gives them a liberty which he knows cannot be used without the most deadly consequences, even that of promoting the very temper and disposition which encouraged the malefactor to commit the crime for which he is imprisoned! This conduct is reproachable in the highest degree. The magistrate ought rather to refuse the licence, and represent the necessity of allowing keepers of prisons salaries suitable to the importance of their office.

'The conversion of a house, which ought to be a scene of sorrow and repentance, into jollity, and carelessness to all events, is one of the chief causes of the evil with which we are so sorely afflicted. If this is not remedied, can any expedient restore good discipline and true economy in prisons? If some prisoners should be thus deprived of a comfort they might be entitled to, it would be far better than granting an indulgence, so pregnant with mischief to the generality.

'By an act of the third of his present majesty, no jailor in Ireland is to sell ale, beer, or any other liquor, by himself or any other person, under the penalty of £5 for every offence; and I am assured it operates happily in preventing the ordinary bad effects. With us the case is different; for every capital prison is a public-house; and though spirituous liquors, commonly so called, are prohibited, yet, under the name of cordials, I am told they pass; or at least that by the force of wine, and malt liquor, all the bad effects of intoxication are continued.

'Among the several grievances which rise in judgment against us, are the fees demanded of malefactors, now softened, but not abolished. The want of medical assistance—the deficiency of baths—inattention to cleanliness—foul air for want of ventilation—want of a change of clean-washed and well-dried garments, with a regular change of linen—where these are wanting, death must be a familiar guest to a prisoner. Even the regular washing of hands and feet is of consequence. A proper regard to diet, according to the apparent wants of prisoners, is necessary to the preservation of life in prisons, more than in other places; and the defect often operates like a plague.'

That a reform in the management of our prisons is necessary, no man of common sense can doubt; and it remains with the wisdom of legislature to provide a remedy for the evil.

Perhaps the keeping prisoners separate from each other, and totally denying all the means of intemperance, would go far towards effecting that reformation which is so much wanted. As matters now stand, the man charged with felony is repeatedly visited by the most abandoned of his acquaintance, and they mutually harden each other in vice. These visits should be very unfrequent, and never permitted but in the presence of the keeper or his deputy, who should be people of the most unexceptionable character, and take care that not an improper word is uttered.

To drop, however, this subject, let us conclude this volume by a fervent wish that the readers of it may carefully and steadily avoid every vice therein recorded, every folly therein exposed. Let honesty be the prevailing, the ruling, principle among us; let us be humbly content in the situation which Providence hath allotted us; not seeking to possess ourselves of the property of others; and paying a devout reverence to that divine command, the authority of which no one will deny:

'Thou shalt not covet thy neighbour's house, thou shalt not covet thy neighbour's wife, nor his man-servant, nor his maid-servant, nor his ox, nor his ass, nor ANY THING that is his.'

PRINTED IN ENGLAND